The Handbook of French Fantasy & Supernatural Fiction

OTHER RELEVANT TITLES FROM BLACK COAT PRESS

by Jean-Marc & Randy Lofficier

The French Fantasy Treasury 1: The World's Edge (ISBN 978-1-61227-544-4)
The French Fantasy Treasury 2: Myths & Legends (ISBN 978-1-61227-545-1)
The French Fantasy Treasury 3: Far Realms (ISBN 978-1-61227-546-8)
Shadowmen: Heroes and Villains of French Pulp Fiction (ISBN 978-0-9740711-3-8)
Shadowmen 2: Heroes and Villains of French Comics (ISBN 978-0-9740711-8-3)
The Handbook of French Science Fiction (ISBN 978-1-64932-161-9)
The Handbook of French Fantastic Cinema & Television (ISBN 978-1-64932-166-4)

by Brian Stableford

The Plurality of Imaginary Worlds: The Evolution of French Roman Scientifique (ISBN 978-1-61227-503-1)
Tales of Enchantment and Disenchantment: A History of Faerie, with an Exemplary Anthology of Tales (ISBN 978-1-61227-838-4)

The Handbook of French Fantasy & Supernatural Fiction

by

Jean-Marc & Randy Lofficier

A Black Coat Press Book

Acknowledgements: Portions of this book have previously appeared in *French Science Fiction, Fantasy, Horror & Pulp Fiction* published in 2000 by McFarland and *The French Fantasy Treasury* (Black Coat Press).

CONSULTING EDITORS:
Henri ROSSI
Brian STABLEFORD
Jean-Luc RIVERA

Copyright © 2022 by Jean-Marc & Randy Lofficier.
Cover illustration Copyright © 2022 by Nathalie lial.

Visit our website at www.blackcoatpress.com

ISBN 978-1-64932-165-7. First Printing. November 2022. Published by Black Coat Press, an imprint of Hollywood Comics.com, LLC, P.O. Box 17270, Encino, CA 91416. All rights reserved. Except for review purposes, no part of this book may be reproduced or transmitted in any form or by any means, electronic or mechanical, including photocopying, recording, or by any information storage and retrieval system, without permission in writing from the publisher. The stories and characters depicted in this novel are entirely fictional. Printed in the United States of America.

TABLE OF CONTENTS

Foreword 7
The Middle Ages 11
    Chansons de Geste 12
    Fabliaux 16
    Poetry 18
    Religious Dramas 19
The Renaissance 23
    The Merveilleux 24
    Occult & Esoterism 26
The Age of Enlightenment 33
    The Fairy Tales 34
    Occult, Esoterism & Proto-fantastique 45
The 19th Century 51
    Romans Noirs 52
    Fantastique Populaire 64
    Fantastique Littéraire 91
        Fantastique Romantique 91
        Fantastique Réaliste 101
        Fantastique Symboliste 108
    Fantasy 114
    Occult & Esoterism 123
    Belgian Fantastique 128
The Belle Époque 133
    Fantastique Populaire 134
    Fantastique Littéraire 148
    Fantasy 152
Between the Wars 159
    Fantastique Populaire 160
    Fantastique Littéraire 165
        The Surréalists 166
        Other Mainstream Authors 169
    Fantasy 177
    Belgian Fantastique 183

- *Jean Ray* 183
- *Fantastique Populaire* 187
- *Fantastique Littéraire* 188
- The 1950s & 1960s 193
  - Fantastique Populaire 195
  - Fantastique Littéraire............................. 206
    - *The New Surrealists* 206
    - *Other Mainstream Authors* 210
    - *Female Authors* 215
  - Fantasy 217
    - *Folklore & Legends* 219
  - Occult & Esoterism 221
  - The YAs 224
  - Belgian Fantastique 227
- The 1970s 233
  - Fantastique Populaire 233
  - Fantastique Littéraire............................. 236
  - The New Surrealists 237
    - *Other Mainstream Authors* 240
  - Female Authors 241
  - Fantasy 243
  - Occult & Esoterism 248
  - The YAs 249
  - Belgian Fantastique 251
- The 1980s & 1990s 255
  - Fantastique Populaire 257
  - Fantastique Littéraire............................. 265
    - *Female Authors* 268
  - Fantasy 269
  - The YAs 277
- Afterword: 2022.. 285
- Index 289

Foreword

When embarking on any study about fantasy and supernatural fiction in literature, it is often customary to start with an attempt to define these genres.

In French, this book would be entitled "*The Handbook of French Fantastique*", the word *fantastique* carrying with it a much larger definition, or "semantic field", than its approximate English equivalent, which is commonly assumed to be "fantasy" despite the fact that the fantastique also includes horror and supernatural literature, often studied separately in English. Because it is easy to lose oneself in complex arguments about definitions, about what belongs to the genre and what does not, we subscribe to Pierre Gripari's simple definition: "The *fantastique* is everything that is not rational".

We do this because we believe that, from their very inceptions, the two genres, *fantastique* and science fiction, reflected two sharply different literary objectives on the part of their writers, as well as filled two sharply different literary needs from the standpoint of their readers. Which is why literary works belonging to fantasy, horror, the supernatural, and the *fantastique* in general, are chronicled and reviewed in here, while science fiction is the subject of our companion volume, *The Handbook of French Science Fiction*.

For the purpose of these handbooks, we shall construe as *fantastique* all of that which appeals to the heart, to the emotions, to the soul. The *fantastique* relies on irrational beliefs, a sense of the *merveilleux*. It stems from faith; faith in established religions as well as in folkloric legends; faith in ancient or modern myths, such as what is commonly known as the occult or, more accurately, what the French dub *ésotérisme* [*esoterica*], meaning that which is hidden, occult, obscure or secret. Faith traditionally opposes science and material progress, which science fiction, naturally, embraces and advocates.

Like religion, the *fantastique*, whether expressed through the forms of drama, poetry or fables, first helped the medieval people begin to illuminate the fearsome darkness in which they lived, before the age of humanism and enlightenment.

Its lighter, more baroque side, mutated into the *merveilleux*, the fairy tales which evolved into 19th century classic fantasy and high fantasy, its romantic, symbolic and surrealistic variants, and later, modern-day heroic-fantasy and sword and sorcery, often following English or American templates borrowed from J. R. R. Tolkien and Robert E. Howard.

The darker side of the *fantastique* evolved into gothic literature, the *romans noirs* and *romans frénétiques*, as well as occult literature and other forms of "classic" *fantastique*, before ultimately branching out into modern horror, called *Horreur* or *Angoisse* in French, and more generally, supernatural fiction. A literary tradition which began following in the footsteps of E. T. A. Hoffmann and Edgar Allan Poe eventually produced a rich catalog of authors ranging from the popular, such as Gaston Leroux and Marcel Aymé in France and Jean Ray in Belgium, to the highly literate such as Michel de Ghelderode or Alain Robbe-Grillet.

These, then, are our terms of reference, the literary canvas against which we propose to paint the history of French *fantastique*.

It should also be understood that, throughout this book, we have used the word "French" in the sense of French-language, that is to say, including Belgian, Swiss and French-Canadian works and/or authors whenever appropriate We have, however, strived to identify such non-French-national works and/or authors.

Finally, no project of this type is ever perfect, or complete. We have tried to be as comprehensive as possible and correct all mistakes that appeared in the McFarland tome.

Nevertheless, in a book of this scope, no matter how careful one is, omissions are still bound to creep in, as well as the occasional mistake. We will be grateful to anyone pointing out such errors or omissions to us, for future reference and inclusion in subsequent reprints. One thing we have not tried to do, however, is update the McFarland tome beyond its original end point, which was the year 2000. We have left the description of French *fantastique* in the 21st century to future genre historians.

Jean-Marc & Randy Lofficier

The Middle Ages
(1100-1500)

French language, and therefore French literature, first took form in the Middle Ages. After the Roman Conquest, the Gaul dialects gave way to Latin, which evolved into several Romance languages, and eventually into something called "Old French".

It is worth noting that this development was not uniform. The language remained divided into the *langue d'oil*, employed in Northern France, and the *langue d'oc*, employed in Southern France. (These terms derived from their respective expressions for *yes*.) As Northern France became politically dominant, so did the *langue d'oil*, even though the *langue d'oc* did not entirely disappear, and still survives today as Provençal or Occitan.

The first texts written in Old French appeared during the reign of Emperor Charlemagne c. 800 A.D. It was under Charlemagne's rule that the feudal ideals of knightly behavior: courtesy, generosity, modesty, loyalty to one's liege, consideration for the weak, etc., first took root. Charlemagne was a great warrior-king, fighting for Christendom against the Saracens. His reign was a time of unique political stability and economic prosperity. Finally, Charlemagne encouraged scholars and writers. All these factors combined to foster a legend-making process which, itself, gave birth to French literature.

Fantasy was virtually defined in the Middle Ages. This was a time when the supernatural was perceived as something perhaps to be preferably avoided, but still not outrageous or unbelievable. It was during the Middle Ages that the old Celtic, Frankish and Germanic myths were translated from the cultural sphere more commonly associated with religion (implying serious belief and worship) into that of popular folklore (implying belief but not worship).

The Catholic Church, as the dominant religion of the times, made sure that the old myths, since they could not be totally eradicated, would remain just that: folklore, the latter being obviously less important than religion. In some cases, such as the Arthurian Romances, it even ensured that the myths were redressed in Christian trappings.

Finally, the Middle Ages were the period during which all the various tales dealings with supernatural concepts such as angels, demons, fairies, witches and warlocks, etc. were consolidated, unified and given modern form. Concepts and characters such as Melusine, Harlequin, Oberon, Morgan Le Fey, etc. which are, today, considered an integral part of fantasy, were first given their definitive shapes at the time.

For purposes of convenience, we have divided medieval French fantasy literature into four sub-genres:

Chansons de Geste

The *Chansons de Geste* (Songs of Deeds or High Feats) were poetic sagas that began as oral literature, sung by wandering minstrels and troubadours, and were an integral part of a vast oral tradition. Starting around the 12th century, they were eventually committed to paper by pious monks working in monastic libraries. About a hundred *Chansons de Geste* are known to have existed. Most dealt with knightly epics and courtly love.

One of the earliest and most deservedly famous *Chanson de Geste* was *La Chanson de Roland* [The Song of Roland] (c. 1100), which told of the desperate fight of Knight Roland, Charlemagne's own son, against the Saracens, and his eventual doom in the Pyrenean Mountains pass of Roncevaux, after having been betrayed by the evil Ganelon. In reality, historical evidence would suggest that Roland was ambushed by Basque brigands, but no minstrel ever let truth stand in the way of a great song!

La Chanson de Roland, like most other *Chansons de Geste*, contained its usual array of supernatural phenomena: celestial visitations, etc. However, it was memorable in that it featured the first, invulnerable magical blade, Roland's sword, Durandal, as well as Roland's magical horn, Oliphant. Heroic-fantasy fans may recall that British author Michael Moorcock sent his famous hero, Elric of Melnibone, to Roncevaux to collect Durandal.

La Chanson de Roland was first "translated" into modern French in 1837 by Francisque Michel. Numerous editions and revisions followed, in 1850, 1872, 1878 and 1887. In this author's opinion, the best modern-language edition is that of Joseph Bédier (1922, revised in 1937).

By the 12th century, as Old French came into being, formally educated poets started expanding their repertoire by using dramas drawn either from classic (i.e.: Roman or Greek) sources, but also, more interestingly, from Celtic or Germanic legends, imported into France by other scholars. The fact that Latin was still the *lingua franca* of the literary elite greatly facilitated international communication. In these new Songs, Christian Miracles were replaced with pagan ones.

One such epic was the popular *Le Roman de Tristan et Iseult* [The Novel of Tristan & Ysolde], which made its first appearance circa 1170 and became an overnight success. (Bédier also provided a modern-language edition of it.) Another natural candidate for the epic treatment was the life-story of King Arthur of Britain, adapted from Geoffrey of Monmouth's 1136 historical tome, *History of the Kings of Britain*.

The most important French poet of the times was Chrétien de Troyes, who became the virtual founder of Arthurian romance. Chrétien de Troyes had already produced a number of more conventional works, such as *Erec et Enide* and *Cligès*, which reused the *Tristan and Ysolde* motif. His first Arthurian saga was *Lancelot, ou Le Chevalier à la Charette* [Lancelot, or The Knight with a Cart] (c. 1177), which related how brave knight Lancelot rescued beautiful Queen Guinevere. *Lancelot*'s success eventually led Chrétien de Troyes to write his masterpiece, *Perceval, ou le Conte du Graal* [Perceval, or The Tale of the Grail] (c. 1182).

In *Perceval*, the eponymous character was a brave but innocent knight, who discovered the accursed land of the *Roi Pêcheur* [The Fisher King, even though it should really be Sinner King], who was the guardian of the Grail and suffered from a mysterious wound that would not heal. Perceval could have healed the King and become the Grail's guardian, but missed his opportunity.

Few people even today realize that, in its original version, *Perceval* was not a Christian work at all. The Grail was not yet *Holy* and bore no relation to the latter version of the cup allegedly used by Joseph of Arimathea to gather Christ's own blood. Instead, *Perceval* drew on a variety of pagan myths and symbols. Some were clearly Celtic in nature and echoed druidic ceremonies; others were more obscure. Some scholars have theorized that *Perceval* contained Greek Mythology from the Mysteries of Eleusis, and even Middle Eastern esoteric influences taken from the cult of Mithra.

In 1215, the Roman Catholic Church held its Council of Lateran, which formally established the dogma of the Eucharist—Christ's flesh and blood being mystically present in the wafer host and wine taken during the Holy Communion. It certainly was no coincidence that, at the same time, Robert de Boron, one of Chrétien de Troyes' continuators, tied together the Arthurian legends of Lancelot and Perceval and placed them firmly within a Christian context. It was De Boron, not Chrétien de Troyes, who established the now well-known origins of the "Holy" Grail, with Joseph of Arimathea and the blood of Christ. He also added the characters of Lancelot, King Arthur, Merlin, and Morgan Le Fey, and, more generally, gave the entire saga the form that we know today.

Between 1215 and 1235, De Boron published five books: *Histoire du Saint-Graal* [The Story of the Holy Grail], *Histoire de Merlin* [The Story of Merlin], *Le Livre de Lancelot du*

Lac [The Book of Lancelot of the Lake], *La Quête du Saint-Graal* [The Quest for the Holy Grail] and *La Mort du Roi Arthur* [The Death of King Arthur] which, taken together, formed the basis for all subsequent Arthurian legends, including the later retelling by Sir Thomas Malory .

Among other *Chansons de Geste* told and/or written during the 13th century, there were three which included strong fantasy elements and deserve to be mentioned here because of the archetypes they virtually created for later genre works.

The first was *Huon de Bordeaux*, an anonymous epic in which Huon, one of Charlemagne's proud knights, met the fairy king Aubéron, whom William Shakespeare would later turn into Oberon for *A Midsummer Night's Dream*, and who was described in there as being the son of Julius Cesar and Morgan Le Fey, Cesar being remembered, in those days, only as a great, almost magical, emperor from a long-buried past. As for Morgan, or Morgane, she was originally a fairy queen named Morgue, whose origins predated that of the Arthurian legends. Aubéron gave Huon a magic ring, and a magic horn which enabled him to summon the legions of fairyland. Huon fought an evil Saracen sorcerer-king, and eventually freed and married the beautiful Esclarmonde.

Amadas et Ydoine, another anonymous epic, was a tale of thwarted love between the beautiful Ydoine, betrothed to the Count of Nevers, and her brave lover, Amadas. It featured witches and sorcery aplenty, and the mysterious character of the *Maufé*, who was either the Devil himself, or one of his Agents. The *Maufé* (a deformation of the French word *mauvais*, meaning bad or evil) was not like the crude and grotesque devils depicted until then in religious dramas. He was, on the contrary, a seductive, clever, charismatic character, imbued with evil supernatural powers, but bound by certain rules. The *Maufé* was the model for all subsequent "Princes of Darkness" types, from *Faust*'s Mephistopheles to the devil played by Jules Berry in the classic film *Les Visiteurs du Soir* [*The Devil's Envoys*; 1942].

Le Paradis de la Reine Sybille [Queen Sybil's Paradise] (c. 1200), credited to Antoine De la Salle, told the story of a knight who discovered a hidden fairyland, ruled by the beautiful Queen Sybil. The Queen and her maidens were succubae of some kind—a clue is that they periodically turn into snakes! As was often the case in such legends, the Knight could only leave the kingdom on certain days. Eventually, he did leave, but the memories of the sexual delights he experienced proved so great a temptation that he chose to return to Queen Sybil's paradise, thereby losing his eternal soul. *Le Paradis de la Reine Sybille* was the template for numerous, similar tales, such as Richard Wagner's *Tannhauser*. It also most clearly and emphatically condemned the pleasures of the flesh, more evidence of the "Christianization" of the old legends.

The *Chansons de Geste* survived throughout the centuries and, in various modernized versions, are still on French bookshelves today. Chrétien de Troyes and Robert de Boron's Arthurian stories are available in modern retellings by Jacques Boulenger and Jean Markalé. The *Huon de Bordeaux* story, as well as numerous others, were collected in a remarkable series of books, the *Contes et Légendes* imprint, written by various authors and still in print today.

Finally, other Arthurian novels, such as *Méliador* by renowned historian Jean Froissart, *Méraugis de Portlesguez* by Raoul de Houdenc, *La Demoiselle à la Mule* [The Lady with a Mule] by Païen de Maisières, *Perlesvaus, Le Livre de Caradoc, Le Chevalier à l'Épée, Hunbaut, L'Atre Périlleux, Gliglois, Le Roman de Jaufré, Blandin de Cornouaille, Les Merveilles de Rigomer* and *Le Chevalier au Papegau* have been collected in *La Légende Arthurienne*, a remarkable anthology assembled by Danielle Régnier-Bohler.

Fabliaux

Another aspect of French medieval fantasy literature were the *fabliaux*, satirical fables which relied on a tradition well-established by Aesop of using anthropomorphic animals in order to poke fun at, or criticize, the world's various ills.

The most famous of these *fabliaux* was, without a doubt, the *Roman de Renart* which chronicled the feud between sly Renart (or Renard, i.e.: the fox) and his rival, the loutish wolf Ysengrin. The animals were portrayed as inhabiting Man's world—Renart stole chickens from human farmers—but also as having a parallel society of their own, ruled by the benevolent King Noble the lion. In *Renart*, the animals were all noblemen, usually barons, and it went without saying that they were all Roman Catholics.

Renart himself was a consummate con artist and totally devoid of scruples, yet not without roguish charm. He periodically landed himself in trouble, was caught, tried, condemned, escaped, fled to his castle Maupertuis, was besieged by his enemies, etc., but, every time, he managed to outwit his foes and came out on top. Through ruse and betrayal, he even usurped Noble's throne when the King was away, fighting a Saracen army composed of exotic animals: such as camels, elephants, etc.

Le Roman de Renart was attributed to poet Pierre de Saint-Cloud who chronicled the first Renart-Ysengrin battles circa 1175. But other writers soon jumped into the act and Renart's saga grew to epic proportions. By the 14th century, *Le Roman de Renart* included over 30 new sections.

Le Roman de Renart was first assembled and put into coherent form by D.-M. Méon, using manuscripts from the 13th, 14th and 15th centuries, preserved in the Royal Library, and was published in a four-volume edition in 1826. There was also a three-volume edition published in 1881-1887. A more modern, and definitive edition is Léopold Chauveau's 315-page volume.

Poetry

French medieval poetry was lyrical, elegant and full of allegorical meanings. As such, it often employed fantasy elements as a mean of literary artifice. The *Roman de la Rose* [The Romance of the Rose] (c. 1230), by Guillaume de Lorris, which celebrated courtly love, showed a young couple venturing into a dreamland where the plucking of a rose symbolized an amorous victory.

Lesser-known works, such as the Celtic ballads of Marie de France (c. 1170), were filled with fantasy: *Lanval* featured a fairy queen; *Yonec*, a lover who turned into a bird (an earlier version of what would become the inspiration for *L'Oiseau Bleu* [The Blue Bird]); *Milon*, an enchanted ring; *Eliduc*, a magic potion; *Bisclavret*, a werewoklf.... Marie de France, who may have been a composite of several poets, was likely the first artist to have sung about the magical doom of the city of Ys, a mythical city off the coast of Brittany which was reputed to have sunk in the 5th century.

Le Jeu de la Feuillée [The Game of Leaves] (c. 1275) by Adam De la Halle was an epic poem which also featured fairy creatures and introduced the character of King Hellequin, patterned after a Germanic storm god. Hellequin was the Lord of the Wild Hunt, the Master of Spells. In the 14th century, Dante Alighieri took the character and renamed him Harlequin. In the original poem, Hellequin was madly in love with Morgue the fairy, the Morgan Le Fey or Fata Morgana of later incarnations.

In the anonymous *Le Livre de la Fontaine Périlleuse* [The Book of the Perilous Fountain] (c. 1425), a young man sought the waters of the Fountain of Life. When he peered into it, an arm made of fire came out and stabbed him. In order to be cured, he then had to undergo a series of mystic tests. The poem was demonstrably written as an allegory of the alchemical *Great Work*, and the young protagonist eventually found enlightenment when he discovered and worshipped the "Hermetic Sun". This was one of the first recorded literary works in which the frontier between the occult and fantasy was easily crossed.

The famous fairy queen *Mélusine* took her modern form from Jehan d'Arras' eponymous 1475 poem. One day of every week, the lovely bride Mélusine sought isolation in order to revert to her natural form. She begged her husband, Raimondin de Lusignan, to not try to find out her secret. Unfortunately, he did and discovered that his wife was half-human, half-reptile. This cost poor Mélusine her soul. She was forced to turn back into a winged serpent and fly away.

Religious Dramas

Classic Roman and Greek theater had all but vanished after the Fall of Rome. Serious drama was reborn during the Middle Ages, somewhat surprisingly, within the folds of the Catholic Church, which sponsored religious dramatizations of the life of Jesus or of the Saints, called *Mystères* or *Miracles*, performed at Easter and Christmas times.

The *Mysteries* and *Miracles* were first performed in Latin, then in Old French. They often took several days to perform and included spectacular stage effects. Among the most noted plays performed during the 12th, 13th and 14th centuries were: *Le Jeu d'Adam* [The Play of Adam]; *La Résurrection du Sauveur* [Our Savior's Resurrection]; *Le Jeu de Saint Nicolas* [The Play of Saint Nicolas] by Jean Bodel d'Arras; the monumental *Le Mystère de la Passion* [The Mystery of the Passion], which took four days to perform, by Arnoul Gréban,the organist and choirmaster of Notre-Dame cathedral; *Les Miracles de Théophile* [Theophile's Miracles], which contained an early variation of the Faust theme; *Les Miracles de Notre-Dame* [The Miracles of Our Lady] by Gautier de Coincy; etc.

Religious drama was eventually codified into a series of prose stories purported to be the "true stories" of the lives of the Saints, which became known as *La Légende Dorée* [The Golden Legends]. Like the *Roman de Renart*, the texts which comprised it were eventually gathered and collected c.1264 by the Dominican monk Jacques de Voragine, a.k.a. Jacques de Varazze, who later became Archbishop of Genoa. They were translated into French in 1900 by the Abbot Jean Baptiste Marie Roze in a modern edition which is still in print today.

Jacques de Voragine

La Légende Dorée

*

GF-Flammarion

LA LÉGENDE ARTHURIENNE

LE GRAAL ET LA TABLE RONDE

PERCEVAL LE GALLOIS OU LE CONTE DU GRAAL
PERLESVAUS, LE HAUT LIVRE DU GRAAL
MERLIN ET ARTHUR : LE GRAAL ET LE ROYAUME
LE LIVRE DE CARADOC
LE CHEVALIER À L'ÉPÉE
HUNBAUT
LA DEMOISELLE À LA MULE
L'ATRE PÉRILLEUX
GLIGLOIS
MÉRAUGIS DE PORTLESGUEZ
LE ROMAN DE JAUFRÉ
BLANDIN DE CORNOUAILLE
LES MERVEILLES DE RIGOMER
MELIADOR
LE CHEVALIER AU PAPEGAU

BOUQUINS

ROBERT LAFFONT

The Renaissance
(1500-1650)

The Renaissance of the 16th century was marked by the emergence of new ideas and literary trends, often as a reaction against what was perceived as the "obscurantism" of the Middle Ages.

Among the factors which contributed to the Renaissance were: the discoveries of new continents by Christopher Columbus, Vasco da Gama, Fernand Magellan, Giovanni da Verrazano and Jacques Cartier, which offered new imaginary vistas in which to locate stories; the scientific and technical discoveries of scientists such as Copernicus and Ambroise Paré; and, finally, Johannes Gutenberg's discovery of the printing press c. 1450, which made the greater circulation of literary works possible.

After the fall of Constantinople in 1453, Greek intellectuals moved to Italy, which quickly became the cultural center of the Renaissance, drawing talent from all over Europe. From the Latin word *humanitas* [culture] then came the humanists, who taught humanism, a school of thought based on the ancient Greco-Roman ideals of wisdom, tolerance and rational thought. One of foremost humanists of the times was the philosopher Erasmus who, although born in Holland, spent a considerable amount of time in France.

The Renaissance bloomed in France during the reign of King Francis I (reigned 1515-1547). As Charlemagne had done before, François 1st created a favorable environment for the development of letters, arts and sciences. He founded several scientific colleges, attracted foreign artists, such as Leonardo da Vinci, to the French Court and, more generally, gave a seal of official tolerance towards the publication of the new philosophy.

It was during the French *Renaissance* that the traditional *fantastique* derived from myths, legends and folklore split into two forms: one which continued the poetic tradition of the Middle Ages and eventually led to the *Merveilleux* and the *Contes de Fées* [Fairy Tales], and the other, the darker side of the same literary coin, dealing with witchcraft, devil worship, sorcery and, generally, all matters pertaining to the Occult, which we have labeled here Occult and Esoteric Literature.

The Merveilleux

From 1550 until 1650, a strange, almost schizophrenic, form of literary cohabitation existed between humanist philosophy, devoted to the material universe, and fantasy; between pagan influences, harking back to the Greeks, and Christian faith.

For example, the great 16th century French poet Pierre de Ronsard, founder of the literary group La Pléïade, this called as an homage to a group of seven 3rd century BC Alexandrian poets who had placed themselves under the protection of this constellation, published a number of works that would, today, be considered as fantasy.

In his earlier *Odes* (1550), Ronsard often drew heavily on the folk tales of his native Vendômois country. Then, at the peak of his literary fame, he devoted several of his more famous *Hymnes* [Hymns] (1552) to subjects such as gods and demons.

Jean-Antoine de Baïf, another member of La Pléïade, celebrated the pagan goddess Hecate and Medea.

In a remarkable poem entitled *Les Sepmaines* (1578), which may well be the first heroic fantasy-type work in French literature, Guillaume Du Bartas described the creation of the world by God in fantasy terms, including scenes of battles between angels and various monsters in the Garden of Eden.

The ensuing *Baroque* period continued to rely heavily on myths drawn from Antiquity, such as Medea, Circe, or the Witches of Thessalia, in an imitation of the increasingly successful pastoral literature coming from Italy and Spain, in which Greco-Roman myths played a strong role.

The classic novel *L'Astrée* (1607-27) by Honoré d'Urfé was obviously inspired by the prose romance of chivalry *Amadis of Gaul*, a neo-*Chanson de Geste* which had been circulating in various forms since the late 13th century, but reached its pinnacle when put together by Spanish writer Garcia Rodriguez Montalvo. *Amadis of Gaul* was originally based on myths derived from the Celtic Arthurian legends, but in its 16th century form, came to embody all the ideals of the now-vanished Age of Chivalry: a virtually invincible, handsome Christian knight who was totally loyal to his God-anointed King and terribly courtly and chaste towards his princess love. What had once been fiery, mystic, raw legend had now become a literary convention, if not a cliché. The true belief was gone; only the sense of wonder remained, the sense of what the French called the *Merveilleux*—the Marvelous.

In the same fashion, *L'Astrée*, with its druid Climante, his magic mirror and his Fountain of Truth, functioned not as a first-degree romance, but a stylized, artificially contrived romance. From *L'Astrée* to famous playwright Pierre Corneille's lesser known but classic tragedies, *Médée* (1635) and *Circé* (1675), wizards and the witches became the popular *deus ex machina* of French literature.

Raymond Lebègue, in his article "*Le Merveilleux Magique en France dans le Théâtre Baroque*" [Magical Marvelous in France in the Baroque Theater], published in the *Revue d'Histoire du Théâtre* (Jan-Mar., 1963), listed no less than seventy-five plays whin which wizards played a major part, often appearing in several plays, written by different authors.

Ismen the Wizard, for example, originally created by Le Tasse, (Torquato Tasso), also appeared in Nicolas Chrétien des Croix's *Les Amantes* [*The Lovers*] (1613). In *La Bague d'Oubli* [*The Ring of Oblivion*] (1628), Jean de Rotrou introduced the sorcerer Alcandre, who then went on to star in Gervais Bazire d'Amblainville's *Arlette* (1638). A number of Jean Racine's plays, such as *Andromaque* (1667), *Iphigénie* (1674) and *Phèdre* (1676) all borrowed elements from Greek mythology.

Operas, too, were prodigious re-users of mythology, folk tales and legends, classic dramas featuring larger-than-life deeds and exacerbated passions. They were the successors of the medieval "mystery" plays and sagas, and the precursor of modern heroic fantasy and space opera films.

Themes borrowed from classic Greco-Roman authors such as Ovid, Apuleius, Ariosto, etc. became the source of inspiration of numerous operas performed at the court of the Louis XIV, the Sun King. Amongst the best authors of fantasy librettos, we have singled out Philippe Quinault (who wrote for composer Jean-Baptiste Lully), d'Albaret, who wrote *Scylla and Glaucus* (1746), Pierre-Joseph Bernard, Louis de Cahusac, Louis Fuzelier, Adrien-Joseph Le Valois d'Orville, Jean-François Marmontel, Antoine Houdar de la Motte, Antoine Danchet and the Abbott Pellegrin, who wrote for composer Jean-Philippe Rameau.

Occult & Esoterism

Using mythical witches was certainly safer than using the real-life witches whose trials were leaving a blazing trail throughout Christendom.

During the Middle Ages, there was generally no difference between a magician and a sorcerer. Merlin, Vivian and Morgan were each considered on their own merits, and their connections, if any, with Christian Dogma were loose and informal. Religious persecution began in the 13th century when the Roman Catholic Church formally defined a sorcerer as a heretic who obtained his powers from a pact with Satan, while a magician was someone practicing the ancient divining arts.

The former was deemed to be anathema and was usually condemned to be burned at the stake, while the latter, while held in dubious regard, was not automatically assumed to have diabolical connections.

In the early part of the 14th century, French King Philip IV the Fair (1268-1314) used trumped up accusations of witchcraft and sorcery to justify the elimination of the powerful Order of the Knights Templar, burning their Grand-Master Jacques de Molay at the stake in 1314. Then, the Black Death struck (1347-1351), which both strengthened and weakened the Church. It strengthened the Church because it seemingly justified its persecution of witches and heretics, and gave it more temporal power; however, spiritually, it weakened it because it revealed its sheer powerlessness before the plague, costing it many of the minds and souls of the common folk. A number of grief-stricken people began to turn away from the powerless Church, and secretly started to worship revamped avatars of old gods, such as the Horned One (which was not Satan, the Fallen Angel, but was treated by the Church as such), or at least looked towards them for succor.

No one will ever know the actual number of real "witches", but undeniably, the pressure was growing and the Church had to react to prevent what it saw as an unacceptable return to pagan worship, or worse. Big scale witch hunts therefore started in the 15th century. Joan of Arc (b. 1412), deemed guilty of sorcery, was burned at the stake in 1431. Gilles de Rais (b. 1404), who later provided inspiration for Charles Perrault's infamous "Blue-Beard", was also tried for sorcerous practices and executed in 1440.

Finally, in 1484, the newly appointed Pope Innocent VIII (1432-1492) published his famous bull, *Summis Desiderantes Affectibus* [Desiring with the Most Profound Anxiety]. In it, the Pope complained that the work of two fanatical, sadistic Dominican inquisitors, Heinrich Kramer and Jakob Sprenger lacked support because—a surprisingly candid admission!—neither the clergy nor the laity were convinced of the extent and seriousness of the "crime" of witchcraft! The Pope went on to warn everyone to support the madmen's investigations, or else "upon him shall fall the wrath of God Almighty." *Summis Desiderantes Affectibus* had the nefarious result of fastening on European powers the duty of fighting the Devil and eradicating witchcraft, justifying the most merciless persecutions, for at least the next two centuries.[1]

So while Humanism and its enlightened creed was spreading throughout Europe in the 16th century, another, darker, evil storm was brewing. In 1486, the same Jakob Sprenger wrote and published the infamous *Malleus Maleficarum*, a.k.a. the *Hammer of Witches*, undoubtedly the most important and sinister work on demonology ever written. While this book was not considered a work of fiction by his author or his readers, it nevertheless belongs squarely in this study to the extent that it catalogued and codified all magical practices known at the time.

From a purely literary standpoint, like any contemporary best-seller, the *Malleus Maleficarum* spawned a large number of imitations. Among French works directly or indirectly deriving from it were:

Jean Bodin's *La Démonomanie des Sorciers* [Demonology of Sorcerers] (1580), *De la Démonomanie* [Of Demonomania] (1587) and *Le Fléau des Démons et ses Sorciers* [The Scourge of Demons and Sorcerers] (1616).

Henri Boguet's *Discours Exécrables des Sorciers* [Awful Discourses of Sorcerers] (1603).

Pierre de Lancre's *Tableau de l'Inconstance des Mauvais Anges* [Table of the Inconstancies of Fallen Angels] (1613) and *L'Incrédulité et Mescréance du Sortilège* [Incredulity and Unbelief of Spells] (1622).

As unpalatable as the fact may be, these books, far more real and awful than H. P. Lovecraft's fictional *Necronomicon*

---

[1] Contemporary chroniclers noted that, towards the end of his life, Innocent VIII was kept alive by blood transfusions from young boys and was thus responsible for the deaths of three lads.

or Marvel's *Darkhold*, are among the true ancestors of today's modern horror fiction.

Fortunately, occult literature was not all demons and witches. The tradition of esoteric writings, originated by the medieval alchemists, remained strong. There was a tenuous line between the non-fictional writings of these proto-scientists, and the transparent, symbolical fictional allegories that they often used to hide their knowledge, in plain sight as it were, and to avoid persecution. We have already mentioned *Le Livre de la Fontaine Périlleuse* as an example of this approach.

Alchemy likely originated with Greek, Egyptian and Middle Eastern scientific traditions brought into Europe through Italy or through the Moorish Conquest of Spain during the 8th century. Indeed, words like elixir, alcohol and alembic all have Arabic roots.

The University of Montpellier, in the South of France, was established in 1181, and became the cradle of alchemy. Among its students and/or teachers were such notorious alchemists as Albert le Grand, a.k.a. Albertus Magnus (1193-1280), who wrote five books about alchemy, including the treatise *De Alchemia*; Raymond Lulle (1235- 1315), who wrote *Ars Magna*; Arnauld de Villeneuve (1240-1313), who wrote *Le Grand Rosaire* [The Great Rosary]; Roger Bacon (1214-1294); etc. The University of Montpellier also counted at one time or another Erasmus, François Rabelais, and even the notorious Nostradamus (1503-1566) among its staff.

Another notorious alchemist of the times was the legendary "gold-maker," Nicolas Flamel, who wrote *Explication des Figures Hiéroglyphiques* and whose mysterious life has since then provided much grist for the fictional mill. Eventually, with such proto-scientists as Paracelsius (1493-1541) and Agrippa de Nettesheim (1486-1535), a branch of alchemy turned into regular science, like medicine and chemistry, while the other remained hidden in the domain of the occult.

A popular misconception was that alchemists sought the secret of the philosopher's stone, which was said to have the power to transmute base metal—usually lead—into gold. The reality was somewhat more complex. The alchemist was dedicated to the *Grand Oeuvre*, a life-long spiritual and chemical process, whose end-result was the production of an elixir of long life. The so-called philosopher's stone was, by all accounts, a reddish powder dubbed "projection powder". A small portion of it, wrapped in paper, was thrown into molten lead and, according to various witnesses, did turn it into gold.

The fact that lead has an atomic weight of 82 in the periodic table of elements, while mercury (a vital element in the alchemical process) is 80 and gold is 79 gives cause to wonder. How could the alchemists, in an age where earth, water, air and fire were considered "elements", connect these three metals together, and imagine methods of transmutation not requiring massive energy bombardments? Today, we would call their methods cold fusion.

In any event, the "philosopher's stone" was but the final test, a chemical proof, in the process leading to the true goal: the elixir of long life. Whether alchemy was fact or fantasy may never be fully known or understood; however, it is worthy to note that, in an age where the average life span was 38 years, all the above-mentioned alchemists lived to reach their 80s.

Marcelle et Georges HUISMAN

CONTES ET LÉGENDES
DU MOYEN-AGE
FRANÇAIS

FERNAND NATHAN, ÉDITEUR - PARIS

LE CABINET DES FÉES

TOME I vol. 1
Contes de
Madame d'Aulnoy

The Age of Enlightenment
(1650-1800)

The 18th century was known to French historians as the *Siècle des Lumières* [Century of Lights], or the Age of Enlightenment. Starting with the accession to the throne in 1643 of the Sun King Louis XIV, France entered a period of political, artistic and scientific *grandeur*, before settling into the decadent reigns of Louis XV (1710-1774) and Louis XVI (1754-1793).

The Age of Enlightenment could be arguably said to have started with René Descartes in 1637 with his *Le Discours de la Méthode*, or in 1687 when Isaac Newton published his *Mathematical Principles of Natural Philosophy*, the basis for a comprehensive, mathematical description of the Universe, which demonstrated the power of science over the material world.

The prevailing modes of Enlightenment thinking were rational thought and skepticism. Throughout the use of reason, Man would master nature and himself. Nothing exemplified this better than Denis Diderot's massive, seventeen-volume *Encyclopedia* (1751-72), a sum of knowledge whose advocated purpose was to disseminate information, reduce superstition and improve the human condition.

Religious persecution and witch hunts finally stopped in 1670, after the personal intervention of Louis XIV, who overruled the local Parliament of the city of Rouen, in an affair where five hundred persons were under suspicion of witchcraft.

In literature, the *baroque* was eventually replaced by classicism during the reign of the Sun King, with its roster of great playwrights. The so-called "Quarrel of the Ancients and the Moderns" (c. 1690) then freed French writers from the need to imitate the literature of antiquity.

The Fairy Tales

Baroque (whether in the form of the novel, the theater or even the operas) was the link between the *Merveilleux* of the Renaissance and the more formalized *Contes de Fées*, or Fairy Tales, of the Enlightenment.

The undeniable popularity of the genre was, in great part, attributable to the fact that Fairy Tales were safe; they did not imperil the soul—a serious concern for a nation which had just come out of an era of great religious persecution—and they appropriately reflected the *grandeur* of the Sun King's reign.

The great precursor in the genre was the Baroness Marie-Catherine d'Aulnoy who, in 1690, introduced in her rambling novel *Histoire d'Hyppolite, Comte de Douglas* [Story of Hippolyte, Count of Douglas] a fairy tale entitled *L'Île de la Félicité* [The Island of Felicity].

Then, in 1695, Marie-Jeanne L'Héritier de Villandon included several fairy tales in her *Oeuvres Mêlées* [Mixed Works].[2] A relative of the better-known Charles Perrault, she was among the most important creators of the fairy tales genre. She originally published four stories in 1696, a year before *Tales of Mother Goose*, then the classic *La Tour ténébreuse et les Jours Lumineux* [The Dark Tower and the Luminous Days published in 1705, as well as an essay written in the form of a letter, in which she casts more light on the detail of her thinking, the process by which the tales came to be written and the various things that she was attempting to achieve. Her stories may well be the source material that inspired *Cinderella* and *Rumpelstiltskin*, amongst others, and are not an adaptation of

---

[2] In *The Robe of Sincerity*, Black Coat Press, ISBN 978-1-61227-732-5.

folklore, but an attempt to recycle literary inventions attributed to the medieval troubadours.

It was in 1697 that Charles Perrault appeared on the scene. Until then, Perrault had been a well-known literary figure, a man who was a champion of sciences, and the author of a decisive article in the so-called "Quarrel of the Ancients and Moderns" (on the side of the latter). Perrault released, first under his son's name, Pierre Perrault Darmancourt (also a folklorist) a book entitled *Histoires ou Contes du Temps Passé* [Histories and Tales of Past Times] which was soon reprinted as *Contes de ma Mère l'Oie* [Tales of Mother Goose]. In it, Perrault had collected a number of popular folk tales and legends, such as *Cendrillon* [Cinderella], *La Belle au Bois Dormant* [Sleeping Beauty], *Peau d'Âne* [Donkey Skin], *Le Petit Chaperon Rouge* [Little Red Riding Hood], *Barbe-Bleue* [Blue-Beard], *Le Chat Botté* [Puss in Boots], and many others. These ancient stories were retold in a style free from affectation, and were always accompanied by a moral, taking a leaf from the popular *Fables* of Jean de La Fontaine. The book proved incredibly successful and immediately spawned numerous imitators. It is worth noting that, unlike some of them, Perrault had not softened or "prettified" his fairy tales. His yarns preserved the cruelty, some would say savagery, and goriness of the original tales. In his stories, sorcery was still very real. A number of his literary successors, on the other hand, chose to emphasize nicer sentiments and tinseltown-like magic.

After Perrault, Baroness Marie-Catherine d'Aulnoy followed suit with a remarkable, three-volume collection simply entitled *Contes de Fées* [Fairy Tales] (1698), and then *Contes Nouveaux ou Les Fées à la Mode* [New Tales or Fashionable Fairies] (1698).[3] Unlike Perrault, Madame d'Aulnoy used her tales for satirical purposes, deliberately aiming them at a more adult readership. As a result, her stories were more complex

---

[3] Published as *Tales of the Fays* (2 volumes), Black Coat Press, ISBNs 978-1-61227-836-0 and 978-1-61227-837-7.

and sophisticated. Her best-remembered tales are *L'Oiseau Bleu* [The Blue Bird], *La Chatte Blanche* [The White Cat] and *Le Nain Jaune* [The Yellow Dwarf], which spawned a popular board-and-card game. *L'Oiseau Bleu* introduced one of the very first "Prince Charmings" in the world of fairy tales.

From the 1690s onwards, Madame d'Aulnoy was an active member of a literary salon where she and the Comtesse de Murat (see below) became the most prolific contributors to the new genre of the *contes de fees*, which they helped invent, shape and develop. Like almost all of the other members of her coterie, she became a renegade female aristocrat writing tales for the select consumption of other renegade female aristocrats about a world the corrupt glamour of which they understood only too well, with a depth of sarcasm that the innocent could not be expected to comprehend.

One should regard these women as significant writers of Decadent fantasy, and one wonders what they might have done had they been allowed to continue with their work. Given that both had extraordinary imaginative range, it is hard to imagine that they would have run out of inspiration, had they not been violently stopped in their tracks. We have to be grateful that they contrived to publish as much as they did during their brief window of opportunity, leaving behind fugitive material that could be recovered once the worst of the repression had blown over.

Considered separately Madame d'Aulnoy and the Comtesse de Murat were great writers of imaginative fiction, but as a competitive collective, they are unique in literary history, and it is as part of that collective endeavor that Madame d'Aulnoy is fully entitled to her classic status today. They were the first to virtually define the boundaries of modern fantasy. After them, magicians, ogres, dragons, dwarves and fairies became fully integrated in the realms of fantasy.

Fairy tales was a genre in which many women excelled. Between 1697 and 1702, some of the best authors included:

Catherine Bernard, one of the originators of the genre, with *The Rose-Bush Prince, Riquet with the Crest*[4] and *The Origins of the Fays* (c. 1696)[5]

Countess Henriette-Julie de Castelnau de Murat, with *Les Contes de Fées* [The Fairy Tales] (1697) and *Les Nouveaux Contes des Fées* [The New Fairy Tales] (1698).[6] The author's early stories are set in the time of the fays, a remote mythical past, but her later ones take place contemporaneously in countries that are only separated pseudo-geographically from France. Her works are remarkable for the imaginative extravagance of their plots; the superbly surreal depiction of magical civilizations, the extreme trials to which she subjects her heroes and heroines, caused by jealous rivals intent on breaking the amorous bond between them, and their often deliberately atypical conclusions.

Charlotte-Rose Caumont de La Force, with *Les Fées: Contes des Contes* [The Fairies: Tales of Tales] (1698).[7] Of all the pioneering writers of *contes de fées*, the author is perhaps the one who took the greatest imaginative license from the freedom to make arbitrary inventions and narrative moves. Her tales tell a story that is very different from the historical fantasies built on Perrault's moralistic tales for children. The morals attached to her tales are certainly not aimed at children. In fact, what distinguishes her tales from those of her most famous contemporaries is their evident moral unease. By far the most famous of her tales is "*Persinette*" which was plagiarized by Friedrich Schultz, who retitled it "*Rapunzel*" (1790).

---

[4] In *The Queen of the Fays*, Black Coat Press, ISBN 978-1-61227-814-8

[5] Black Coat Press, ISBN 978-1-61227-821-6.

[6] Published as *The Palace of Vengeance*, Black Coat Press, ISBN 978-1-61227-774-5.

[7] Published as *The Land of Delights*, Black Coat Press, ISBN 978-1-61227-760-8.

Comtesse D.L., with *La Tyrannie des Fées Détruites* [The Tyranny of the Fays Abolished] (1703).[8] The mysterious Comtesse disappeared from view, censored out of history, and to this day, she has only been replaced in the official record by a phantom who probably originated as a spelling mistake. In her own peculiar fashion, however, she was a heroine. Her story's representation of marriage as a matter of innocent young women falling into the brutal hands of disgusting Ogres who abuse them is only par for the course, but what is unusual is the conclusion, in which the bold Prince, eager to do battle against the monsters guarding the cave where his beloved princess is being held captive, is told to put away his sword, this particular rescue being women's work. When the rescue is complete, the prince is graciously permitted to continue adoring the princess, provided that he never lays a finger on her, while she enjoys a perfect bliss with her steadfast female best friend, under the tutelage of their benign protectress, the fay Clementine.

Several men also left their mark in the genre included:

Chevalier Louis de Mailly, with *Les Illustres Fées* [The Illustrious Fairies] (1698),[9] which showed how the fairy tales quickly became suited to very different narrative purposes.

Jean de Préchac, with *Contes moins Contes que les Autres, Sans Paragon et la Reine des Fées* [Tales Less Talish Than Others, Without Paragon and Queen of Fairies] (1698),[10] which deliberately subvert not merely their narrative strategy, but also their entire mythology, and are allegories of French history as seen through the prism of faerie.

Marie-Antoinette Fagnan, with Kanor (1750), *Minet-Bleu et Louvette* (1752) et *Le Miroir des Princess Orientales* [The Mirror of Oriental Princesses] (1755),[11] which demon-

---

[8] Black Coat Press, ISBN 978-1-61227-792-9.
[9] In *The Queen of the Fays*, q.v.
[10] In *The Queen of the Fays*, q.v.
[11] Published as *The Enchanter's Mirror*, Black Coat Press, ISBN 978-1-61227-820-9.

strates that the fantastic can be a useful instrument in the advancement of Enlightenment, because rather than in spite of its absurdity. The author's sardonic narrative points out the absurdity of the fairy tales, and emphasizes that the age of the fays, if ever there was one, reached its twilight long before history became possible. Her work as a whole asserts that fays are not, and never could be, up to the task of providing miracles, because the inevitably corrupting effects of their power would always lead them to indifference toward human suffering, if not to the malevolence of causing it. That, rather than any scientific skepticism relating to the workability of magic, is the Enlightenment that hammered the nails into the coffin of the genre, and although the final nail had yet to be added, that coffin was already sealed by 1755.

Among other writers who made a contribution to the genre were the renowned Jean-Jacques Rousseau, Swedish diplomat Count Carl Gustaf Tessin, Charles Duclos and François-Augustin de Paradis de Moncrif, two members of the French Academy, and the exiled defrocked nun Marianne-Agnès Falques, who assisted William Beckford on *Vathek*.[12]

As the *contes de fées* suffered a decline in fashionability in the 1750s, they began to rely on hybridization with Oriental and Medieval fantasies. The tales continued to be replete with fays, ogres, magic swords and other motifs, but they also revolved around a series of moral dilemmas, provided with fanciful magically-aided resolutions, although reflecting real philosophical debates of the times.

Not coincidentally, the classic *Thousand and One Nights* was first "translated" into French at that time, with some stories quite possibly having been made up from thin or nonexistent sources, as no earlier Arabic manuscripts of *Aladdin* and *Ali-Baba* are known to exist. Its "author/translator" was Antoine Galland who, from 1704 to 1717, increased both the

---

[12] All in *The Origins of the Fays*, Black Coat Press, ISBN 978-1-61227-821-6.

popular appeal of these fantasy tales and their sense of disconnection from reality.

As was the case with the *Féeries*, the Oriental Fantasy tradition created by Galland was continued with much success by a number of imitators, who all claimed to have "translated" other "Oriental" collections, such as:

François Petis de la Croix, with *Les Mille et Un Jours* [The Thousand And One Days] (1710-12).

Abbott Jean-Paul Bignon, with *Les Aventures d'Abdalla, Fils d'Hanif* [The Adventures of Abdallah, Son of Hanif] (1712-14).

Chevalier Louis de Mailly again, with *Voyage et les Aventures de Trois Princes de Serendib* [Voyage & Adventures of the Three Princes from Serendib] (1719).

Thomas-Simon Gueulette, with *Les Mille et Un Quarts d'Heures* [The Thousand and One Quarters of an Hour] (1723), *Les Mille et Une Heures* [The Thousand and One Hours] (1759) and *Les Mille et Une Soirées* [The Thousand and One Evenings] (1765).

In the same vein were the *Arlequinades*, plays featuring famous characters from the *Comedia Dell'Arte*, many of which incorporated the popular fantasy concepts of the times. In addition to the already mentioned Nolant de Fatouville's *Arlequin, Empereur de la Lune* [Harlequin, Emperor of the Moon] (1684), we shall mention several other titles including some by the popular playwright and novelist Alain-René Lesage such as *Arlequin, Roi de Serendib* [Harlequin, King of Serendib] (1713), *Arlequin Mahomet* (1714), and *L'Île des Amazones* [Amazon Island] (1718). Lesage is better remembered today for his three-volume, historical swashbuckling novel, *Gil Blas de Santillane* (1715, 1724, 1735).

To each action, a reaction: in *Zadig* (1747), Voltaire mocked his contemporaries' predilection for the *Féeries,* while making use of the same literary devices.

After a twenty-or-so years' pause, a second wave of fairy tales hit the market in the mid-1700s, this time written by authors such as:

Catherine de Lintot,, whose stories *Timandre and Bleuette, Prince Sincere* and *Tendrebrun et Constance* (1735)[13] show a marked evolution in the genre, each being more substantial, and more imaginatively innovative than its predecessor. Although they clearly attempt to take up where Madame d'Aulnoy and the Comtesse de Murat had been forced to leave off, in terms of their imaginative extravagance, their use of metamorphoses and their quirky employment of allegory exhibit a further development in the direction of the calculatedly absurd and the surreal. These are not the only works of the period to extrapolate its licensed disorder to the chaotic brink of surrealism, but they do so more self-consciously than most. The stories gathered herein provide an intriguing kaleidoscopic pattern and can justly be reckoned to be more than the sum of their parts.

Marie-Madeleine de Lubert,[14] whose first fantastic tale, published in 1737, was the striking original *Tecserion* in which the eponymous king of the Land of Ostriches is madly in love with Belzamire, Princess of Flowers, who herself dotes on the King's nephew, Melidor. The story is replete with elaborate descriptions of strange societies, including one located on Venus. The fascination extravagantly displayed in her stories with the metamorphoses of humans into animals is reflected in the ambiguous naming of realms and individuals. Such metamorphoses are a common motif within the genre, but no other writer ever deployed it with the same intensity and fascination as this author. Both *Princess Camion* and *Prince Frozen and Princess Sparkling* (1743) strike a better balance between surreal extravagance and narrative discipline, but remain flamboyant and intent on defying conventional expectations. There is justice in the fact that *Princess Camion* is now her best known work by virtue of the availability online

---

[13] In *Funestine*, Black Coat Press, ISBN 978-1-61227-812-4.
[14] *Princess Camion*, Black Coat Press, ISBN 978-1-61227-796-7.

of a video of a 2014 dramatization by a French theater company.

Comte Anne Claude Philippe de Caylus, was one of the major writers of the "second wave" of fairy tales produced in the 1730s and 1740s, when the publication of unlicensed works became far too abundant for effective suppression by the authorities. He displayed a flair for the bizarre that continually edged into the surreal, and never entirely forsook the spirit of parody in which he had commenced. His tales collected in *Les Féeries Nouvelles* [New Fairy Tales] (1741), *Les Contes orientaux* [Oriental Tales] (1743) and *Cinq contes de fees* [Five Fairy Tales] (1745),[15] expand on the notion that the fays have a council which regulates their activity and Faerie comes to refer to the polity of the fays, a kind of parallel world in which fays and other supernatural beings live. His collection of tales set in a land where faerie has determined the people must change sex every year on their birthday also aspires to the status of a *conte philosophique*. The real strength of his longer stories lies in their many phantasmagorical elements.

Abbott Joseph de La Porte penned the *Bibliothèque des Fées et des Génies* [Library of Fairies and Djinns] (1765), and even encyclopedist Denis Diderot tackled the genre.

But the one author with the most long-lasting impact was the talented Jeanne-Marie Leprince de Beaumont, whose classic *La Belle et la Bête* [Beauty and the Beast] (1757) has transcended the ages. Madame Leprince de Beaumont authored forty collections of tales (dubbed *"Magasins"*, or Stores), published in London between 1750 and 1780. *La Belle et la Bête* was, itself, based on an earlier tale by Gabrielle-Suzanne Barbot de Villeneuve, included in her collection *Les Contes Marins ou La Jeune Américaine* [Sea Stories or The Young American Girl] (1740).[16]

---

[15] *The Impossible Enchantment*, Black Coat Press, ISBN 978-1-61227-809-4.
[16] *Beauty and the Beast * The Naiads*, Black Coat Press, ISBN 978-1-61227-626-7.

The *Beauty and the Beast* by Madame de Villeneuve was first published in 1740 and later abridged and rewritten by Madame Leprince de Beaumont.The main interests of the original tale lie two sections, one in which the Beast explains how he came to be transformed and why it was forced to act as he did in regard to the Beauty; and the other in which the fay who contrived his liberation from his curse explains how and for what motives an evil rival placed her in that elaborate necessity. This original account of the organization and politics of the world of Faerie is of considerable interest, as well as completing the explanatory schema of the enigmatic fundamental tale.

The Naiads, published 100 years after Madame de Villeneuve's death, is one of the earliest fantasy novels. It is set in a distant past in a fictitious realm with a religion based on elemental spirits. While it uses the stock motifs of the fairy tale, featuring a Prince Perfect who falls in love with a shepherdess, unaware that she is really a Princess, as well as a wicked stepmother and an ugly sister bent on persecuting the beleaguered heroine, it also looks behind those motifs and provide them with elaborate explanatory schemas, such as the strange story of the Mill of Misfortune and the revelation of the Prince's true identity by the Gnome Queen.

Nicolas-Edmé Restif de la Bretonne also contributed to the genre with *Les Contes Bleus* published in *Le Nouvel Abeilard* (1778-89).[17] This volume contains two fantasy tales, "*Les Quatre belles et les quatre bêtes*" [The Four Beauties and the Four Beasts] and "*Le Demi-Coq*" [The Demicock], both featuring the character of the Enchantress Ouroucoucou. Written between 1775 and 1785, they are fascinating examples of a particular phase in the evolution of fantasy fiction, and of one exceptional author's contribution to that progress.

In the four-volume *Les Veill. es du Marais ou Histoire du grand Prince Oribeau Roi de Mommonie, au pays d'Evinland*

---

[17] In *The Four Beauties and the Four Beasts*, Black Coat Press, ISBN 978-1-61227-602-1.

& *de la Vertueuse Princesse Oribelle de Lagenie* [The Story of the Great Prince Oribeau, King of Mommonia, in the country of Evinland, and the Virtuous Princess Oribelle of Lagenia] (1785),[18] Restif pretends having found a tale in the "ancient annals" of Ireland, one "recently translated by Nicholas Donneraill of the County of Cork, descendant of the author," In addition to narrating the educational journeys of Prince Oribeau and his mentor O'Barbo, the book features three separate fairy tales, "*Mellusine*," "*Sireneh*" and "*The Fay Ouroucoucou*," connecting the genealogy of the fay to the imaginary history of the story, and the known history of the world, in a fashion that is as ambitious as it is ambiguous. The book also provides a detailed account of the metaphysics of Faerie, explaining its location and its contiguity with the perceived world. "*Mellusine*" and "*Sireneh*" are transfigurations of well-known legends, while "*The Fay Ouroucoucou*" is an allegorical apologue similar to the dream stories of Louis-Sébastien Mercier.

This overabundance of material eventually led an enterprising publisher, the Chevalier Charles-Joseph de Mayer, to gather the best tales of the times in a prodigious, forty-one volume anthology entitled *Le Cabinet des Fées* [The Fairies' Cabinet], published in Amsterdam and Geneva between 1785 and 1789. *Le Cabinet* thus has the honor of being the first specialized fantasy imprint ever published.

Jacques Cazotte, who had started as a writer of fairy tales such as *La Patte du Chat* [The Cat's Paw] (1741) and *Les Mille et Une Fadaises* [A Thousand and One Silly Stories] (1742), soon tired of the increasingly precious and effete *Féeries* of latter years, and eventually ended up writing much darker tales such as *Le Diable Amoureux* [The Devil in Love] (1772) (see below). In his *Ollivier*, a poem written in 1773, the inhabitants of an island who lost the power of speech use music to express themselves.

---

[18] *The Story of the Great Prince Oribeau*, Black Coat Press, ISBN 978-1-61227-601-4.

In this fashion, the literary evolution of the *Féeries* paralleled that of French Royalty, with the decadence and corruption of Louis XV replacing the aristocratic grandeur of Louis XIV. Cazotte well embodied the transition between the *Contes de Fées* and a darker and grimmer *fantastique*.

Eventually, the French Revolution came and, in an act tantamount to a literary execution, guillotined the heads of, if not the fairies and the little people, but many of the people who had become so much associated with this *Ancien Régime* genre.

Occult, Esoterism & Proto-fantastique

Even in the Age of Enlightenment, there were those who strenuously opposed the scientific and "positive" spirits of the times.

As the spiritual influence of the Catholic Church waned, thinkers dreamt of new universal faiths. Many of these based their thinking on occult knowledge handed (or allegedly handed) down through the ages, from the far-flung Orient to the Knights Templars and, finally, to the Freemasons and the Rosicrucians who flourished during the Enlightenment.

The line between proto-scientists like Franz Mesmer (1734-1815), real philosophers like Emanuel Swedenborg (1688-1772), "illuminists" like Louis-Claude de Saint-Martin, the author of *L'Homme de Désir* [The Man of Desire] (1790), in which a man reached total unity with the universe, and more mysterious figures such as the notorious alchemist/seer Count de Saint-Germain (1710-1784?) and his Masonic disciple, Giuseppe Balsamo, a.k.a. Cagliostro (1743-1795), was indeed a fragile and argumentative one.

The impact of these philosophers on the *fantastique* was, nevertheless, unquestionable, as their ideas acted as the starter which inflamed the imagination of many writers. Eventually, as had been the case during the Middle Ages when religious concepts slowly evolved into fantasy, a number of esoteric theories and writings were bowdlerized and trivialized to become merely adjuncts of the *fantastique*.

This transition was perfectly illustrated by the fact that writer Alexandre Dumas used both Saint-Germain and Cagliostro as fictional characters in his novels, *Joseph Balsamo* and *Le Collier de la Reine* [The Queen's Necklace].

Savinien de Cyrano de Bergerac's letters, *Pour et Contre les Sorciers* [For and Against Sorcerers] (1663), made fictional use of real-life alchemists.

In 1670, the Abbott Nicolas-Pierre-Henri de Montfaucon de Villars published the thinly disguised occult fiction, *Le Comte de Gabalis* [The Count of Gabalis] sub-titled *Entretiens sur les Sciences Secrètes* [Conversations about Secret Sciences]. Interestingly, the latter was reprinted in 1788 by Charles-Georges-Thomas Garnier in his *Voyages Imaginaires* imprint, proving again how thin the delineation between the genres was. Having disclosed secret knowledge allegedly led to the Villars' murder by Rosicrucians in 1675.

In 1707, Alain-René Lesage penned a famous play about the demon Asmodeus, *Le Diable Boîteux* [The Lame Devil], inspired by a Spanish novel by Luis Velez de Guevara.

In 1731, the Abbott Jean Terrasson wrote *Séthos, Histoire ou Vie Tirée des Monuments, Anecdotes de l'Ancienne Égypte* [Sethos, Stories and Life Drawn from Monuments & Anecdotes from Ancient Egypt], whose pseudo-Egyptian and occult themes were later plagiarized by Mozart himself for his famous opera *The Magic Flute* (1791), which also incorporated the composer's Masonic beliefs and other Masonic imagery.

One of the most interesting esoteric novels of the times was *Le Diable Amoureux* [The Devil in Love] (1772) by Jacques Cazotte, sub-titled "*un roman fantastique*" [a novel of the *fantastique*] perhaps the first time in literary history that a work had been so clearly labeled. That alone marked it as one of the most important precursors in the genre. Its hero, Alvaro, a young Spanish nobleman, conjures up the Devil who assumes the shape of Biondetta, a seemingly innocent, beautiful young woman. Biondetta eventually succeeds in drawing Alvaro into her bed, at which point she reverts to her true form, that of a hideous demon. However, thanks to his strong faith and subsequent confession, Alvaro saves his soul from eternal damnation.

Le Diable Amoureux was truly the first modern French horror novel. In it, the supernatural was not treated as a phantasmagory, or for satirical or philosophical purposes. It was intended to be real and to induce fear in the reader. Even though Cazotte was not a member of any occult societies, *Le Diable Amoureux* nevertheless drew much attention from occult circles because of its mystic and esoteric contents. Indeed, an 1845 reprinting was prefaced at great length by noted occultist/writer Gérard de Nerval.

Another work in the same vein was *Vathek*, a novel written directly into French in 1787 by English-born writer William Beckford. A Byronesque figure steeped in occult knowledge and sexual perversions, the author allegedly wrote his novel non-stop in three days and two nights in a state of trance prefiguring the Surrealists' automatic writing. *Vathek* told the story of the damnation of the eponymous Caliph who succumbs to the charms of the Giaour, a sorcerer ogre, and ends up worshipping the Oriental demon Eblis. Vathek is eventually fated to suffer eternal damnation, his heart forever ablaze in his chest.

Other examples of the proto-*fantastique* worth mentioning were:

La Poupée [The Doll] (1747), by Jean Galli de Bibbiéna, in which a porcelain doll turns into a young woman.

Valérie (1792), by Jean-Pierre Claris de Florian, in which the eponymous heroine is a ghost.

That same year, Louis-Claude de Saint-Martin penned *Le Crocodile, ou La Guerre du bien et du mal, arrivée sous le règne de Louis XV: poème epiquo-magique en 102 chants* (1792),[19] a brilliant epic, one of those rare books of which one

---

[19] *The Crocodile*, Black Coat Press, ISBN 978-1-61227-568-0.

can say that no one ever wrote anything else like it. The eponymous "Crocodile" is an attempted saboteur of the Divine Plan, an instrument of the Adversary, who claims to have created and shaped the universe—but who is, after all, a liar. As for the divinity, He remains invisible, but is described as a jeweler whose wife supervises a Society of Independents, the members of which never meet but are always in session. Add to these concepts a plague of books, which reduces human knowledge to a soggy pulp; the sunken city of Atalante, where everything stopped dead at the moment of its submersion; and the fact that the ultimate hope of a beleaguered Paris in the face of diabolical catastrophe is an aging Jew armed with a little box, and the cocktail is, to say the least, original and appealing to the connoisseurs of the bizarre.

Finally, in 1813, the very strange *Le Manuscrit Trouvé à Saragosse* [Ms. Found in Saragosa] was published in Paris. It did not properly belong to the *Roman Noir* genre so popular at the time, and reviewed in our next chapter, being more like a work of proto-*fantastique* (hence its inclusion here). Like *Vathek*, it was written directly into French by a non-French writer, the Polish count and scientist Jan Potocki. In it, a young captain stops at a Spanish inn and hears tales-within-tales of horrific nature. *Le Manuscrit* features a pair of sisters who are either vampires or succubae, as well as an assortment of ghosts and demons and the character of the Wandering Jew which by then had been popularized by Lewis' *The Monk* (1796). It also virtually created the archetypes of bandits living in secret underground caverns, and gypsies being the practitioners of contemporary versions of the medieval witches' Sabbaths, which would later become perennially popular staples of works of pulp fiction by 19th century authors. Paradoxically, *Le Manuscrit* featured another modern characteristic: its macabre imagery was contrasted by the author's deliberate attempt (through his hero) to find rational explanations for his horrible adventures, such as drug-induced nightmares, before diving again mercilessly into the murky waters of the *fantastique*.

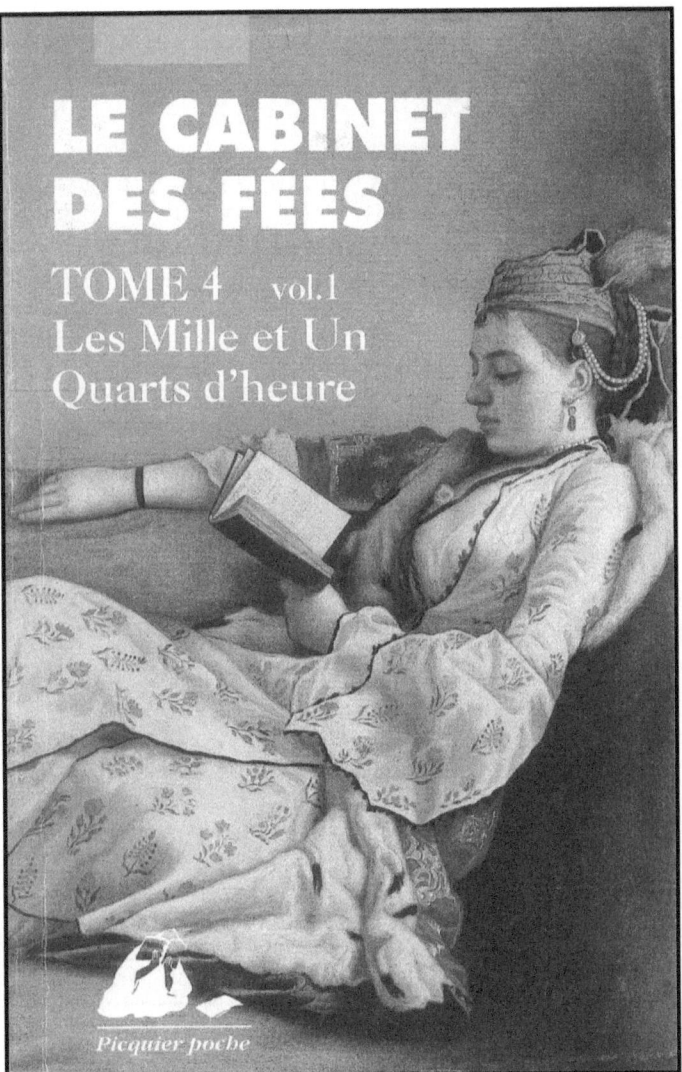

LE CABINET DES FÉES

TOME 4   vol.1
Les Mille et Un
Quarts d'heure

Picquier poche

EUGÈNE SUE

LES MYSTÈRES DE PARIS

RODOLPHE
le justicier

Tome I

The 19th Century

The 19th century was a period of great turmoil in French history. After the French Revolution, France successively experienced Napoléon's First Empire, a Monarchic Restauration, a Second Republic, a Second Empire and a Third Republic. During the First and Second Empires, periods of proud, military glory alternated with crushing, humiliating defeats.

It was in this ever-boiling cauldron of historical upheaval that French literature exploded into a bouquet of heretofore unknown and abundant colors—and so did the *fantastique*.

French literature of the 19th century was dominated by three currents: the *romantisme* [romanticism], the *réalisme* [realism, or naturalism] and the *symbolisme* or *décadent* [symbolism, or decadence] which, while distinctive in terms of works, nevertheless intermingled in the lives of their respective writers. For example, Honoré de Balzac, a founder of realism, also had his romantic period; Victor Hugo and Gérard de Nerval, to name but two, moved easily between romanticism and symbolism. Therefore, we were forced to use a certain degree of arbitrariness when choosing where to classify an author's works.

In addition to the literary currents mentioned above, the French *fantastique* of the 19th century was influenced by a number of powerful, visionary foreign authors: The English Gothic writers, especially Ann Radcliffe, Matthew Lewis and Charles-Robert Maturin; the German writer, E. T. A. Hoffmann and the composer Richard Wagner; and the American writer, Edgar Allan Poe.

Finally, it is worth noting that it was during this incredibly rich century that we started seeing the formation of a clear split between the more lurid and exploitative forms of the *fantastique* which catered to the masses and are dubbed here *fan-*

tastique populaire, which involved into horror fiction, and the more literary and refined works of both major and minor mainstream writers, dubbed *fantastique littéraire*, as well as the first emergence of classic fantasy.

Our overview of the century begins with the gothic novels.

Romans Noirs

As the 19th century was about to begin, the English gothic novels hit the French literary scene with a bang. Their extravagant and macabre nature tapped into the emotions released during the French Revolution, and eventually helped the genre to seamlessly evolve into the more modern forms of the *fantastique*.

Horace Walpole's *The Castle of Otranto* had already been published in 1765, but it was Ann Radcliffe, with her *The Mysteries of Udolfo* (1794), and Matthew Lewis, with *The Monk* (1796), which both proved enormously successful in their French translations, that inspired an entire new wave of French authors, imitation being the sincerest form of flattery. A subsequent, but no less influential, author was Charles-Robert Maturin, whose *Melmoth the Wanderer* (1820) was praised by distinguished writers such as Charles Baudelaire and Balzac, the latter even writing a sequel to it.

This became known in France as the *romans noirs* [black novels], or *romans frénétiques* [frantic novels], the first subgenre of popular horror literature.

One of the first French writers to borrow from the English gothics was the infamous Donatien Alphonse François, Marquis de Sade, an indomitable rebel and notorious *débauché* whose erotic novels *Justine* (1791) and *Juliette* (1798), although they contained no true fantastic elements, were clearly gothic in inspiration, and obviously anticipated the trend towards the gothic in French literature. Also, by becoming the first of the *écrivains maudits* [accursed writers], the author started another modern trend, that of pushing the envelope, challenging the mores of the times, thumbing his nose at society, daring his literary successors to further explore and test the boundaries of what is acceptable in the genre.

Also in 1798, Jacques-Antoine Reveroni Saint-Cyr imitated De Sade with *Pauliska, ou la Perversité Moderne* [Pauliska, or Modern Perversity]. But the first real French *roman noir* is usually considered to be *Coelina, ou l'Enfant du Mystère* [Coelina, or The Child of Mystery], written in 1799 by François-Guillaume Ducray-Duminil, which was quickly turned into a successful stage play by Guilbert de Pixérécourt, himself the author of over a hundred plays in the gothic vein, such as *Le Château des Appenins* [The Castle in the Appenins] (1799) and *Le Solitaire de la Roche Noire* [The Hermit of the Black Rock] (1806).

In the same vein, Charles Pigault-Lebrun wrote *Les Barons de Flesheim* [The Barons of Flesheim] (1798).

From 1800 onward, French enthusiasm for the *roman noir* grew by leaps and bounds. One of the most notable examples was the anonymous *Fantômes Nocturnes ou La Terreur des Coupables, Le Théâtre des Forfaits, Offrant par Nouvelles Historiques des Visions Infernales de Monstres Fantastiques, d'Images Funestes, de Lutins Homicides, de Spectres et d'Échafauds Sanglants, Supplices Précurseurs des Scélérats* [Nocturnal Ghosts or The Terror of the Guilty, Theater of Evil Deeds, Offering Through Historical Stories Infernal Visions of Fantastic Monsters, Nefarious Images, Murderous Goblins, Specters & Bloody Scaffolds, Tortures Worthy of the Worst Villains] (1821) (the title pretty much spells it out!).

Two years earlier, in 1819, John William Polidori's notorious vampire tale, *The Vampyre*, falsely attributed to Lord Byron, starring the vampire Lord Ruthven, had been translated and published in France. It proved hugely successful and was immediately copied by Cyprien Bérard, who authored *Lord Ruthwen ou les Vampires* [The Vampire Lord Ruthwen] (with a "w") (1820),[20] in which the mysterious Lord Ruthwen travels to Venice and strikes again, killing the beautiful Bettina and torturing her lover, Léonti, who swears to avenge her. He joins vampire hunters Aubrey and Nadoor Ali to search for the elusive monster. This was the first (unauthorized) sequel to continue the story of a successful, ground-breaking character. Also drawing upon *The Thousand and One Nights* for inspiration, Bérard wove stories of mystical Venice, Arabian Nights and Vampire legends into one exotic and suspenseful tale of revenge against the Undead. It was a significant stepping-stone in the evolution of the modern image of the vampire, foreshadowing the other major thread of subsequent vampire fiction: the seductive female vampire.

The character of the vampire, which had previously been mocked by Voltaire in his *Dictionnaire Philosophique* (1764), had now become a Byronesque romantic icon which took the literary establishment by storm. Bérard's novel was then promptly adapted into a stage play entitled *Le Vampire* by Charles Nodier the same year.[21] An inventive and talented writer, the author had already begun his literary career by penning popular *romans noirs* such as *Les Proscrits* [The Proscribed] (1802), *Le Peintre de Salzbourg* [The Painter of Salzburg] (1803) and *Les Méditations du Cloître* [The Meditations of the Cloister] (1803). But his true genre career began when he wrote the play *Le Vampire* in 1820. Another genre play by Nodier worthy of mention here is *Le Monstre et le Magicien* [The Monster and the Magician] (1826),[22] co-written with Antoine Béraud and Jean Toussaint-Merle, which revisits the legend of Mary Shelley's *Frankenstein* by recasting the legendary scientist as a sorcerer and his creature as a silent killer from Hell.

---

[20] Black Coat Press, ISBN 978-1-61227-004-3.
[21] In *Lord Ruthven the Vampire*, Black Coat Press, ISBN 978-1-932983-10-4.
[22] In *Frankenstein Meets the Hunchback of Notre-Dame*, Black Coat Press, ISBN 978-1-932983-38-8.

Lord Ruthven (with a "v") quickly returned in 1821 in a vaudeville play by Eugène Scribe, also entitled *Le Vampire*,[23] and yet again in Alexandre Dumas' play *Le Vampire* (1851),[24] in which the implacable Lord Ruthven comes face-to-face with an even more fearsome enemy, Zizka, a female Ghoul of great necromantic powers.

The 1868 play *Douglas le Vampyre* [25] by Jules Dornay was a transparent attempt to give an origin to the famous character. The story takes placed in Scotland, in 1648. Sir William Clifford expects to receive the vast Ruthven estates after the death of the old Lord, but a young man suddenly appears, claiming to the be the new Lord, and also claiming the hand of the beautiful Anna Clifford in marriage.

In 1823, the Théâtre de la Gaité in Paris featured a play by Théodore de Banville entitled *Polichinelle Vampire*.

In 1825, in *La Vampire*,[26] Étienne-Léon de Lamothe-Langon, a writer known for writing fake memoirs, told the story of Edouard Delmont, a young officer from Napoléon's Great Army who promises to marry Alinska, a Hungarian girl. But once back in France, he goes back on his vows and marries someone else. Several years later, Alinska suddenly reappears in his life, transformed into an avenging vampire. She threatens to kill his wife and children unless he honors the vows he made to her. What makes Alinska stand out in the ranks of implacable female vampires is that she is not a predator, but the instrument of a higher power, working for God as the tool of Divine Wrath. It is worth noting that this story predates Bram Stoker's *Dracula* (1897) by seventy-two years!

---

[23] *Being Lord Ruthven* in *Lord Ruthven the Vampire*, q.v.
[24] *The Return of Lord Ruthven*, Black Coat Press, ISBN 978-1-932983-11-1.
[25] *Lord Ruthven Begins*, Black Coat Press, ISBN 978-1-935558-43-9.
[26] *The Virgin Vampire*, Black Coat Press, ISBN 978-1-61227-032-6.

Lamothe-Langon also penned an impressive number of gothic novels with lurid titles. His *L'Ermite de la tombe mystérieuse* [The Mysterious Hermit of the Tomb] (1816),[27] one of the best *roman noirs*, in which the evil Arembert consigns his father to a dark dungeon, and has his brother assassinated in order to get his hands on the vast family estate of Saint-Felix. But unbeknownst to him, his brother has survived and returns in the guise of a strange Hermit, intent on persecuting Arembert using all the tricks that the darkest phantasmagoria can provide. The action takes place during the bloody Albigensian crusade of the 12th century. The author attempts to blend Gothic horror and chivalric romance, depicting the genocidal participants of the crusade as if they were knights of medieval romance, while adding Gothic villains and castles replete with subterrains and garish hauntings into the mix. The resulting work does have a surreal charm that transcends the limits of the genres it tries to amalgamate. *L'Ermite de la tombe mystérieuse* pioneers untrodden territory, exhibiting a bold defiance of literary conventions, and displaying an admirably zestful iconoclasm.

Other titles in the same vein included *Le Monastère des Frères Noirs* [The Monastery of the Black Friars] (1825) and *La Cloche du Trépassé* [The Bell of the Trespassed] (1839). But the one most worthy of mention here is *Le Diable* [The Devil] (1832), about the charming yet corrupt Chevalier Draxel, evil incarnate, one more literary archetype shaped in the cauldron of gothic literature.

In 1820, the great Honoré de Balzac, justly famous for a series of novels called *La Comédie Humaine* [The Human Comedy] (1842-46), but still an aspiring writer, paid his dues to the *roman noir* by becoming a renowned and prolific writer of popular gothic novels such as *Falthurne* (1820), about a virgin prophetess who knows occult secrets dating back to Ancient Mesopotamia. In 1822, under the pseudonym of "Lord R'Hoone" (an anagram of Honoré), the author wrote

---

[27] Black Coat Press, ISBN 978-1-61227-734-9.

L'Héritière de Birague [The Heir of Birague], *Jean-Louis, ou La Fille Trouvée* [Jean-Louis, or The Found Girl] and *Clotilde de Lusignan*. Then, under the pseudonym of "Horace de Saint-Aubin", he penned *Le Vicaire des Ardennes* [The Vicar of the Ardennes], inspired by *The Monk*, *Annette et le Criminel* [Annette and the Criminal] (a.k.a. *Argow le Pirate*) (1824) and *Wann-Chlore* (a.k.a. *Jane la Pâle*) (1825).

More significant is *Le Centenaire, ou Les Deux Beringheld* [The Hundred-Centenarian, or The Two Beringheld], this one inspired by *Melmoth*, published in 1822. In it, the author does not use the convenient cliché of a pact with the Devil, but instead draws on his own occult knowledge, specifically, Rosicrucian beliefs, to create the character of a four hundred year-old vampire who, in order to prolong his existence, does not drain blood, but the essence of life itself.

Maturin's influence on Balzac was even more pronounced in *L'Élixir de Longue Vie* [The Elixir of Long Life] (1830) and *La Peau de Chagrin* [The Skin of Sorrow] (1831). In the former, the protagonist, Don Juan Belvidero, is not only obsessed with the secret of immortality, but he is also a monster of pride who feels only contempt for mankind and for God. In the latter, the author focuses on the theme of the destruction of the precious life essence. The power and consequences of the unchecked passions which imbue these two novels become his trademark, a theme which he later put to good use in the more realistic settings of his *Comédie Humaine* novels.

Even after Balzac had become a respected and successful mainstream writer, and even though he is credited as the creator of realism and naturalism, he still chose to incorporate mystical and philosophical speculations in some of his works. His knowledge of, and interest in, the occult, and especially his search for "higher" planes of existence, manifested itself in some of his latter novels, which anticipated the *symboliste* school (see below). Among these were *Louis Lambert* (1832), which featured a man seeking higher dimensions; the aptly-named *La Recherche de l'Absolu* [The Search for the Absolute] (1834), whose hero was an alchemist; and *Seraphita* (1835), a novel clearly inspired by Emmanuel Swedenborg's philosophy about a perfect, angelic hermaphrodite—a recurring theme in the *symboliste* movement.

Finally, in *Melmoth Réconcilié* [Melmoth Reconciled] (1835), Balzac took the last, logical step. Reusing Maturin's character, and drawing from the "illuminist" philosophies of Louis-Claude de Saint-Martin, he concocted a yarn that showed Melmoth a path to salvation.

Having begun his literary career with *Falthurne* and ending it with *Seraphita*, Balzac could be said to have completed his personal initiation. He left behind the negative energies of the *roman noir* and instead focused on the positive aspects of his personal spiritual quest. A remarkable literary journey by any standards.

In 1821, the Vicomte Charles-Victor d'Arlincourt combined Walter Scott's sense of historical epic with Ann Radcliffe's gothic passion, and penned the genre's first historical gothic novel, *Le Solitaire* [The Hermit], a *roman frénétique* with genre elements. It postulated that, from a Swiss hideaway, the hidden hand of Charles le Téméraire (who in reality died in 1477) continued to secretly control all the major events of history until the early 1500s. In many ways, it was the first modern conspiracy novel! The public loved it, and it soon spawned several imitations.

The celebrated Victor Hugo, who went on to write *Les Misérables* (1862), paid his dues to the *roman noir* by penning *Han d'Islande* [Han of Iceland] (1823), a bloody tale featuring two monstrous heroes, one a Viking warrior who drank blood from his victims' skulls, and the other a semi-mythical bear. In 1826, in *Bug-Jargal*, the author told the story of a native revolt on the island of Saint-Domingue and included the description of a terrifying witch doctor. Hugo was also influenced by Walter Scott when he penned his classic *Notre-Dame de Paris* [*The Hunchback of Notre-Dame*] (1831), which contained numerous horrific elements as well as one of the first "classic" monsters after Frankenstein and Lord Ruthven. His penultimate novel, the morbid and romantic *L'Homme qui Rit* [*The Man Who Laughs*] (1869) was about Gwynplaine, a horribly disfigured man who lived in 17th century England. Its 1928 film version, starring Conrad Veidt, was credited as the model for *Batman*'s notorious villain, the Joker. *L'Homme qui Rit* showed a marked return to Scott's influence and the *roman noir*. Gwynplaine is a sublime, horrific figure, matching that of the earlier Quasimodo. He is the son of a 17th century English nobleman who rebelled against the King. As a result, the King ordered the boy's mouth to be sliced open to his ears, and the boy himself to be sold to gypsies. When he grows up, Gwynplaine's hideous grin turns him into a tragic circus freak, known as the "Man Who Laughs", who hates the society which inflicted such a monstrous and unfair punishment upon him.

Similar themes were explored in the lesser known *Le Monstre* [The Monster] (1824) and *Le Damné* [The Damned] (1824) by Eugène de Lamerlière, as well as in the medieval gothic novel, *Danse Macabre* (1832)[28] by Paul Lacroix, Alexandre Dumas' best collaborator also known by his pseudonyms "P.L. Jacob", "Le Bibliophile", or "Bibliophile Jacob". Set in 1438, the novel stars the sinister Macabre, who lives in the cemetery of the Saint-Innocents in Paris, sleeping in a coffin with his wife Giborne. He has amassed a fortune through producing the eponymous play in a ghastly theater made of bones, and selling clothes stolen from the dead. His partner, Benjamin, falls in love with the wife of a nobleman, and plots to get rid of her husband, setting in motion a series of events marked by death, torture and disease against the background of the most sinister ossuary of all time. *Danse macabre* is not just a novel of great historical interest; it remains a powerful narrative, possessed of admirable intricacy and dramatic tension, as well as holding a horrific impact undiminished by time. Even today, its raw ferocity remains unmatched.

---

[28] Black Coat Press, ISBN 978-1-61227-205-4.

In 1829, *L'Âne Mort et la Femme Guillotinée* [The Dead Donkey and the Guillotined Woman] by literary critic Jules Janin was hailed as a new masterpiece of the macabre, often verging on the pastiche, but was criticized by others for being just too bloody and horrible. *Gore* as a subgenre of horror fiction had arrived.

Excessive amounts of gore had already been featured in the works of Philarète Chasles, such as *Le Père et la Fille* [The Father and the Daughter] (1824) and *La Fiancée de Bénares* [The Fiancée from Benares], but it was Janin who made it popular and enabled it to reach new audiences, anticipating the "Grand-Guignol" theater by sixty-eight years.

Imbued with a sense of light-hearted cynicism, the author penned a vast number of eccentric and sometimes improvised fantastic and horror stories, now mostly forgotten. His *Contes Fantastiques & Contes Littéraires* (1863)[29] include stories about a dead man kept alive by magnetism (published several months before Poe's "*The Facts in the Case of M. Valdemar*", fake folk legends, paradoxical ghost stories in the vein of Hoffmann, and surreal reflections on the supernatural nature of music. Janin was probably closer to Poe in spirit, although his ambition took him in a different direction.

Eugène Sue's earlier works were all traditional *romans noirs*, borrowing themes from Ann Radcliffe and Fenimore Cooper: tales of grisly murders, blood-thirsty pirates and high adventure, such as *Kernock le Pirate* (1830), *Atar-Gull* (1831), *La Salamandre* (1832), *Paula Monti* (1842) and *La Morne au Diable* [The Devil's Morn] (1842) His *Latréaumont* (1837) was an historical gothic novel which inspired Isidore Ducasse to choose the pseudonym of Lautréamont.

The almost sadistic description of the slow, pernicious influence of evil was particularly well handled by writer Frédéric Soulié who, in 1832, published his first *roman noir*, *Les Deux Cadavres* [The Two Corpses], which was followed

---

[29] *The Magnetized Corpse*, Black Coat Press, ISBN 978-1-61227-248-1.

by *Le Vicomte de Béziers* [The Viscount of Beziers] (1834) and, in 1838, by his masterwork, *Les Mémoires du Diable* [The Devil's Memoirs]. In it, the author combined the techniques of the *roman noir* with the passions of Sade (the reading of *Justine* is actually used as a means of torture in the novel!) to orchestrate a series of crimes, murders, adulterous and incestuous liaisons, which all took place under the malevolent eye of a dandified Satan. The prolific Soulié wrote over one hundred other novels, many of which dealt with Napoleon's First Empire.

Bloodthirstiness was also a trademark of Pétrus Borel, who wrote *Champavert, Contes Immoraux* [*Immoral Tales*] (1833), an anthology featuring macabre, morbid and gory tales. Some of these featured the first modern exploration of the theme of the werewolf, adding one more "classic" monster to the gallery listed above. A romantic who was nicknamed the "Lycanthrope" by his friends, the author became one of the most outrageous purveyors of romans noirs. His *Madame Putiphar* (written in 1833, but published only in 1839) is often listed as one of the true masterpieces of French gothics. It, too, anticipated what eventually became the "Grand-Guignol". At the same time, it proved to be one of the last *romans noirs* of the period, the genre having run out of blood (as it were) and being progressively replaced by more classic forms of the *fantastique*.

Le Mutilé [The Mutilated Man] (1832), by Xavier-Boniface de Saintine is about a poet whose tongue and hands are cut off to prevent him from expressing himself. The author was a prolific dramatist who collaborated in more than 200 plays with Eugène Scribe and a noted figure of the Romantic Movement.

L'Histoire de Jonathan le visionnaire [Jonathan the Visionary] (1823)[30] is a collection of fantasy tales told by a mysterious immortal called Jonathan (who is only featured as an active narrator in a few of them). It includes the story of an

---

[30] Black Coat Press, ISBN 978-1-61227-751-6.

Antediluvian Civilization, which retells the history of a civilization from Ethiopia, only a few distant echoes of which survive today. Ranging from prehistorical fantasy to post-apocalypse, it provides a prophetic indication of the manner in which our own civilization might degenerate. The fact that scientific and technological progress is presented here as a symptom of social disease makes Saintine's vision more modern and radical than any of his contemporaries.

La Seconde Vie [The Second Life] (1864)[31] was Saintine's swan song. This collection of fictitious dreams, hallucinations and metaphysical fantasies examine the nature of dreaming from a viewpoint infused by contemporary psychological science, when the phenomena of dreams and hallucinations had begun to attract serious attention, but had not yet reduced to Freudian analyses. *The Second Life* is a remarkable book, as much in its self-indulgence as in its strangeness, covering a remarkably wide spectrum, while always retaining a firm moral anchorage. It is one of the finest and most ambitious 19th century extensions of the tradition of *contes philosophiques*.

Other successful works in the genre at the time included:

Césaire (1830) by Alexandre Guiraud, a member of the French Academy.

Le Manteau d'un Sous-Lieutenant [The Sub-Lieutenant's Coat] (1832) by Auguste Jeancourt.

L'Écuyer Dauberon [The Squire Dauberon] (1832) by Mélanie Waldor.

In 1832, Jacques Boucher de Perthes, a famous archeologist who, in a five-volume treatise entitled *De la Création* [*Of Creation*] (1838-41), first postulated the then-controversial theories about the real age of Mankind, published *Nouvelles*, a collection of short stories including "*Paola*", the tale of a 300-year-old vampire countess.

---

[31] Black Coat Press, ISBN 978-1-61227-750-9.

Les Contes de Sainte-Pélagie [Tales of Sainte-Pelagie] (1833), by Alphonse Choquart, a collection of gothic and supernatural tales told by prisoners of the famous jail.

Les Roueries de Trialph [Trialph's Lies] (1833), by Charles Lassailly.

Le Cimetière d'Ivry [The Ivry Cemetery] (1834), by Émile Arthaud & Adolphe Poujol.

The grim *Album d'un Pessimiste* [Album of a Pessimist] (1835), by Alphonse Rabbe.

Ugolino (1835), by Aloysius Block.

La Nonne Sanglante [The Bloodied Nun] (1835), in which a ghostly nun seeks revenge on the former lover who sealed her fate, by the prolific Albert Bourgeois, who penned well over two hundred melodramas, among which *Les Pilules du Diable* [*The Devil's Pills*] (1867), in which a witch turns a man into a turkey!

Le Magicien [The Magician] (1838), by Alphonse Esquiros, who later became a senator.

Une Promenade de Bélial [Belial's Walk] (1848), by Alfred de Poittevin.

Les Nuits du Père Lachaise [The Nights at the Père Lachaise] (1845), about the famous Parisian cemetery, *Les Veuves du Diable* [The Devil's Widows] (1858) by Léon Gozlan.

After so much blood, so much gore and so much evil, the *roman noir* began to justifiably display signs of exhaustion and gave way to more modern forms of the *fantastique*.

On the one hand, it continued along the paths of popular fiction, published in inexpensive formats and catering to large audiences. This tradition of *fantastique populaire*, which had begun with the pre-Revolutionary imprints of *Le Cabinet des Fées* and the *Voyages Imaginaires*, continued and gained momentum with the publication of the more lurid and exploitative samples of the *romans noirs*. The more brutal, gorier, brand of horror, as exemplified by the notorious performances of the "Grand-Guignol" theater in Paris (which began in 1897), was published in small, inexpensive pamphlets, labeled *"horreur"* or "*épouvante*". In the true tradition of popular fiction, they were considered cheap thrills, good only for the barely educated masses.

At the other end of the literary spectrum, the *roman noir* was alchemically transformed by the influences of Hoffmann and Poe, and evolved into a more poetic and literary form of the *fantastique*, which attracted major authors, such as Gustave Flaubert, Honoré de Balzac, Victor Hugo, Théophile Gautier, Prosper Mérimée, George Sand, Gérard de Nerval and Guy de Maupassant, to name but a few amongst the more famous.

Thus did the *fantastique* gain entrance, even if sometimes through the back door, in "classic" French literature, forming a sub-set referred to here as the *fantastique littéraire*.

Fantastique Populaire

The pioneer, and one of the most successful representatives ever, of the *fantastique populaire* was Eugène Sue, whose *Les Mystères de Paris* [*The Mysteries of Paris*] was serialized in 1843 in the daily newspaper *Le Journal des Débats* and later inspired *Les Misérables*. *Les Mystères de Paris* was the popular soap of its times, a hugely popular social-gothic serial pitting the mysterious Prince Rodolphe and the beautiful Fleur-de-Marie against the villainous Maître d'École [*Schoolmaster*], Chourineur [*Stabber*] and La Chouette [*Owl*] in the darkness-filled mazes and haunts of the Paris underworld. Its initial serialization in a daily newspaper—hence the label "*roman feuilleton*" (*feuille* [leaf] being a newspaper's page)—rather than publication in the more traditional and higher-brow book form, was a clear evidence of the distinction between popular entertainment and works with more respectable literary and cultural aspirations.

Sue wrote in a style which was a captivating combination of gothic melodrama and social realism. He was one of the first French writers to denounce some of the social ills that accompanied the Industrial Revolution.

With *Le Juif Errant* [The Wandering Jew], serialized in 1844-45, the author penned his first, full-blown *fantastique* novel. In it, the Wandering Jew and his sister Herodiade meet every hundred years across the Straits of Bering. Throughout the centuries, they have waged a secret war against the powerful Jesuits, using men and even real-life historic events—such as the cholera epidemic which struck Paris in 1832—as chess pieces in their time-spanning game.

The character of the Wandering Jew had previously appeared in Simon Tyssot de Patot's *La Vie, les Aventures et le Voyage de Groenland du Révérend Père Cordelier Pierre de Mésange* [The Life, Adventures & Trip to Greenland of the Rev. Father Pierre de Mesange] (1720)[32] and Jan Potocki's *Le Manuscrit Trouvé à Saragosse* [Ms. Found in Saragosa] (1805). But the seminal novel about the character was, without a doubt, Edgar Quinet's *Ahasuérus* (1834). The story begins with the Creation of the world and moves rapidly to the Last Judgment. But it does not end there, as have previous literary visions of the Apocalypse, but goes beyond it, in order to pass judgment on the verdict. In this startingly original epic, the Last Judgment is not only appealed, but set aside, reweighed and found wanting. The verdict passed on the human race by the Eternal Father is supplemented by a very different judgment delivered by Christ, of a particular individual cursed to be a witness to the unfolding of human history: Ahasuerus, the Wandering Jew. Having overturned the traditional Last Judgment and substituted one more in keeping with modern ideas, the author continued his narrative to provide a further vision, which passes judgment not on humankind, but on God himself in a curious and strangely poignant coda.

The Wandering Jew returned in Alexandre Dumas' *Isaac Laquedem* (1853), an unfinished historical novel originally

---

[32] In *The Strange Voyages of Jacques Massé and Pierre de Mésange*, Black Coat Press, ISBN 978-1-61227-370-9.

serialized in the newspaper *Le Constitutionnel*. The author planned it to make it his major work, a complete fresco of the history of humanity. Under cover of fiction, the novel would also have offered a meditation on ancient and modern myths. However, it quickly came up against the hostility of Catholic circles. The newspaper was forced to stop its publication in March 1853. Apart from a few partial editions, it remained in oblivion until two complete editions appeared, in quick succession, in 2005. and in 2006.

The prodigious Alexandre Dumas, known worldwide for his classic *Les Trois Mousquetaires* [The Three Musketeers] (1844) (and its sequels) and *Le Comte de Monte-Cristo* [The Count of Monte-Cristo] (1845), was the undisputed master of French popular fiction. Some of his early works, such as *Le Château d'Eppstein* [The Castle of Eppstein] (1844) and *Le Trou d'Enfer* [The Hell Hole] (1851), were *romans noirs*. Like Balzac, Dumas had a strong interest in, and knowledge of, the occult. One of his earliest works was a collaboration with Gérard de Nerval entitled *L'Alchimiste* [The Alchemist] (1839). Later, his *Joseph Balsamo* (1846) starred the eponymous freemason who was shown using the mediumistic powers of a young virgin to pave the way for the destruction of the French Monarchy and the advent of the Revolution. In its sequel, *Le Collier de la Reine* [The Queen's Necklace] (1849), Balsamo was replaced by Cagliostro, who was now pulling the strings.

Dumas was gifted with a prodigious imagination and was a born storyteller. He was also finely attuned to the trends and fashions that were popular in the marketplace. The success of Hoffmann's *Tales* and of *The Thousand and One Nights* undoubtedly influenced him to team up with Paul Lacroix (see above) to publish *Les Mille et Un Fantômes* [*A Thousand and One Ghosts*] (1849), an anthology of macabre tales, linked by the now-classic device of guests sharing ghostly tales at a dinner party. Among its contents was a story about a vampire who preyed on a girl and was eventually destroyed by being nailed in his coffin with a consecrated sword.

One of the stories, A wry, sarcastic fable of supernaturally-punished infidelity, was expanded into a novella by Lacroix and became *Les Mariages du père Olifus* [The Marriages of Père Olifus] (1849),[33] which remains entertaining as well as intriguing, and deserves to be reckoned one of the flawed classics of its genre. It tells the picaresque story of a sailor, Père Olifus, who first marries a mermaid, then embarks upon a series of voyages to a semi-mythical Far East where he enjoys various economic opportunities, but remains plagued by the vengeful astral form of the mermaid wife he left behind.

Vampires sold books and Dumas returned to the theme with the play *Le Vampire* (1851) featuring Lord Ruthven (see above). Finally, in 1857, he penned one of the first modern werewolf stories—and still one of the best—*Le Meneur de Loups* [*The Wolf Leader*], the tale of a man who became a werewolf after a pact with the devil.

After Dumas, the most famous author of serialized novels was Paul Féval. He, too, penned several popular swashbuckling novels, such as *Le Loup Blanc* [The White Wolf] (1843),[34] a Breton *Monte-Cristo*-like tale, featuring the first masked crimefighter in popular literature (long before *The Scarlet Pimpernel* or *Zorro*); its prequel *La Louve* [The She-Wolf] (1856),[35] featuring the first female swashbuckler in popular literature; and the classic *Le Bossu* [*The Hunchback*] (1857),[36] in which the hero, Lagardère, a prodigious swordsman, disguises himself as a hunchback to take revenge against his enemies.

In terms of genre elements, *Les Mystères de Londres* [*The Mysteries of London*] (1844)[37] was an obvious attempt at

---

[33] *The Man Who Married a Mermaid*, Black Coat Press, ISBN 978-1-61227-612-0.
[34] Black Coat Press, ISBN 978-1-61227-832-2.
[35] Black Coat Press, ISBN 978-1-64932-008-7.
[36] Black Coat Press, ISBN 978-1-64932-066-7.
[37] The stage play adaptation, *Gentlemen of the Night*, is available from Black Coat Press, ISBN 978-1-932983-81-4.

cashing in on *Les Mystères de Paris*. The story begins in 1810 when young Irishman Fergus O'Breane, whose family was destroyed by the British, swears revenge. He is arrested after a duel and deported to Australia. He escapes and becomes a pirate, traveling to China, India, the Americas, and even meeting an exiled Napoléon in Saint-Helena. Fergus returns to London twenty years later as a wealthy Portuguese nobleman, the Marquis de Rio Santo, socialite by day, leader of the criminal empire of the Gentlemen of the Night by dark. Féval made the story even more sensational by including a lurid tale of revenge against the despicable Godfrey of Lancaster, Lord Whitemanor, then threw in a mad scientist performing human experiments, and a scheme to rob the Bank of England! Fergus O'Breane was a determining influence on *The Count of Monte-Cristo*, written the following year.

Les Revenants [Revenants] (1852)[38] takes place on the windswept moors of Brittany. Renegade priest Gabriel Le Brec and Count Filhol de Treguern embark on a scheme to defraud an insurance company by faking the death of the latter. This sets in motion a danse macabre of murders, betrayals, people who change their names, lost birth certificates, false testimonies, an Ann Radcliffe-type romance, a struggle between Good and Evil and an impossible phantasmagoria of living men who pretend to be dead and dead men who return to claim vengeance. The plot boils down to a duel between two insanely obsessive sorcerers, Commander Malo Treguern and Dowager Françoise Le Brec. Were it not for Féval's repeated assurances that Malo has Destiny and God on his side, while the Dowager is the Devil's pawn, the reader would surely be at a loss to know which of the two to root for.

La Fille du Juif Errant [The Wandering Jew's Daughter] (1863)[39] features not just one immortal, but several, who battle fiercely throughout the ages, until the daughter of one of them falls in love with a young French nobleman. The novel antici-

---

[38] Black Coat Press, ISBN 978-1-932983-70-8.
[39] Black Coat Press, ISBN 978-1-932983-30-2.

pates later developments in popular fiction, starring an invulnerable (but flawed) hero who stops bullets and blades with his body and gives succor to the wounded, and featuring a transfer of souls between two characters.

Féval never shrank from using classic fantastic concepts because of fear of rejection by the public. Written in 1856—over 40 years before Dracula—*La Vampire* [The Vampire Countess][40] features the perversely charismatic vampire Countess Addhema and her lover Count Szandor, in a supernatural murder mystery in which the prime investigator is Napoléon's old sword master now head of the Paris Morgue, Jean-Baptiste Séverin. Addhema—or Countess Gregoryi as she is known then—is, first and foremost, the vampire-as-libido-run-wild, but she is also the vampire-as-gold-digger too, and she may well have something of the vampire-as-muse to complete her mystique.

Féval followed it with *Le Chevalier Ténèbre* [The Knight Darkness] (1860),[41] which relates the criminal exploits of two brothers, Ange and Jean Ténèbre, one a vampire, the other a ghoul—or maybe there are merely two very clever con artists? Written almost 40 years before Dracula, the brothers Ténèbre are the Eternal Adversaries against which Eternal Champions and Thousand-Faced Heroes are pitched.

Finally, the outrageous *La Ville Vampire* [Vampire City] (1867),[42] completed the trilogy. In it, Féval parodied Ann Radcliffe, even turning her into his fictional hero! *La Ville Vampire* opens with the news of a vampire plaguing the English countryside where Ms. Radcliffe lives. To save one of her cousins, the indomitable novelist (or her fictional counterpart) gathers a group of fearless vampire hunters—the first in literary history—comprised of Merry Bones the Irishman, Grey Jack, the faithful old servant, the revenge-driven Doctor Mag-

---

[40] Black Coat Press, ISBN 978-0-9740711-5-2.
[41] *Knightshade*, Black Coat Press, ISBN 978-0-9740711-4-5.
[42] Black Coat Press, ISBN 978-0-9740711-6-9.

nus Szegeli, and Polly Bird, one of the vampire's earlier victims.

Radcliffe and her band travel to the vampire city of Selène, located in Serbia. Normally invisible to mortal eyes, Selène (or The Sepulchre) is a giant necropolis carved from black marble which is eternally in mourning, enveloped by perpetual gloom, lit by a lunar twilight that never gives way to day or night. There are immense amphitheaters capped with domes like mosques, and minarets reaching for the sky, a circus of colossal proportions, surrounded by a triple rank of white marble cloisters. Arranged there, in mysterious order, are the sepulchral dwellings of the vampire race which the wrath of God has placed in the margins of our world. The sons of that people, half-demon and half-phantom, are living and dead at the same time, incapable of reproducing themselves, but also deprived of the blessing of death. Their womenfolk are ghouls, also known as *oupires*. Some have sat on thrones and terrified history. There, the vampire hunters succeed in tearing out the heart of the Vampire Lord Goetzi and burning it, thus putting an end to the undead menace. They then make their escape from the accursed city.

La Ville Vampire is remarkable because of the modernity of its concepts. It is arguably the first true, popular vampire epic, unabashedly commercial, without any literary pretensions. The book's tremendous success only proved the justness of Féval's commercial instincts. With the aid of hindsight, one can easily see in *La Ville Vampire* the ultimate literary ancestor of *Buffy the Vampire-Slayer*. Although Radcliffe is not permitted by her gentlemanly author actually to slay any vampires with her own hand, she is nevertheless the prime mover of the expedition, and she watches with a distinctly proto-feminist fascination as the Irish hero carefully excises the heart from the breast of Goetzi.

With these novels, Féval helped the gothic novel merge with the *fantastique*. But his masterpiece was unarguably *Les Habits Noirs* [*The Black Coats*] a huge, sprawling saga comprised of eleven interconnected novels featuring occult conspiracies and a mysterious criminal secret society working behind the scenes and pursuing nefarious goals.

Technically, the series began with *Bel Demonio* (1850),[43] which was later retroactively incorporated into it by the author. Ther novel takes place in the Spoleto region of Italy between 1625 and 1655. In it, Ercole Vitelli murders his cousin, Francis Vitelli, who is the legitimate heir of the wealthy Monteleone family, under the eyes of Francis' son, Andrea. Fifteen years later, Andrea returns seeking revenge, posing as "Demonio," the leader of a ring of bandits.

Féval loosely rewrote, expanded and gave a sequel to *Bel Demonio* with *Les Compagnons du Silence* [The Companions of the Silence] (1857).[44] This time, the story takes place in 1808, when the three children of Mario Monteleone, grandmaster of the Iron Knights, a secret society in Southern Italy, are kidnapped by a mysterious enemy. In 1815, Mario himself is arrested and executed. The Iron Knights then morph into the Companions of the Silence, which have sworn to avenge Mario, but eventually turn to crime. In 1823, a mysterious stranger walks into their midst, claiming to be the notorious bandit Bel Demonio, but in fact, he is Mario's eldest son, Fulvio. He then takes over the Companions and embarks on a mission of vengeance, while defying the traps laid for him by the diabolical Chief of Police, Johann Spurzheim. The two novels function as the backstory of the vast criminal conspiracy of the Black Coats.

The peak of development that Féval attained in *Les Compagnons du Silence* was so splendidly theatrical, that future exercises in a similar vein had no option but to take a step back and find new directions of development. If the heroes are cast in the same mold as the character of Monte-Cristo, and revenge lies at the heart of the plots and keeps the action going, Féval cannot hide his fascination for the criminal masterminds at the center of it all.

---

[43] Black Coat Press, ISBN 978-1-61227-708-0.
[44] Black Coat Press, ISBN 978-1-61227-706-6.

With the next volume in the series—still a foreshadowing of things to come—*Jean Diable* [John Devil] (1861)[45] Féval pioneered the modern crime thriller, creating here both the first police detective (Gregory Temple, the first Scotland Yard Detective in fiction) and the first arch-criminal (John Devil, a proto-Fantômas) in popular fiction. In the 1820s, Chief Superintendent Gregory Temple of Scotland Yard is mystified by the actions of a faceless crime leader who calls himself "John Devil", a nickname previously used by master thief Thomas Paddock. The new John Devil turns out to be Thomas Brown, the son of Helen Brown, a former accomplice of Paddock. Helen has married a French nobleman, the Marquis Armand de Belcamp. Tom Brown is the brother of Belcamp's legitimate son, Henri de Belcamp. *Jean Diable* is a remarkable criminal thriller, in which the reader never truly learns if the crimes attributed to Tom Brown, who dies on the gallows, were not in fact committed by his brother, Henri, who commits suicide.

The most interesting character in *Jean Diable* is Gregory Temple, who proclaims himself the world's premier "detective" which appears to be the first use of the word in that context, and is the author of the book *L'Art de Découvrir les Coupables* [The Art of Unmasking Criminals]. Temple investigates crimes by covering a blackboard with scribblings he calls his "deductive calculations" or his "detection machine". Temple uses his prodigious abilities to discover the secret identity of the elusive mastermind and tries to capture him before his adversary can use armored warships to free Napoleon from Saint-Helena. John Devil then plots to conquer India, making the book the first techno-thriller in popular literature.

Féval then embarked on the series proper: In the first volume, *Les Habits Noirs* [The Parisian Jungle] (1863),[46] he merely rehashes his plot for *Le Bossu*, but in a mid-19th century setting. However, unlike *Le Bossu*, which featured a single

---

[45] Black Coat Press, ISBN 978-1-932983-15-9.
[46] Black Coat Press, ISBN 978-1-934543-03-0.

adversary, the author had the brilliant idea of inventing an all-powerful international brotherhood of criminals, a 19th century Mafia, led by the mysterious Colonel Bozzo-Corona, the Moriarty-like godfather of a criminal empire over a century old. The Colonel's right-hand man is Monsieur Lecoq, also nicknamed Toulonnais L'Amitié, a character inspired by the real-life master criminal turned Prefect of Police, Vidocq, who also inspired Balzac's Vautrin, and whose "memoirs" inspired Poe's Dupin. The story starts in 1825 and stars metal-worker André Maynotte who is framed by Lecoq for a crime he did not commit. Maynotte eventually escapes from prison and returns in 1842. Using various disguises, he succeeds in exposing the real villains and proving his innocence. At the end of the story, Féval made the mistake (like Arthur Conan Doyle killing off Holmes and Moriarty) of having the Colonel die of old age, surrounded by the members of the High Council of the Black Coats, and had Maynotte kill Lecoq, before retiring to Australia with his wife. This first volume introduces us to the code words used by the Black Coats: "*Il fait jour*" [It's daylight] means to commit a crime; "*fera-t-il jour demain?*" [Will there be daylight tomorrow?] therefore means, "will a crime be committed tomorrow?" The ritual reply is "It will be daylight from midnight to noon if it's the will of the Father." Conversely, "*il fait nuit*" [It's night] means that things are going badly for the gang and that they should flee. "*Coupez la branche*" [cut a limb] means killing the member responsible for the failure and who could, if captured, betray the rest of the gang. Finally, "*payer la loi*" [pay the law] means to always frame an innocent for the crime to be committed.

The leader of the Black Coats is Colonel Bozzo-Corona, a very old man who lives on the rue Thérèse in Paris with his granddaughter, Fanchette, and whom his neighbors think is a saintly old gentleman. The truth is that he rules with an iron fist over a gang whose size was estimated by Féval at 2000 men, women and children in Paris alone. Only members of the High Council know the Colonel's true identity. They include: the Colonel's right-hand man, Lecoq; the Countess de Clare,

Marguerite Sadoulas; Docteur Samuel; the banker J.-B. Schwartz; and Count Corona, who is married to Fanchette. The Colonel is called the "*padre d'ogni*" [all-father]. He calls his lieutenants "my dear children" and they, in turn, call him "father"—with a note of fear in their voices. The similarities with both the Mafia and Freemasonry are obvious.

The huge success of *Les Habits Noirs* prompted Féval to write a second story, *Cœur d'Acier* [Heart of Steel] (1865),[47] which was not a sequel, but the tale of another member of the High Council previously seen only in a cameo, the beautiful Marguerite Sadoulas. Marguerite becomes Countess of Clare by marrying the brutish Count Joulou du Bréhut de Clare, who is besotted with her. Marguerite plots to steal the enormous fortune of the Clare Inheritance. The story takes place between 1832 and 1843. Marguerite's adversaries are Dr. Abel Lenoir, whose brother was killed by Joulou, and the mysterious M. Coeur [Mr. Heart], a.k.a. Coeur d'Acier, who is later revealed to be Roland Fitz-Roy, Duke de Clare, the legitimate heir. In the end, Roland exposes and defeats Marguerite and regains his title and wealth. Once again, Féval made the mistake of having Marguerite shot by a remorseful Joulou at the end of the book.

The next volume was entitled *L'Avaleur de Sabre* [The Sword Swallower] (1867).[48] The story takes place much later, between 1852 and 1866, and chronicles what looks like the end of the Black Coats. In 1852, twelve-year-old Saladin, son of Similor, one of the Black Coats' henchmen, kidnaps baby Justine de Vibraye and entrusts her to a circus performer, the kind, towering bearded lady and lion tamer, Leocadie Samayoux, a.k.a. Maman Leo. By 1866, Saladin has now become the Marquis Franz de Rosenthal, and Justine the rope dancer, Miss Sapphire. Saladin, nicknamed the Sword Swallower, is also the leader of the Black Silk Hoods, a new gang formed from the remains of the Black Coats, who have fallen

---

[47] Black Coat Press, ISBN 978-1-935558-05-7.
[48] Black Coat Press, ISBN 978-1-61227-024-1

prey to in-fighting after the Colonel's death. Eventually, Justine's real father, Justin de Vibraye, saves her from Saladin's clutches, and marries her off to young Hector de Sabran.

Féval had now painted himself into a fictional corner. In order to keep exploiting the huge success of the Black Coats he had to reinvent the entire series, which he did in the fourth volume, entitled *La Rue de Jerusalem* [Salem Street] (1868),[49] named after the headquarters of the Sureté. In this volume, he wisely went back in time to tell stories that took place before the previous two volumes, which enabled him to re-use the charismatic Colonel, Lecoq and Marguerite de Clare again, without worrying about their deaths. The novel takes place between 1834 and 1838. In it, the Black Coats use a fake Louis XVII, a pretender to the throne of France, to steal the fortune of Mathurine Goret de Champmas. In the end, the Pretender betrays the Colonel. The Black Coats' merciless executioner, Coyatier the Marchef, whose hand even other criminals are afraid to shake, seals the traitor alive inside a wall. This novel also introduces the character of Clampin, nicknamed Pistolet, a young private detective whose methods are precursors to those of Rouletabille and Archie Goodwin.

It is in Chapter IX of Part I of *La Rue de Jerusalem* that Féval first told his readers the back story of the Black Coats, connecting the saga to no less than four of his earlier novels: the historical swashbucklers *Bel Demonio* and *Les Compagnons du Silence*, *Les Mystères de Londres* and *Jean Diable*. Until then, it could be theorized that he had not yet decided to embark on a vast, historical criminal saga, to rival *Balzac*'s *Human Comedy*.

Having found his stride, Féval wrote the fifth book in the series, *L'Arme Invisible* [The Invisible Weapon] (1869),[50] arguably the best in the saga. The story takes place in 1838, just after *La Rue de Jésusalem*. The Black Coats are worried about young magistrate Remy d'Arx who is investigating them. The

---

[49] Black Coat Press, ISBN 978-1-932983-46-3.
[50] Black Coat Press, ISBN 978-1-932983-80-7.

Colonel decides to use what he calls his "invisible weapon". That turns out to be Fleurette, a young girl raised by Maman Leo. Remy falls in love with Fleurette, but then discovers that she is his biological sister, and commits suicide. In the second volume, Fleurette, Maman Leo and her friend, Echalot, strike back at the Black Coats. The Colonel, surprisingly, helps Fleurette save her true love, young Maurice, who was framed by the Black Coats and was about to be sent to the gallows. Fleurette and Maurice leave France, never to return. In a parallel plot, the Colonel thwarts a scheme by the members of the High Council to kill him and steal his treasure.

The theme of the treasure moves to center stage in the sixth volume, *Les Compagnons du Trésor* [The Companions of the Treasure] (1872),[51] completed after the war of 1872. The story begins in 1835 and ends in 1843. The so-called "Companions of the Treasure" are none other than the members of the High Council, more intent than ever on killing the Colonel and stealing his treasure. Féval engages in a bit of retroactive continuity by rewriting the Colonel's death scene as it was described in the first volume, and showing us that there was, in fact, far more to it than we knew. In this book, the Colonel is apparently murdered by his own son, Count Julian, who then goes on to impersonate him, like Moriarty's younger brother impersonates the older Professor in John Gardner's series. The death scene seen in Volume 1 is, therefore, revealed to have been an elaborate charade staged by Julian, who becomes the new Colonel, and thereafter seems to return from the dead. But the real Colonel somehow reaches from beyond the grave and uses Julian's own son, architect Vincent Carpentier, and grandson, Reynier, to set in motion a deadly trap. In the end, all of the conspirators are dead, except for Reynier and his girlfriend.

The final volume, *La Bande Cadet* [The Cadet Gang] (1875),[52] bridges the gap between the 1843 events told in *Les*

---

[51] Black Coat Press, ISBN 978-1-934543-26-9.
[52] Black Coat Press, ISBN 978-1-935558-45-3.

Compagnons du Trésor, and the 1852 events that began in *L'Avaleur de Sabres*. Féval continues to indulge in some retroactive continuity, revisiting the events of *Coeur d'Acier* and revealing that Marguerite de Clare is still alive in 1853, ten years after she was presumably killed at the end of that volume. The Clare fortune is now in the hands of Clotilde, who has been masquerading as the aerialist Lirette. Meanwhile, the deadly Cadet Gang, led by Cadet L'Amour, has stepped into the vacuum created by the destruction of the High Council in the previous volume, and now seeks the Treasure of the Black Coats. But Cadet L'Amour is thwarted by the Colonel, who once again mysteriously returns from the grave (whether this is the real Colonel, Julian or Reynier is unclear). In the end, Cadet L'Amour dies.

A few months after writing *La Bande Cadet*, Féval stopped writing crime novels and the various plotlines he had hinted at were left unfinished. For example, he had announced further revelations about Saladin's future criminal career (as outlined in *L'Avaleur de Sabres*) and promised to tell the story of the "last, deadly battle" between Dr. Lenoir and the Colonel. Sadly, these stories were left untold. By its methods, themes and characters, the saga of *Les Habits Noirs*, while only marginally a genre work, was another precursor of today's conspiracy thrillers.

Charles Rabou was one of the founders of the prestigious *Revue de Paris* and a friend of Balzac, whose unfinished novels he completed after the latter's death. He was also a master of the *roman noir* with *L'Allée des Veuves* [Widows' Alley] (1845). Together with Balzac and Philarète Chasles, he compiled a notable anthology of dark and fantastic tales entitled *Contes Bruns* [Brown Tales] (1832). His masterpiece, however, was a series of novels which began with *Le Cabinet Noir* (1849),[53] that tells the story of the Hulet family which, for generations, has headed the government's spy network, the

---

[53] *The Secret Bureau*, Black Coat Press, ISBN 78-1-61227-510-9.

"Secret Bureau", that intercepts and opens all private mail. The first book follows the ambitious Henri Hulet as he tries to avoid the fatal destiny marked out for him, then switches to the resourceful Gregorio Matiphous, as he attempts to thwart the diabolical schemes of the villainous Marquis de Lupiano, leader of the mysterious Sleepers' Club.

The next book, *Les Frères de la Mort* [The Brothers of Death] (1856),[54] follows the doomed destinies of the Hulets and their relentless enemy, the Marquis de Lupiano, now the leader of the Brothers of Death, from the execution of Charles I of England to the secret terror spread by the Apostles of Nuremberg, while Gregorio Matiphous is now accused of having murdered the mysterious Ephraim, founder of the Illuminati.

In the third volume, *La Fille Sanglante* [The Bloodied Girl] (1857),[55] we discover how the downfall of Napoleon and the return of the Bourbon King Louis XVIII to power in 1815, plays havoc with the lives of the saga's many protagonists. Gregorio Matiphous is now trapped in a web of schemes of his own making. The artisan of his downfall, the former bandit Rempailleux, succeeds in replacing the last of the Hulet family which, for generations, has headed the Secret Bureau.

Finally, in the fourth and final tome, *Le Marquis de Lupiano* (1858),[56] we finally learn the origins of the mercurial Marquis and his connection to the Hulets. The secret master of the various conspiracies, such as the Sleepers' Club, the Brothers of Death and the Red Brotherhood, now plots to change the course of history by freeing Napoleon from Saint-Helena. We also learn of the final fate of Gregorio Matiphous, the cunning Maltese who fell in love with Georgiana, the so-called "bloodied girl". We see how the web of fate that has trapped the Hulets for generations collides with the bandit Rempailleux, who is now the head of the Secret Bureau. *Le Cabinet Noir* is an important link between the works of Jules

---

[54] Black Coat Press, ISBN 978-1-61227-592-5.
[55] Black Coat Press, ISBN 978-1-61227-675-5.
[56] Black Coat Press, ISBN 978-1-61227-761-5.

Janin and Frédéric Soulié on the one hand, and Paul Féval and Ponson du Terrail on the other.

In 1861, Léon Gozlan penned *Le Vampire du Val-de-Grâce* [The Vampire of the Val-de-Grâce] (1861),[57] featuring the mysterious Doctor Salomon Kanali and his family who arrive in a Paris ravaged by a cholera epidemic. The man is an embalmer who claims to have the power to resurrect the dead. But his wife fears that her daughter is being wooed by the same vampire who once destroyed her mother. Vampire of Val-de-Grâce (1862) is a horror story and a mystery, unique in its excess and its bizarre absurdity. It teasingly refuses to confirm or deny the existence of vampires, but play extravagantly with the idea, while merrily exploiting its sinister fascination.

Finally, one could hardly cover the field of 19th century *roman feuilleton* without including Pierre-Alexis de Ponson du Terrail, who wrote several genre novels located at the intersection of the *roman noir* and the *fantastique*.

La Baronne Trépassée [The Dead Baroness] (1852),[58] takes place in 1723. The fearless Baron de Nossac returns from a daring military mission in Eastern Europe when, crossing the forests of Bohemia, he is captured by the legendary Black Huntsman, a 900-year-old wraith who is none other than the Devil's own son. Held prisoner at the Huntsman's enchanted castle, the Baron is then seduced by a female vampire who resembles his dead wife. The reader never learns if the title character was truly dead or not, and if she was dead, did she return to life as a vampire? The ending offers no rational explanation, making the book a significant contribution to the development of modern horror fiction and a foreshadowing of literary things to come, bringing together for the first time two major modern archetypes: the seductive female vampire and the Son of the Devil.

---

[57] Black Coat Press, ISBN 978-1-61227-123-1.
[58] Black Coat Press, ISBN 978-1-932983-55-5.

L'Auberge de la Rue des Enfants Rouges [The Inn of the Street of the Red Children] (1867)[59] is another milestone in the development of supernatural crime fiction. Its hero, the cunning police agent Mr. Porion, a.k.a. Père Cinnamon, does not employ his detective skills to pursue a vampire-like serial killer intent on bleeding children, but rather to protect him, while simultaneously serving other predatory aristocratic interests, such as providing the lecherous King Louis XV with a steady supply of virgins. The novel may seem eccentric to modern eyes because the genre has undergone many refinements, but it remains fascinating as an example of its evolution. The Police Agent contains examples of deductive detection applied to a criminal investigation, as well as foreshadowing what became the "police procedural". The Police Agent boldly asks: if the police and the criminals are on the same side, possessed of all the power and legal authority, who can play a heroic role, and how can he possibly prevail, escaping torture, murder and annihilation?

With *La Femme Immortelle* [The Immortal Woman] (1869),[60] Ponson penned another masterpiece of early vampire fiction. In 1675, a female vampire possessing the secret of immortality was burned alive. Forty-five years later, during a dinner at the table of the French Regent, her then-lover, Marquis de la Roche-Maubert, discovers that another guest, Chevalier d'Esparron, is in love with the same immortal woman. However, her attraction to him is not to satisfy her hunger for blood, but to implement one of the greatest secrets of alchemy: the transmutation of lead into gold! The vampirism in the book is not real, rather it is quickly identified as a trick but certain characters maintain a belief in it through the entire length of the novel. The book is actually a tale of revenge, but the lore included is interesting. The vampire is said to feed from the neck and, when her old lover tells his tale, he says

---

[59] *The Police Agent*, Black Coat Press, ISBN 978-1-61227-593-2.
[60] Black Coat Press, ISBN 978-1-61227-175-0.

that she tried to pass off the pinprick at his neck by suggesting that one of her hairpins had scratched him. The novel suggests that the vampire can make another immortal by slowly draining every drop of their blood and then "infuse [their] veins with a young and generous blood. For that, it will be sufficient to give you a kiss every night." Both the scratch and the kiss bring aspects of the later *Dracula* to mind. Interestingly there is a mention of the vampire's hair having moved from black to blonde, reminiscent of *The Vampire Countess*.

Ponson is best remembered today as the author of the saga of *Rocambole* (or *Les Drames de Paris* [The Dramas of Paris]), comprising twenty-five volumes published between 1857 and 1867. Rocambole's importance to popular fantastic fiction cannot be underestimated, as it represents the transition from the, by then, old-fashioned *roman noir* to modern superheroic fiction, in the sense that it created and virtually defined all the archetypes of modern superheroes and supervillains. The fact that the word *rocambolesque* has become common in French to label any kind of fantastic adventure, is the best testament of which the author could have dreamed.

Rocambole was an adventurer who began on the wrong side of the law, but ended up doing good, just like his literary descendants, Raffles, Arsène Lupin and the Saint. As was the case with Sherlock Holmes, The Shadow and Doc Savage, Rocambole eventually gathered around him a group of dedicated assistants, selected from various slices of society, ready to drop everything to help their "Master". He often operated in the shadows, pulling strings from behind the scenes. Finally, he mastered the so-called skills of the Orient and inherited the secrets of "ancient Tibet" and equally exotic lost civilizations. In short, Rocambole became more than a mere man, he was the first modern, literary superhero.

The first novel, known as *L'Héritage Mystérieux* [The Mysterious Inheritance] (1857) began with a prologue taking place in 1812 during the Russian retreat of Napoléon's great army. There, we meet Captain Armand de Kergaz, a French nobleman from Britanny, who is murdered by his young Italian aide-de-camp, Paolo de Felipone. Armand and his wife, Hélène, had a son also named Armand. Then, in 1816, after her husband's death, Hélène married Paolo, not suspecting his role in her husband's death, and had another son, Andrea. Paolo, of course, got rid of baby Armand to clear the path for Andrea to inherit the Kergaz' rich estate of Kerloven. Hélène died soon after finding out the truth. The story then moves to 1840 when a grown-up Armand de Kergaz II eventually returns. His mother long dead, he is still able to expose Paolo who confesses his villainy on his deathbed, enabling him to reclaim his birthright. The thoroughly evil Andrea is forced to flee to England, but not before swearing revenge: "It will be between the two of us now, my virtuous brother," Andrea tells Armand. "We shall see who shall win–you the philanthropist or I the villain. Heaven or Hell... And Paris shall be our battlefield!"

While in England, Andrea becomes a major figure in the British criminal underworld and takes the alias of the Irish baronet, Sir Williams. Sir Williams returns to Paris in 1843, and soon a prodigious battle of wits begins between him and Armand. Armand is trying to find the legitimate heir to the Kermouaret inheritance, a young woman named Hermine, while Sir Williams tries to steal the money by marrying her. Among the many protagonists of this saga, the one who stands out the most is the beautiful Baccarat, a courtesan, a daring and resourceful adventuress, who does not hesitate to interfere in the affairs of men and, at first, straddles the line between helping Armand and joining forces with Sir Williams.

Another, at first minor, protagonist is an extremely resourceful boy, an orphan, whose origins are unknown, who is the adopted son of Maman Fipart, a horrible, old crone who owns an inn where villains from the Paris underworld gather. That boy is named Rocambole. When we first meet him, Ponson claims that he is 14. But as the character became Sir Williams' protégé, he showed so much potential and displayed so much charisma that the author aged him in the course of a few chapters, and he suddenly became 16! The true hero of

L'Héritage Mystérieux is, nevertheless, the fearless Armand who, at the end, defeats his half-brother and marries the lovely Jeanne de Balder. Baccarat eventually chooses good over evil and becomes a nun. Rocambole, too, switches sides for money and helps Armand expose Andrea.

The next novel, *Le Club des Valets de Coeur* [The Club of the Jack of Hearts] (1858), begins five years later, circa 1848-49. Andrea has convinced Armand of his repentance and lives with him. Armand has even put him in charge of his private police to fight a gang of thieves known as the "Jack of Hearts." But in reality, Andrea is as rotten as ever, and he is the secret leader of the Jack of Hearts, ably assisted by Rocambole, now posing as the Viscount of Cambohl. The plot revolves around earning a bounty promised by a Hindu woman named Dai Natha if the gang can break up the marriage of her lover, the Marquis Van Hop. New characters include the Jack of Hearts' pretty boy, Cherubin, a beautiful courtesan and hypnotist named Turquoise, whom Andrea uses in his schemes to bring about Armand's downfall, and Sarah, a teenage medium. Sir Williams' evil plans are derailed by the return of Baccarat, who at first pretends to be bad again, but who, in reality, has joined forces with the brave Russian Count Stanislas Artoff to expose Andrea. In the end, the villain is defeated, Van Hop, Dai Natha and Cherubin are killed, and Turquoise goes mad. Rocambole again betrays Sir Williams to Armand, who was, until the very end, refusing to believe in his half-brother's villainy. Taken prisoner by Count Artoff, Sir Williams is forcibly blinded, his tongue is cut out, his face disfigured, and he is exiled to live among the savages of South America. Baccarat marries Count Artoff. Rocambole, who has struck a bargain with Armand, goes to London with 200,000 francs and Sir Williams' address book.

Rocambole returns to Paris two years later, in 1851, in *Les Exploits de Rocambole* [The Exploits of Rocambole] (1859). He is more a villain than ever: a ruthless, brilliant schemer, motivated purely by greed. He steals and murders without remorse, but with a wicked sense of humor and banter that will become characteristic of future heroes like Arsène Lupin and the Saint. This time, Rocambole's goal is to impersonate the Marquis Albert de Chamery and marry a wealthy Spanish heiress, Concepcion de Sallandrera. As luck would have it, he comes across the disfigured Sir Williams who has returned to Europe from the New World under the alias of Walter Bright, a British sailor allegedly disfigured by the Indians, and takes him under his wing. Sir Williams becomes Rocambole's evil mentor and advises him in his schemes. To cover his tracks, Rocambole does not hesitate to kill even his own adopted mother, Maman Fipart, whom he strangles with his own hands. Ultimately, Rocambole realizes that only one man who knows his true identity remains: Sir Williams himself. So he regretfully pushes him to his death. Yet, after the death of the "savage", Rocambole becomes mortally afraid–he remembers all too well his mentor's dying curse: "I am the genius who presided over your lucky star... When I am no more, your star will fall..."

And fall it does in the last part of the story, also known as *La Revanche de Baccarat* [The Revenge of Baccarat], which takes place in 1852. For it is the then-Countess Artoff who, back in Paris, pieces together the puzzle and comes to the conclusion that the Marquis de Chamery is none other than her old foe, Rocambole. She manages to enlist the help of Rocambole's henchman, Zampa, locates the real Albert, who was prisoner in Cadiz, marries him to Concepcion, and ultimately captures Rocambole in a Spanish castle. Baccarat's punishment is horrible: Rocambole's handsome face is burned with acid; he is then dispatched to the gallows of Cadiz to take Albert's place, then transferred to the hard-labor camp of Toulon (where Jean Valjean had been imprisoned thirty years or so before). The novel ends with a tragic scene: during a charitable visit to the labor camp, Albert's sister, Blanche de Chamery, a woman Rocambole loved as if she had been his true sister, now married to Fabien d'Asmolles, fails to recognize Rocambole in the bedraggled, disfigured convict he has become. "She did not recognize me," laments Rocambole. "All I have suffered until now was nothing. That is the true punishment!"

Les Exploits de Rocambole was a huge success, causing the sales of *La Patrie* to go through the roof. But Ponson had left his charming yet utterly villainous anti-hero in a desperate predicament. Something had to be done.

Rocambole's return was trumpeted the following year in *Les Chevaliers du Clair de Lune* [The Knights of Moonlight] (1862), a *Count of Monte-Cristo*-like tale which began c. 1854-1855. Yet, the entire, long, first chapter of this complicated saga does not even feature the hero. Once again, the plot revolves around a complex inheritance. Four young men, Gontran de Neubourg, Lord Blackstone of Galwy, Arthur de Chenevières and Albert de Verne decide to join forces, dubbing themselves the "Knights of Moonlight". Their purpose is to help a mysterious young woman, first known only as Domino, but whose identity is later revealed to be Danielle de Main-Hardye, to avenge her murdered parents and reclaim her inheritance from the evil Ambroise de Mortefontaine. Two other characters are the brave but crippled French Army Captain Charles de Kerdrel, nicknamed Grain-de-Sel, and the courtesan Saphir. Where is Rocambole? He barely appears in the novel. His face is still scarred, he now wears blue or green-tinted glasses—a disguise Arsène Lupin uses in *L'Agence Barnett*—and walks with a pronounced limp. He did not escape from Toulon but was pardoned thanks to Fabien and Blanche's efforts—they recognized him after all! Now financed by Armand de Kergaz and the Countess Artoff, Rocambole uses his talents for the cause of good, to make up for his evil past. But his role in the novel is not that of a man of action–that part is reserved to the four Knights of Moonlight–but rather of a schemer, a man who pulls the strings behind the scenes. Baccarat is also totally missing from the novel.

This was emphatically *not* what the readers wanted, and the sales of *La Patrie* fell accordingly. The editors asked Ponson to switch gears in a hurry, and the novel was wrapped up hurriedly in a brief epilogue tagged at the end of the third and final section entitled *Le Testament de Grain de Sel* [The Testament of Grain-of-Salt]. Then, the author did something extraordinary: after a three-year interval, he went back to the point when Rocambole was prisoner at the hard labor camp of Toulon, and started the story over, thereby erasing *Les Chevaliers du Clair de Lune* from the continuity of the series, without bothering to pretend it had been a dream or anything–just as the television series *Dallas* did over a century later.

So Rocambole, now known as Convict No. 117, returned in a new saga aptly entitled *La Résurrection de Rocambole* [The Resurrection of Rocambole] (1866), for it was a literary resurrection as well as the tale of a moral redemption. The first part of the book shows Rocambole, no longer disfigured, escaping from the labor camp of Toulon after ten years of captivity–so the events now take place in the present, when the novel was written, and experiencing a Saint Paul-like moral epiphany. He decides to become a force for good and gathers around him a small cadre of associates who call him Master: the repentant, hulkish convict Milon, and the fiercely loyal Vanda. Rocambole's first task is to protect two orphaned young women, first Antoinette, then her sister Madeleine, from the schemes of the evil Karle de Morlux and his partner-in-crime, the Russian she-devil, Countess Wasilika Wasserenoff. Rocambole's new secret identity is that of Major Avatar, a respected Russian nobleman. During the course of the adventure, his path again crosses that of Baccarat, a.k.a. Countess Artoff, who eventually comes to accept his redemption when she sees him deliberately let Madeleine, whom he dearly loves, marry Yvan Potenieff. Then and only then, Baccarat knows that Rocambole has exorcised the ghost of Sir Williams, and whispers in his ear a single word: "Redemption!" In a short epilogue entitled *La Vengeance de Wasilika* [The Revenge of Wasilika], Rocambole, having put his affairs in order, wants to kill himself–even Milon and Vanda fail to persuade him otherwise. But then, Blanche de Chamery, whom he loved as a sister, comes to tell him the Wasilika has kidnaped her son, and Rocambole is once again resurrected.

Rocambole saves the child and kills Wasilika, but is mortally wounded. The book ends on a cliffhanger, with Milon saying, "Rocambole is dead!" and Vanda replying, "No, God would not will it! *Rocambole still lives!*"

From that point forward, the publication of a new *Rocambole* serial was heralded with much advance publicity and caused the sales of newspapers to go through the roof. Ponson was crowned king of the *roman feuilleton*. He left *La Patrie* and gave his next *Rocambole* novel to *La Petite Presse*, who had offered him a small fortune for the rights.

Rocambole made his much-heralded return in *Le Dernier Mot de Rocambole* [The Last Word of Rocambole] (1867), another complex saga sprinkled with fantastic elements. Rocambole infiltrates a gang of thieves known as the "Destroyers". During the course of a burglary, he comes across a gang of Thugees from India who have arrived in France via England, and seek to kidnap virgins to serve their goddess, Kali. Rocambole travels to London with Milon, Vanda and several reformed Destroyers, including young Marmouset, to fight the Thugees. Their target is Gypsy, a girl raised among the gypsies, but whose real identity is Anna Blesingfort. Gypsy's inheritance was stolen by her aunt, nicknamed "Milady", who is the mistress of Ali-Remjeh, the Thugees' leader. Rocambole saves Gypsy; the British government loans him a ship and he captures Ali-Remjeh and Milady. He pardons the woman and delivers the Thugee leader to the British. He then goes to India, leaving his friends behind.

In the second part of the story, Marmouset comes across a mysterious woman known as the "Beautiful Gardener" who grows deadly plants in her garden. Several members of a club of idle rich, the so-called "Club of Corpses," have broken into her house and discovered the wax statue of one of their members, Maurevers. He was also a friend of Turquoise, a character from *The Club of The Jack of Hearts*, and has mysteriously vanished. The Beautiful Gardener is Roumia, a gypsy woman, who kidnapped Maurevers because he killed his half-brother, Perdito, who was her lover. Roumia captures Marmouset and

Vanda. But then, Rocambole returns from India, accompanied by his new friend, Nadir, leader of the heroic Sons of Shiva, enemies of the evil Kali-worshipping Thugees. Rocambole defeats Roumia, who sees the error of her ways and frees Maurevers.

We learn that, while in India, Rocambole joined forces with Rajah Osmany. With the help of Nadir, he defeated Osmany's villainous minister, Sir Edward Linton. But Linton escaped, taking with him the Rahjah's young son. He has returned to Europe, and Rocambole is hot on his trail. The story moves back to London. There, Roumia helps Rocambole defeat Linton, but in turn the villain has arranged for Rocambole to be arrested by the British police. Roumia, Marmouset, Milon and Vanda capture Linton, and get the Rajah's son and his treasure back.

Le Dernier Mot de Rocambole was a huge commercial success, and only confirmed Ponson's reputation. Its final section was entitled *La Vérité sur Rocambole* [The Truth About Rocambole] and was a strange departure, almost a semi-autobiographical novel in which Ponson wrote about himself, and the life of a writer of serials, and explained how he had become Rocambole's biographer! In it, he states that he had heard only rumors about Rocambole when he wrote *L'Héritage Mystérieux* (therefore, that story was mostly made up), then the real Rocambole contacted him and recounted his true adventures. Ponson then lost contact with Rocambole again after he was captured, which is why he was forced to invent *Les Chevaliers du Clair-de-Lune*. But Rocambole renewed his acquaintance with him after he escaped from Toulon. Since then, Ponson claims he has written only true stories, as conveyed to him by Rocambole himself. He ends by stating that he just learned that Rocambole has escaped from a British jail, and that new adventures are on their way.

The following installment of the saga was entitled *Les Misères de Londres* [The Miseries of London] (1868) and again took place in England. In it, the name of Rocambole is never mentioned; he is merely known as the fearsome Man in

Grey. His allies are Irish priest Samuel, and the beggar Barclay nicknamed "Shocking", because it's his favorite expression. The stakes are to locate the last heir of a wealthy Irish family, Ralph, who was raised in the gutters of London in transparent Dickensian fashion. Rocambole's enemies are Lord Palmure and his daughter, the beautiful Miss Ellen, who stand to inherit, and their associate, the diabolical Reverend Peters Town. After many complicated plots, Rocambole finally outwits Miss Ellen, but is recaptured by the police. As he is taken away, Ellen Palmure realizes she was in love with him

The adventures of Rocambole continued with *Les Démolitions de Paris* [The Demolitions of Paris] (1869). Rocambole is prisoner in Newgate. Miss Ellen goes to Paris to enlist the help of Rocambole's old gang: Vanda, Milon and Marmouset. One presumes that Nadir is now back in India, happily married to Roumia. But Lord Palmure and Peters Town, a.k.a. Patterson, have sworn revenge. Their henchman, James Wood, captures Ellen near a construction site–hence the title–but she is rescued by a young bricklayer dubbed the Limousin, because he comes from that part of France. Shocking also comes to Paris to seek help for Rocambole. Eventually Wood is defeated, the gang gets back together and travels to London. Ellen is reconciled with her father, who regrets his evil ways. With Samuel's help, the gang prepares to spring Rocambole, but runs afoul of a similar scheme by Irish patriots. The story ends with a huge explosion in the tunnels under Newgate.

Rocambole's exploits were abruptly interrupted in the midst of the last saga, *La Corde du Pendu* [The Rope of the Hanged Man] (1870), by Ponson's sudden death during the German invasion of 1871. Everyone has now escaped safe and sound from Newgate. While in jail, Rocambole met a man, Tom, who was a servant working for the Pembertons. He discovered a sinister plot by Evandale Pemberton, who stole the fortune and title of the rightful heir, his half-brother, William. Tom killed Evandale, but poor William is still locked up in Bedlam. Rocambole decides to help him, but runs afoul of his old enemy, Peters Town (Patterson), now working for Sir

Archibald, Evandale's father-in law. Marmouset springs William out of Bedlam. Rocambole and Shocking capture Patterson. Vanda seduces Sir Archibald and takes him to France. But Patterson's criminal organization is hot on the trail of the heroes... Then the story stopped.

Writer Constant Guéroult penned two Rocambole sequels, *Le Retour et la Fin de Rocambole* [The Return and the End of Rocambole] (1875) and *Les Nouveaux Exploits de Rocambole* [The New Exploits of Rocambole] (1880), in which Rocambole now lives in Paris with Vanda and Milon under the alias of Mr. Portal. In it, he defeats criminals planning to commit crimes using his name... but no explanations are given as to the end of the previous adventure.

Another sequel, entitled *Les Bâtards de Rocambole* [The Bastard Children of Rocambole] (1886), by Jules Cardoze followed. The story is mostly about Rocambole's illegitimate children and takes place while he is prisoner in Toulon. In perhaps the first case of crossover fiction, the author mentions the Black Coats, Alexandre Dumas' Mohicans of Paris, Rocambole's earlier *Valets de Cœur*, Eugène Sue's *Ravageurs* (from *Les Mystères de Paris*) and the *Etrangleurs* (from *Le Juif Errant*).

In a series of eight novels devoted to Rocambole's grandson, *Le Petit-Fils de Rocambole*, written by Frédéric Valade (1922-33), we learned that in 1886, before his death, an 80-year-old or so Rocambole married Ellen Palmure and has now groomed his grandson Edward to take over his crime-fighting career. Edward is assisted by Ursule (Milon's daughter), a new Vanda (the daughter of the previous Vanda and a brother of Count Artoff) and Mistigris, the son of Marmouset. The villains include first the Irish-German spy O'Sullivan, and later the beautiful Olivia, daughter of O'Sullivan's right-hand man, Faradol. The series ends c. 1907.

A new series of five YA novels by Michael Honaker, beginning with *Rocambole et le Spectre de Kerloven* [Rocambole and The Spectre of Kerloven] (2002-05), pits Rocambole against a resurrected Sir Williams and the Black Coats, and takes place soon after *La Résurrection de Rocambole*.

Fantastique Littéraire

On the more respectable side of the literary fence, the 19th century *fantastique* literature after 1830 was dominated, as mentioned above, first by the influence of E. T. A. Hoffmann, and then by that of Edgar Allan Poe. The former's famous *Tales* had been translated in a twenty volume-collection published between 1829 and 1833 by publisher Renduel and had an immediate and huge effect on French writers. They were so successful that it is not an exaggeration to say that the mid-1800s belonged to the *fantastique romantique*.

Fantastique Romantique

The first of the French authors of the 19th century to become a disciple of E.T.A. Hoffmann, was Charles Nodier, whose manifesto "*Du Fantastique en Literature*" [Of the Fantastic in Literature] (1830), was enthusiastically endorsed by poets Gérard de Nerval and Alfred de Musset. After dramatizing Polidori's *The Vampire* (1820) (see above), the author wrote a horror story, *Smarra, ou les Démons de la Nuit* [Smarra, or the Demons of the Night][61] (1821), in which a Byronesque hero travels through enchanted forests before eventually confronting an evil vampire, perhaps the first mixture of traditional and modern fantastic elements under a single cover. Then, in 1825, he published *Infernaliana*, an anthology of stories about the Devil and demonic possession. In 1837, he wrote *Ines de la Sierra* and, finally, in 1839, *Lydie*, two more

---

[61] In *Trilby* * *The Crumb Fairy*, Black Coat Press, ISBN 978-1-61227-455-3.

romans noirs. But his heart was not with that genre and he soon moved on to writing fantasy (see below).

Before joining the ranks of France's leading romantic poets, Gérard de Nerval, one of the first symbolist and surrealist writers in French literature, translated Johann Wolfgang von Goethe's *Faust* (1827). He then embarked on the writing of a series of fantastic tales, all exhibiting a strong Hoffmannesque influence: *"Soirée d'Automne"* [Autumn Evening], *"Le Portrait du Diable"* [The Devil's Portrait], *"La Reine des Poissons"* [The Queen Of The Fish], *"Le Monstre Vert"* [The Green Monster], *"La Main Enchantée"* [The Enchanted Hand], etc., all collected in *La Main de Gloire* [The Glory Hand] (1832). In 1839, the author collaborated with Alexandre Dumas on the play *L'Alchimiste* [The Alchemist]. In it, the alchemist Fasio continues his great work while his wife Francesca languishes at home, jealous of a courtesan, La Maddalena, and pursued by the assiduities of the powerful Podesta. The old loan shark Grimaldi wants to drive him out and Fasio makes some gold coins to gain for a few days' respite. The laboratory then explodes. While measuring the extent of the damage, Fasio discovers a passage between his cellar and the one where Grimaldi hides his gold. He secretly witnesses the murder of Grimaldi by Lelio, his nephew, a ruined gambler who has come to claim his share of the inheritance. Discovered by Lelio, Fasio is offered a large part of the old man's fortune. He first resists the temptation, then yields. Fasio and Francesca then go on to live in a real palace. The former alchemist is believed to have been enriched by his art. He invites the fine Florentine society to a masked ball. La Maddalena appears. Deceived by Podesta about her husband's behavior, Francesca flees and finds refuge in the alchemist's workshop where Podesta joins her. Convinced that without his gold, he will no longer be loved by the courtesan, she reveals to the magistrate the origin of the fortune. The latter then discovers Grimaldi's corpse and has Fasio arrested, tried and condemned. Francesca implores in vain Podesta. As Fasio is taken to be executed, Lelio denounces himself to the authorities as the only culprit. The play was first staged on April 10, 1839 at the Théâtre de la Renaissance. Embroidering on an unconventional romantic canvas, Renaissance Italy, secret underground laboratories, masked balls, etc., the two authors were freely inspired by a play by Henry Hart Milman, *Fazio, a tragedy* played in 1815, itself adapted from a short story by the Italian Anton Francesco Grazzini, *La storia di Fazio*.

Mentally unhinged after a lover's death, Nerval developed an interest in mystical beliefs. After a journey through Egypt and the Middle East in 1843, he became fascinated by ancient religions, such as the cults of Isis, Cybele and Mithra, as well as various esoteric secrets such as the Illuminati and the theories of reincarnation, dreams and the means of communication with supernatural realms. In *Voyage en Orient* [Voyage to the Orient] (1851), he wrote an account of his journeys, in which he included some adapted Arabic legends such as "*The Tale of Caliph Hakem and the Queen of the Morning*". In *Les Illuminés* [The Illuminati] (1852), he penned a series of biographies of Jacques Cazotte, Nicolas-Edmé Restif de la Bretonne, Cagliostro and other famous adepts.

Committed to an asylum several times, Nerval nevertheless managed, during his intervals of sanity, to become one of France's most renowned poets. After being institutionalized, his work began taking on an increasing visionary quality, with *Aurélia* (1853-54), *Les Filles du Feu* [The Daughters of Fire] (1854), which included the stories "*Sylvie*" and "*Pandora*" (1854). All were obsessive visions, dreams or nightmares, deeply steeped in oriental mythologies, and dealing with the themes of damnation and salvation of the soul. They reflected with admirable lucidity a man's descent into madness, and his morbid, yet beautiful, exploration of the land of the dead. *Aurelia* also featured one of the first, modern variations on the theme of the doppelganger. Nerval's fantastic poetry was collected in *Les Chimères* [Chimeras] (1854). A year later, his body was found mysteriously hanging from a lamppost near the Chatelet in Paris. Perhaps he had at last met his dreaded doppelganger?

Delphine de Girardin was the daughter of famous writer and playwright Sophie Gay. She began writing at an early age, publishing two books of poems in 1824 and 1824, and a popular collection of children's stories in 1833. She later married writer-journalist Emile de Girardin (and became an important figure in the Romantic Movement. Her Romantic fantasies include *Le Lorgnon* (1831), about a pair of glasses that enables their wearer to read thoughts, and *La Canne de M. de Balzac* [Balzac's Cane] (1836),[62] in which the famous author allows a young man down on is luck to borrow the eponymous object, which confers upon its owner the gift of invisibility.

Gustave Flaubert, the author of the classic *Madame Bovary* (1857), combined romanticism and realism. Some of his early works nevertheless featured alchemists, pacts with the devil and all the traditional elements of gothic and supernatural fiction. Between 1835 and 1838, he wrote a series of fantastic short stories, such as *"Bibliomanie"*, *"Voyage en Enfer"* [Voyage to Hell] (1835), *"Rêve d'Enfer"* [A Dream of Hell] (1837), *"La Danse des Morts"* [The Dance of the Dead] (1838), etc. Of greater interest was *Smarh* (1839), a *Faust*-like novel clearly labeled as *fantastique*, the title of which was probably borrowed from Nodier's *Smarra*. The author returned to the Faustian theme with *La Première Tentation de St. Antoine* (1849), revised in 1874 as *La Tentation de St. Antoine* [The Temptation of St. Anthony], an extravagant Christian fantasy in which he tried to reconcile science and religion.

Théophile Gautier, a leading writer of the Romantic movement, is today better remembered for his swashbuckling novel *Capitaine Fracasse* (1863). Like many, the author first embraced the *fantastique* with classic gothic stories heavily influenced by Hoffmann. *Albertus* (1832) was a novel in verse about an artist who damned himself for the love of a witch. The concept of impossible love, often love between the living and the dead, became a recurrent theme throughout his career.

---

[62] Both in *Balzac's Cane*, Black Coat Press, ISBN 978-1-61227-368-6.

In *La Morte Amoureuse* [The Loving Dead] (1836), he told the story of a young priest who falls in love with a beautiful female vampire, but is eventually forced by his superior to kill her. *La Morte Amoureuse* was a remarkably modern precursor to the romantic vampire novels of Chelsea Quinn Yarbro and Ann Rice, in that its vampire was not a soulless creature of the night, but a loving, sensitive and incredibly erotic woman.

Like his friend Nerval, Gautier exhibited a strong interest in the occult, metaphysics and oriental philosophies. His numerous journeys inspired *Arria Marcella* (1852), a time travel love story which took us back to the days of ancient Pompei; *Jettatura* (1856), the story of a man victim of a curse. Both *Avatar* (1857) and *Spirite* (1866) are *roman spirites* which dealt with the theme of life after death. The former featured an exchange of souls and bodies, made possible by using Doctor Miracle's forbidden oriental knowledge. The latter told of the romantic liaison between a young man and his ghostly lover. The author also translated Rudolf Erich Raspe's *Baron Munchausen's Narrative of His Marvellous Travels and Campaigns in Russia* (1875) into French.

Prosper Mérimée, a writer and journalist well known for his *Colomba* (1840) and *Carmen* (1845), took some of the exotic concepts already developed by Nerval and Gautier, and added his own dose of realism, and even of skepticism. His first excursion into the genre was *La Guzla* (1827), a literary hoax comprised of ballads about murder, revenge and vampires, allegedly translated from the Illyrian by "Hiacynthe Maglanowich". The book even included a pseudo-academic study of vampirism! In 1829, his *Vision de Charles X*, a tale about a Swedish King cursed with second sight, looked so authentic—even though it was mostly made up—that it confirmed his talent of journalist of the *fantastique*. In 1830, the author traveled to Spain and wrote about witchcraft. His *Les Âmes du Purgatoire* [The Souls of Purgatory] (1834) retold the famous Don Juan legend.

Mérimée's eye for realistic details, even when describing fantastic events, was particularly notable in his *La Vénus d'Ille*

(1837), which became an immediate classic. In it, a young man falls in love with a pagan statue and makes the mistake of giving her a wedding ring. The statue eventually comes to life and crushes her groom. The author used no spells and no fancy mysticism to explain the incredible event, just pure fantasy. *Lokis* (1869) reversed the roles: this time, it was the bride who was devoured by her husband, a monstrous "werebear". Two of his latter works, *La Chambre Bleue* [The Blue Room] (1872) and the posthumous *Djoumâne* (written in 1870; published in 1873), based on a North African legend, also showed Mérimée's fascination with the supernatural. He also translated Alexander Pushkin's *Queen of Spades* (1834), and wrote a study about Russian fantasy writer, Nikolai Gogol.

Louis Ulbach was one the fieriest Romantics, notorious for his pugnacious diatribes against Emile Zola published in *Le Figaro*. *Prince Bonifacio* (1864)[63] is a bold *conte philosophique*, which sets out to mock politics in the scathing fashion of Voltaire and Jonathan Swift, mimicking the form of folk tales, but substituting pseudoscientific speculation for magic, and adding an element of satire directed against "mad scientists." The author also penned several historical stories that flirt with supernatural themes, some that are innovative endeavors on the margins of the *roman scientifique*, and likely rewritten *Le Prince des Sots* [The Prince of Fools] (1887).[64] A unfinished novel based on an unproduced play by Gérard de Nerval. During the Reign of French King Charles VI, a fierce struggle for power develops between the king's brother, Louis d'Orléans, and his cousin, Jean de Bourgogne. When the latter instigates the murder of the former in 1407, the conflict degenerates into a civil war between Burgundians and Armagnacs. In the midst of this blood-drenched background, a mysterious comedian and proto-anarchist nicknamed the "Prince of Fools" schemes to save the innocent, punish the villains,

---

[63] Black Coat Press, ISBN 978-1-61227-228-3.
[64] Black Coat Press, ISBN 978-1-61227-872-8.

and undermine the aristocratic order invisibly and subtly through the medium of plays.

Like Nodier and Nerval, George Sand also wrote an essay, entitled "*Essai sur le Drame Fantastique*" [Essay on Fantastic Drama], in which she perceptively stated that "the world of the *fantastique* is neither outside, nor above, nor below, but inside us." After penning two *romans noirs*, *Consuelo* (1842) and *La Comtesse de Rudolstadt* (1844), the author found her own voice in a series of rustic novels which drew their inspiration from the folklore of her native Berry: *La Mare au Diable* [The Devil's Pond] (1845), *La Petite Fadette* [Little Fadette] (1849) and *François le Champi* (1849). However, her *Légendes Rustiques* [Rustic Legends] (1858) and *Contes d'une Grand-Mère* [Grandmother's Tales] (1872) represented an attempt at recreating the Fairy Tale genre in rustic trappings.

Folklore was also the main source of inspiration of Émile Erckmann and Alexandre Chatrian, an Alsatian writing team who signed their works Erckmann-Chatrian. They are known today mostly for their richly drawn novels about life in the French countryside. Their first novella, however, "*Science et Génie*" [Science and Genius] (1850), told the story of an alchemist who invented a potion that could turn people into stone. They then embarked on a series of rustic horror stories, often incorporating the theme of men transforming into beasts. Their stories were collected in four volumes: *Les Contes Fantastiques* [Fantastic Tales] (1847), which included the classic short story "*L'Araignée Crabe*" [The Crab-Spider], about a blood-sucking lake monster with the body of a spider and the head of a man; *Contes de la Montagne* [Mountain Tales] (1860); *Contes du Bord du Rhin* [Rhine Tales] (1862); and finally, *Contes Populaires* [Popular Tales] (1866). Erckmann-Chatrian also wrote the novel *Hughes-le-Loup* [Hugh-the-Wolf] (1863), about a noble family, victims of a werewolf curse, combining the then-popular theme of lycanthropy with story elements taken from the *roman noir*.

It is difficult to determine exactly when Samuel-Henri Berthoud, who anglicized the spelling of his familiar name as an affectation when he elected to sign his literary works "S. Henry Berthoud", first met other leading members of the Romantic Movement; although he was certainly acquainted with Jules Janin and Petrus Borel by 1833.

By the time his third novel, *Mater dolorosa* [Mother of Tears] (1834), appeared, he had completed publication of the work that won him his first real success, the three volumes of *Chroniques et traditions surnaturelles de la Flandre* [Chronicles and Supernatural Traditions of Flanders] (1831-34). The collection does include some genuine items of folklore, only slightly modified in giving them literary form, but it also contains a considerable number of works that do not even bother to mimic the form of folktales, simply being items of modern supernatural fiction based on the kinds of materials found in folktales, and at least some of those that do mimic folktales are original compositions—"fakelore" rather than "folklore."

Such mixtures are not unusual in collections of that sort, but Berthoud is further removed from being an authentic folklorist than the most prominent Romantic contributors to the field, including the brothers Grimm in Germany, Robert Hunt in England and Anatole Le Braz in France. In a single-volume reprint of the collection published as *Légendes et traditions surnaturelles de Flandres* (1862), he added the novella *Asrael et Neptha*, originally published separately in 1832, to the series—a move serving to re-emphasize the fact that its contents are far more readily considered as literary works that draw some inspiration from Flanders folklore than attempts to record the folklore in question in anything resembling its "original" anecdotal form. *Asrael et Neptha*[65] is the most revealing and the purest of the author's fantasies, and a significant early contribution to what became the great Romantic and Symbolist tradition of "literary satanism," in which writers deliberately adopted a stance removed from orthodox Christianity in order to reappraise the character of Satan. As might be ex-

---

[65] *The Angel Asrael*, Black Coat Press, ISBN 978-1-61227-613-7.

pected of a devout writer, Berthoud shows no sympathy for Satan, who remains an archetype of vitriolic nastiness, but in his characterization of the rebel, like John Milton, he cannot help but express a certain admiration for his overweening pride and vaulting ambition. Berthoud's God owes his status not to any intrinsic virtue, but merely to his victory in the War in Heaven, which Satan unhesitatingly attributes to chance.

Other collections of supernatural stories, eccentric scientific fantasies, featuring real or imaginary scientists, and ground-breaking visions of the prehistoric past and the future, include *Contes Misanthropiques* [Misanthropic Tales] (1831), *Le Cheveu du Diable* [The Devil's Hair] (1833), *L'Anneau de Salomon* [Solomon's Ring] (1850), *Le Dragon Rouge, ou L'Art de Commander au Démon et aux Esprits Infernaux* [The Red Dragon, or The Art of Commanding the Devil & the Infernal Spirits] (1861) and *Le Baiser du Diable* [The Devil's Kiss] (1861).[66] They show Berthoud as writer of considerable ability, often displaying pioneering surges of imagination who came close to inventing science fiction as early as the 1840s.

His "*L'Ange de Williams*" [William's Angel] (1838),[67] based on the story of William FitzOsbert, who led a popular uprising by the citizens of London in the spring of 1196, and was executed, is a semi-mythical retelling of this incident, that includes the characters of Robin Hood and Richard the Lionheart.

Berthoud became an important pioneer of the *conte cruel*, and one of the first writers to experiment with that would later be called "stream-of-consciousness" narration. His work would have been just as difficult for contemporary readers to assess as for modern ones, but its esotericism should not be allowed to detract from his achievement, which is as remarkable for its fervor as for its uniqueness.

---

[66] Many stories collected in *Martyrs of Science*, Black Coat Press, ISBN 978-1-61227-229-0.
[67] Black Coat Press, ISBN 978-1-61227-875-9.

Of all the writers who used regional folklore as a source of inspiration, none was more famous or influential than Anatole Le Braz, whose many works were entirely devoted to the preservation of the "soul" of ancient Britanny. The author was praised and recognized by the French Academy. His works included a novel, *Le Gardien du Feu* [The Guardian of the Fire] (1900), several collections such as *Pâques d'Islande* [Icelandic Easter] (1897) and *Le Sang de la Sirène* [The Blood of the Mermaid] (1901), and numerous books preserving the rich heritage of Britannic folk tales, such as the classic *La Légende de la Mort chez les Bretons Armoricains et en Basse Bretagne* [The Legend of Death Among Armorican Britons & in Lower Britanny] (1893), *Vieilles Histoires du Pays Breton* [Old Tales From Britanny] (1897), *La Terre du Passé* [Land of the Past] (1902), *Le Théâtre Celtique* [Celtic Theater] (1905) and *Contes du Soleil et de la Brume* [Tales of Sun and Mist] (1913).

Jules de La Madelène's *Les Années en Peine* [The Years of Pain] (1857) was a collection of fantastic tales including "*Rosita*" and "*La Dernière Heure d'un Stradivarius*" [A Stradivarius' Last Hour].

Armand Silvestre, with *Contes à la Brune* [Misty Tales] (1889), *Histoires Abracadabrantes* [Alakazam Tales] (1893), *La Planète Enchantée* [The Enchanted Planet] (1896) and *Contes Irrévérencieux* [Irreverent Tales] (1896).

Nobel prize winner Frédéric Mistral's classic *Mireille* (*Mireio*) (1859) was an epic poem written in the Provençal language of Southern France; it featured a good witch and various spirits. It was later adapted into an opera by Michel Carré.

Indeed, one cannot complete this overview of the *fantastique romantique* of the 1800s without mentioning the field of Operas, where Hoffmann's tales and other fantastic stories were much in demand. Among the most notable works were:

La Damnation de Faust [Faust's Damnation] (1846) by Hector Berlioz.

La Poupée de Nuremberg [The Nuremberg Doll] (1852) (music by Adolphe Adam) by Adolphe de Leuven and Amédée de Beauplan.

Faust (1859) (music by Charles Gounod) and *Les Contes d'Hoffmann* (1881) (music by Jacques Offenbach) by Michel Carré and Jules Barbier.

Le Sabbat [The Sabbath] (1877) (music by Emmanuel Chabrier) by Armand Silvestre.

Le Roi d'Ys (1888) about the legendary sunken city off the coast of Britanny (music by Édouard Lalo) by Alfred Blau and Louis de Gramont, and *Esclarmonde* (1889) (music by Jules Massenet) by Alfred Blau alone.

Of all opera writers, few were as prolific in the genre as Eugène Scribe, whose works included *La Dame Blanche* [*The White Lady*] (1825) based on a story by Walter Scott (music by François-Adrien Boieldieu); *Robert le Diable* [Robert the Devil] (1831) (music by Giacomo Meyerbeer); *Le Cheval de Bronze* [The Brass Horse] (1835) (music by Daniel Auber); *Le Lac des Fées* [The Fays' Lake] (1839) (music by Daniel Auber); *La Part du Diable* [The Devil's Share] (1843) (which took place on the planet Venus) (music by Daniel Auber); *Le Juif Errant* [The Wandering Jew] (1852) (music by Fromental Halévy, written with Jules-Henri Vernoy de Saint-Georges) (1852) and *La Chatte Métamorphosée en Femme* [The Cat Who Turned Into A Woman] (music by Jacques Offenbach, written with Anne-Honoré-Joseph Duveyrier, a.k.a. Mélesville) (1858).

Even the ballet reflected the fantastic mood of the times, as demonstrated by the prodigious success of Eugène Lami's *La Sylphide* (1832), starring Marie Taglioni, or that of Théophile Gautier's *Giselle* (1842).

Fantastique Réaliste

And then came Edgar Allan Poe and the landscape suddenly changed. The American author's stories were translated and collected in 1856 by the notorious poet Charles Baudelaire. While Hoffmann appealed to the imagination, Poe used a merciless, inescapable form of logic. Where Hoffmann relied on metaphysics, Poe used mathematics. Unlike the romantics and their unbridled fears, Poe provided a logical, almost rational, approach to the supernatural. He also cast a much darker light than Hoffmann, in the sense that his stories rarely offered any hope or salvation. Finally, he also made the genre more respectable, to the extent that his works proved popular and influential, even amongst so-called "mainstream" authors, some of whom began to write stories in the same vein.

Guy de Maupassant, one of the most famous writers of the naturalist school, is often held to be one of the greatest French short-story writers ever. A literary disciple of Gustave Flaubert, Maupassant wrote, throughout his life, about thirty genre stories or novellas, from the macabre *"La Main Coupée"* [*The Severed Hand*] (1875) to *"Qui Sait?"* [Who Knows?] (1890). The author followed in the footsteps of Poe, and clearly anticipated H. P. Lovecraft. Like the writer from Providence, he was obsessed with the notion of insanity and slow descent into madness. He, himself, suffered from congenital syphilis. His brother was retarded and, before being eventually committed in 1888, had allegedly told Maupassant, "It is you who are mad; you are the crazy one in the family." Indeed, by his mid-thirties, the author began to suffer from chronic neuralgia, compounded by his use of drugs and his latent psychoses. He started to hallucinate the presence of mysterious, hostile, invisible beings, and became haunted by the idea of death. He was finally committed in 1892 and died shortly afterwards.

During his last years, Maupassant wrote a number of short stories reflecting those fears: In *"Sur l'Eau"* [On the Water] (1881), a simple boat ride takes its protagonists into another, invisible alien universe. *"Apparition"* (1883) features a man who does not believe in ghosts and whose sanity is severely shaken when he was confronted with a true, supernatural phenomenon. *"Lui?"* [Him?] (1883) and *"L'Auberge"* [The Inn] (1886) deal with hallucinations. *"Un Fou?"* [A Madman?] (1884) with schizophrenia before its nature became known or understood.

His masterpiece was *Le Horla* (1887), which was the basis for the 1963 film *Diary of a Madman*, starring Vincent Price. In it, it is revealed that Man shares the Earth with invisible beings of great powers to whom we are only cattle, and who are fated to be our successors. With its pseudo-scientific and psychoanalytic explanations, *Le Horla* was in the same vein as Edward Bulwer-Lytton's (1803-1873) *The Coming Race* (1871), and anticipated Charles Fort's *The Book of the Damned* (1919) and Eric Frank Russell's *Sinister Barrier* (1943). The origin of the word "Horla" was never fully explained, but could derive from "*hors-là*" [out there] or from the local *patois* word "*horzain*" [stranger].

Unlike his predecessors, Maupassant dealt with the *fantastique* in a casual, natural, and yet immensely disturbing fashion. He did not rely on devils, witches or other outside supernatural forces, but on the objective, fundamental alienness of the universe in which we live, blissfully ignorant of its deadly nature. For him, like for Lovecraft, to get a glimpse of the true reality is to risk madness, death −or worse.

Charles Asselineau, a writer better known for his literary studies and his friendship with Baudelaire, with *La Double Vie* [*The Double Life*] (1858),[68] a collection of supernatural stories (including the classic "*Le Mensonge*" [The Lie]) on the theme of dreams, glimpses into life beyond death and other posthumous experiences.

The eclectic Auguste de Villiers de l'Isle-Adam was another naturalist writer whose *Contes Cruels* [Cruel Tales] (1883) and *Nouveaux Contes Cruels* [New Cruel Tales] (1888)[69] seemed directly inspired by Poe and shared the same sensibilities and taste for the macabre. In these collections, we meet a unique and colorful cast of extraordinary characters

---

[68] Black Coat Press, ISBN 978-1-61227-079-1.
[69] Many included in *The Scaffold*, Black Coat Press, ISBN 978-1-932983-01-2.

such as Akedysseril the Queen of India, Mayeris the big game hunter who capured the sacred white elephant, Maryelle the courtesan, Catalina the gypsy toast of Santander, Mahoin the brigand, the murderous Doctor Hallidon and Tomolo Ké Ké the Antipodean who traversed the Earth. Like Poe, the author was also tempted by science fiction. His *Tribulat Bonhomet* (1887)[70] used ornate literary twists in a horror tale involving possession by a "Vampire Soul".

Few writers have ever been able to draw from that particular well as prolifically and consistently as Catulle Mendès, and there are only a precious few whose work could be assembled into a kaleidoscopic display of phantasmagorical materials. Most of his short fantastic fiction was collected in collections such as *Les Contes du rouet* [Tales of the Spinning Wheel] (1885), *Lesbia* (1886), *Pour les belles personnes* [For Beautiful People] (1886), *Pour lire au couvent* [For Reading in a Convent] (1887), *L'Envers des feuilles* [The Other Side of Leaves] (1888), *La Vie serieuse* [The Serious Life] (1889), *La Princesse nue* [The Naked Princess] (1890), *La Messe rose* [The Pink Mass] (1893), *L'Homme orchestre* [The Orchestra Man] (1896) *Arc-en-ciel et sourcil rouge* [Rainbow and Red Eyebrow] (1897) and *Le Carnaval fleuri* [The Carnival With Flowers] (1904).[71] His stories dealt with anomalous events and altered states of consciousness that might or might not have supernatural causes. Other writers had written stories of the same kind, but the author's work in that vein is particularly interesting, not merely by virtue of its profusion and its uncommon imaginative range, but also because of its macabre humor and its straightforward disturbing aspects. That combination of effects made his contribution to the field of the *fantastique* unique and fascinating.

---

[70] In *The Vampire Soul*, Black Coat Press, ISBN 978-1-932983-02-9.
[71] Many included in *The Exigent Shadow*, Black Coat Press, ISBN 978-1-61227-849-0, and *Don Juan in Paradise*, Black Coat Press, ISBN 978-1-61227-848-3.

Jules Lermina, a writer also known for his science fiction stories (reviewed in our companion volume, *The Handbook of French Science Fiction*), penned several volumes of Poe-inspired stories: *Histoires Incroyables* [Incredible Stories] (1885), *Nouvelles Histoires Incroyables* [New Incredible Tales] (1888) and *L'Élixir de Vie* [The Elixir of Life] (1890),[72] a novel about a man who must steal others' life-forces in order to remain alive.

Jean Richepin, with *Les Morts Bizarres* [The Bizarre Deaths] (1876); *Cauchemars* [Nightmares] (1892); *Théâtre Chimérique* [Chimerical Theater] (1896); *Le Monstre* [The Monster] (1896); *Le Coin des Fous* [The Crazy Corner] (1921); and *Contes sans morales* [Tales Without Morals] (1922). [73] Of all the late 19th century writers of *contes cruels*, the author was the cruelest when it came to the treatment of his characters, not so much in the nasty fates to which they were often delivered—which are typical of the entire genre—but in the merciless way in which he describes and characterizes them. Mad scientists, parrots from Atlantis, witches, madmen, monsters, korrigans, demons, magical paintings and a water sprite trapped in a mirror are but a few of the amazing characters featured in his collections which map out the frontier between madness and nightmare.

Gaston Danville, with *Contes de l'Au-Delà* [Tales from Beyond] (1893). The author's characters are haunted by memories, unconscious impulses and the poignant emotions provoked by those internal spurs. He based his accounts of delusion and obsession on what he took to be sound theories of positivistic psychology which added an extra dimension of cruelty to his fiction and an extra dose of intensity to his eroticism.

---

[72] In *Panic in Paris*, Black Coat Press, ISBN 978-1-934543-83-2.
[73] Many included in *The Crazy Corner*, Black Coat Press, ISBN 978-1-61227-142-2.

Some lesser known genre writers of the period in that vein include:

Angelo de Sorr with *Le Vampire* (1852),[74] a nested series of *contes cruels* aggregated into a quintessentially Romantic *roman frénétique*, and one of the most excessive and convoluted works of that kind. Some of the scenes featuring the necrophiliac vampire Lord Lodore or the one in which a young man tries to pimp his sick sister to a resurrectionist are masterpieces of the grotesque. The author, the son of a family of vine-growers in Bordeaux, made his debut as a novelist in 1848 and eventually went on to build a substantial career, working as a writer for various periodicals and eventually publishing more than a dozen novels, as well as becoming a successful publisher himself.

"Claude Vignon," the nom-de-plume of the sculptor Marie-Noémi Cadiot, once briefly married to the occultist "Éliphas Lévi", with *Minuits, Récits de la Veillée* [Midnight, Tales of the Watch] (1856), [75] remarkable in mapping out an evolutionary spectrum of Gothic and post-Gothic fantasies that exemplifies certain key phases within the evolution of Romantic fantasy. Two are set in Germany, one in the Middle Ages and one in the sixteenth century and are described as "legends." The others are pure Gothic melodrama, deliberately brutal in their supernatural improvisations and their deployment in unusually stark moral fantasies.

Henri de Saint-Georges' talent as one of the most consummate playwrights of his times helped maintain the readability of his stories. *Les Nuits Terribles* [The Terrible Nights] (1821) is a collection of three stories which combine both lewd and horrific elements in a strident and successful fashion. In *Les Yeux Verts* [The Green Eyes] (1872),[76] young Albert

---

[74] *The Vampires of London*, Black Coat Press, ISBN 978-1-61227-264-1.
[75] Black Coat Press, ISBN 978-1-64932-084-1.
[76] Both in *The Green Eyes*, Black Coat Press, ISBN 978-1-61227-651-9.

Dumesnil wonders if the soul of his recently departed uncle has not reincarnated itself in the old man's cat, Freyschutz. The text is carefully ambiguous in its presentation of the narrator's account, always leaving open the possibility that the strange circumstances are the results of obsessive delusion and hallucination. *The Green Eyes* has a casual verve that sets it apart from other contemporary exercises in the same genre.

Ernest Hello, with *Contes Extraordinaires* [Extraordinary Tales] (1879).

Louis Lemercier de Neuville, with *Contes Abracadabrants* [Alakazam Tales] (1880).

Edmond Thiaudière's *Trois Amours Singulières* [Singular Amours] (1886)[77] is a collection of three novellas which are the result of the author's interest in psychological science and represents a significant contribution to the evolving subgenre of "case study" fiction. What he calls "singular amours" explores unusual instances of passion, in the hope that the peculiarities of the phenomenon might be brought out more clearly by the contemplation of its extremes. The three examples offered in the book provide an interesting spectrum, from a fascinating account of a psychological haunting, to a study of obsessions couched as a mystery story, and remarkable narrative of psychological dependency.

Léon Bloy, with *Sueurs de Sang* [Blood Sweat] (1893) and *Histoires Désobligeantes* [Uncomfortable Stories] (1894), two collections of short stories that incorporate the horrific elements from the *roman noir* with modern supernatural concepts, by

Laurent Montesiste, with *Histoires Vertigineuses* [Vertiginous Tales] (1896).

A special mention should be made of humorist Eugène Mouton, whose *Nouvelles et Fantaisies Humoristiques* [Humoristic Short Stories] (1872) and *Fantaisies* [Fantasies] (1883) were Swiftian, macabre, dark-humored stories mixing the fantastique with the burlesque, such as *"Histoire de*

---

[77] Black Coat Press, ISBN 978-1-61227-730-1.

l'Invalide à la Tête de Bois" [Tale of the Invalid with a Wooden Head], the story of a soldier with a transplanted wooden head.

Poe's influence was felt not only on the *fantastique* but also on science fiction, through Jules Verne, who greatly admired him, to the point of writing his own sequel to *The Narrative of Arthur Gordon Pym*, *Le Sphinx des Glaces* (1897), but also on a number of other sf authors such as J.-H. Rosny Aîné and Maurice Renard who crossed the line between *fantastique* and science fiction, borrowing the American author's rational, lucid, and logical approach to the supernatural. Examples of this type of *fantastique réaliste* can be found in Renard's collection *Fantômes et Fantôches* [Ghosts and Puppets] (1905) and Rosny's *La Sorcière* [The Witch][78] (1887); *La Jeune Vampire* [The Young Vampire] (1920),[79] in which a London girl is possessed by an extra-dimensional entity which mutates her body and turns her into a living vampire; and *L'Assassin Surnature* [The Supernatural Assassin] (1923),[80] about a murderous wraith.

Fantastique Symboliste

Towards the later part of the 19th century, the morbid fascination for the supernatural that was obvious in the works of Poe combined with the decadent and erotic influences of the works of Lord Byron and Oscar Wilde, and the esoteric operas of German composer Richard Wagner, to fuel the growth of the *fantastique symboliste*, also dubbed *fantastique décadent*.

A Symbolist Manifesto was published by Jean Moréas in the daily newspaper *Le Figaro* on September 18th, 1886. But

---

[78] In *The Young Vampire*, Black Coat Press, ISBN 978-1-935558-40-8.
[79] *The Young Vampire,* q.v.
[80] In *The Young Vampire*, q.v.

the true precursor of the *fantastique symboliste* was without a doubt Charles Baudelaire. A renowned poet and the French translator of Poe, the author was prosecuted for obscenity and blasphemy for his morbid poetry, which included verses about lost civilizations, ghouls, vampires, etc. His oeuvre, steeped in the macabre and the *fantastique*, was collected in *Les Fleurs du Mal* [The Flowers of Evil] (1857). Rejecting the posings of the romantics, the poet anticipated the symbolists' and, later, the surrealists' spiritual quests. He virtually revolutionized poetry and influenced the creation of the symbolist movement. Indeed, the leaders of that movement attended his funeral and adopted him as their guide and inspiration.

Another *avant-garde poète maudit* of the decadent movement was Isidore Ducasse, who used the pseudonym of Lautréamont (a name borrowed from a fictional character created by Sue). His poems, collected in *Les Chants de Maldoror* [The Songs of Maldoror] (1869), owed their inspiration to both the Marquis de Sade and Lord Byron, as well as the gothic excesses of the *roman noir*.

Baudelaire and Lautréamont were among the first to fully focus on the exploration of evil and the dark recesses of the human soul. Jules-Amédée Barbey d'Aurevilly, a devout catholic, novelist and renowned literary critic, was critical of the naturalist school (e.g.: Émile Zola), but a great admirer of Baudelaire. His novels were tales of terror in which morbid passions were acted out in bizarre crimes, often told against the bloody background of the French Revolution. In *Les Diaboliques* [The Diabolical Women] (written in 1858, published in 1874, no relation to the famous thriller or film adaptations thereof), the author broke new ground, describing with a minutia of psychological details the diabolical nature of perversity, sadism and eroticism. Throughout his other works, such as *L'Ensorcelée* [The Spellbound] (1854), *Le Chevalier des Toches* [The Knight of Toches] (1864) and *Une Histoire sans Nom* [A Nameless Story] (1881), Barbey exhibited a profound belief in the existence of pure evil, and its ability to take possession of the human soul. His works later inspired such classic writers as Georges Bernanos and André Mauriac. His nearest English-language counterpart, Robert Louis Stevenson, did not publish his *Strange Case of Dr. Jekyll and Mr. Hyde* until 1888.

Joris-Karl Huysmans continued Barbey's obsession with the description of evil by creating new dramatic templates for old concepts, such as the Devil, the witches' black mass, etc. What Ira Levin did with *Rosemary's Baby*, the author achieved in *À Rebours* [Backwards] (1884) and *Là-Bas* [Over There] (1891), which became the "manifestos" of the symbolists and the decadents. The character of the Duke des Esseintes, who felt only contempt for the century in which he lived, and instead chose to go to a magical land, perfectly embodied the secret desire of the decadents to turn back the clock to another, mythical time.

Another major writer of the *fantastique décadent* was Rémy de Gourmont, also a renowned literary critic, whose face was hideously marred by lupus. His *Lilith* (1892) was a Satanic play. His darkly horrific tales were collected in *Proses Moroses* [Morose Prose] (1894); *D'un Pays Lointain* [From a Far-Away Land] (1898); and *Histoires Magiques* [Magical Stories] (1902). His *Le Pèlerin du Silence* [The Pilgrim of Silence] (1896) took place in Persia and related an initiatic journey. In the short story *"Péhor"* (included in *Histoires Magiques*), the eponymous incubus crawls his way up through the belly and the throat of his female victim and, as she expires, drinks her soul directly from the inside of her mouth.

The works of Jean Lorrain, also a writer of plays and operas, reflected a similar, lifelong obsession with the nature of evil, corruption and decadence in all its varied forms. In his novels, the supernatural was only one of the means through which the human soul could be degraded. The writer's books included *Buveurs d'Âmes* [Soul Drinkers] (1893); *Un Démoniaque* [A Demoniacal] (1895); *Sensations et Souvenirs* [Feelings and Remembrances] (1895); *Une Femme par Jour* [A Woman A Day] (1896); a kabbalistic novel *La Mandragore* (1899); and *Histoires de Masques* [Stories of Masks]

(1900). His masterpiece was *Monsieur de Phocas* (1901), a novel featuring the character of Claudius Ethal, who like the Duke des Esseintes, cultivates and feeds on evil, except that, unlike the Duke, Ethal is not handsome but a grotesque Mr. Hyde, a Toulouse-Lautrec-like misfit, a manifestation of the author's tortured soul.

Marcel Schwob was another master of the *fantastique symboliste* of the late 19th century. His collection *Coeur Double* [Twin Hearts] (1891) was dedicated to Stevenson, and explored the nature of terror. The author focused on the horrid reality hidden behind the masks of the ordinary. His other collection, the justifiably famous *Le Roi au Masque d'Or* [The King in the Golden Mask] (1892) was dedicated to J.-H. Rosny Aîné and contained some short stories that could be equally considered science fiction or horror. The title piece was about an Oriental King who wore a gold mask and lived surrounded by priests, concubines, jesters and eunuchs, all wearing gold masks. One day, the King took off his mask and discovered that he was a leper; he then blinded himself and abandoned his throne to travel to a City of Lepers, with a still-loyal woman by his side, unaware that she, too, is a leper...

Some of Anatole France's earlier works included several Christian-themed fantasies, such as *L'Étui de Nacre* [The Mother-Of-Pearl Casket] (1892) and *Le Puits de Sainte Claire* [The Well of Saint Clara] (1895).

Symbolist poetry took an increasingly elliptical and esoteric style with Arthur Rimbaud, Paul Verlaine, and Stéphane Mallarmé. Mallarmé's poems *Hérodiade* (1864) and *L'Après-Midi d'un Faune* [The Afternoon of a Faun] (1876), in turn, influenced composer Claude Debussy and Belgian poet Maurice Maeterlinck, whose play *Pelléas et Mélisande* (1892), with its dream-like atmosphere, was perfectly representative of this current of symbolist thought.

Another famous symbolist writer was Paul Adam, who wrote *Volontés Merveilleuses* [Marvelous Wills] (1888-90), a trilogy comprised of *Être* [To Be], *En Décor* [In the Background] and *Essence de Soleil* [Essence of the Sun], in which a sorceress used dark forces to escape from her father.

Élémir Bourges penned several elaborate, dark and esoteric novels, including the classic *Le Crépuscule des Dieux* [The Twilight of the Gods] (1884) and *La Nef* [The Ship], a metaphysical epic which took him almost twenty years to write (1904-1922).

Gustave Kahn was at the heart of the Symbolist Movement and a pioneer and champion of free verse and one of the editors of the prestigious *Mercure de France*. His *Le Conte de l'Or et du Silence* [The Tale of Gold and Silence] (1898)[81] can be construed as an exercise in the further development of the archetypal images subsequently categorized and explored by Jung. It is not only the author's most overtly extravagant symbolist novel, but one of the most overtly extravagant symbolist novels ever attempted, mingling parables, Old Testament and visionary fantasies, throwing in a couple of mock-folktales and a fantasy story for good measure. Kahn's knowledge of and attitude to symbolism was colored by his Jewish heritage, and it was natural for him to deploy symbolist methods in his reexamination of Old Testament mythology and the supposed modifications introduced by the subsequent reinterpretation of much of that mythology by the New Testament.

Camille Mauclair was one of the younger recruits of the Symbolist Movement. He penned several stories such as "*Couronne de Clarté*" [Crown of Clarity (1895) and "*Le Poison des pierreries*" [The Poison of Precious Stones (1903) in the Symbolist style, remarkable for their sheer bizarrerie and flamboyant imagery,[82] as well as two novels, *Le Soleil des Morts* [The Sun of the Dead] (1898) and *L'Ennemie des Rêves* [*The Enemy of Dreams*] (1900).

Some lesser-known genre writers of the period in that vein include:

---

[81] Black Coat Press, ISBN 978-1-61227-063-0.
[82] In *The Virgin Orient*, Black Coat Press, ISBN 978-1-61227-502-4.

Édouard Dujardin, with *Les Hantises* [The Hauntings] (1886).

Bernard Lazare, with *Le Miroir des Légendes* [The Mirror of Legends] (1892).

Paul Claudel, with *La Ville* [The City] (1892) was a social and religious allegory taking place in a fantastical, godless city.

Alfred Le Bourguignon, with *La Chouette* [The Owl] (1893).

Joseph de Gobineau, with *Nouvelles Asiatiques* [Asian Short Stories] (1896).

The symbolist movement eventually reached its peak in the early 1900s before declining and, eventually, giving way to Surrealism after World War I.

A special note should be made of two special writers who, while not symbolists or decadents, appeared to anticipate the currents of thoughts that eventually led to Surrealism after World War I:

Xavier Forneret, with *Un Oeil entre Deux Yeux* [One Eye Between Two Eyes] (1838) and the short fiction *Le Diamant de l'Herbe* [The Diamond in the Grass] (1840), who anticipated the formal word games of the surrealists.

Aloysius Bertrand, with the strange prose poem *Gaspard de la Nuit* [Gaspar of the Night] (1842),[83] subtitled "dark fantasies *à la* Rembrandt and Callot", a text which combines the haunting gothic imagery of Hoffmann with the colorful romantic verve of Victor Hugo. In it, we meet Scarbo the vampire dwarf, Ondine, the faerie princess of the waters, and an unforgettable assortment of lepers, alchemists, beggars, swordsmen and ghosts. *Gaspard de la Nuit* inspired Baudelaire, Rimbaud, Mallarmé, the Surrealist Movement and composer Maurice Ravel, who wrote a suite of virtuoso piano pieces patterned after it. This ground-breaking collection of prose ballads was published a year after the author's death at 34.

---

[83] Black Coat Press, ISBN 978-0-9740711-2-1.

Fantasy

What had begun with the pre-Revolutionary imprints of *Le Cabinet des Fées* [The Fairies' Cabinet] and the *Voyages Imaginaires* continued and gained momentum with the public, eventually producing the first works of classic fantasy.

Charles Nodier created a more romantic type of fantasy and helped steer the genre in new directions. His horror story, *Smarra, ou les Démons de la Nuit* [Smarra, or the Demons of the Night][84] (1821), already mentioned, is a dark fantasy saga, in which the Byronesque hero encounters fairies and vampires, perhaps the first mixture of traditional and modern fantasy elements under a single cover. After a trip to Scotland to tour the scenes of Walter Scott's books, Nodier wrote *Trilby, ou le Lutin d'Argail* [Trilby, or the Brownie of Argyle] (1822),[85] a novel based on an old Scots legend in which a woman is psychically enslaved by a supernatural creature. He then went on to pen several fairy tales, such as *L'Histoire du Roi de Bohême et de ses Sept Châteaux* [The Story of the King of Bohemia and of his Seven Castles] (1830), *Le Songe d'Or* [The Golden Dream] (1832),[86] a tale in the vein of *The Arabian Nights*, and *Trésor des Fèves et Fleur de Pois* [Bean-Treasure and Peaseblossom] (1833). In *La Fée aux Miettes* [The Crumb Fairy] (1832),[87] he succeeded in further breaking down the walls between fantasy and reality. The reader is ultimately left to wonder whether the main protagonist Michel is mad—or in touch with a higher plane of reality. With *La Fée aux Miettes*, the author can rightfully lay claim to being one of the world's

---

[84] In *Trilby * The Crumb Fairy*, Black Coat Press, ISBN 978-1-61227-455-3.
[85] In *Trilby*, q.v.
[86] In *The French Fantasy Treasury Volume 3: Far Realms*, Black Coat Press, ISBN 978-1-61227-546-8.
[87] In *Trilby*, q.v.

first high fantasy writers, sixty years before William Morris' (1834-1896) *The Wood Beyond the World* (1890).

Forty-three years before Jules Verne, and ninety-three years before Edgar Rice Burroughs, Jacques Collin de Plancy, remembered today for his *Dictionnaire Infernal* [Encyclopedia of Demons and Demonology] (1818), penned *Voyage au Centre de la Terre, ou Aventures diverses de Clairancy et de ses companions, au Spitzberg, au Pôle-Nord, et dans des pays inconnus, traduit de l'anglais de Hormidas Peath par M. Jacques Saint-Albin* [Journey to the Center of the Earth; or, Various Adventures of Clairancy and His Companions in Spitzbergen, at the North Pole and in Unknown Lands, translated from the English of Hormidas Peath by Jacques Saint-Albin] (1821),[88] which is both an adventure story and a utopian fantasy. In it, an expedition is mounted to discover the hypothetical opening at the Earth pole, the existence of which was popularized by Tyssot de Patot's *Pierre de Mésange* (1720), Ludwig Holberg's *Nils Klim* (1741) and Giacomo Casanova's *Icosameron* (1788). There, they discover an alien world located inside the Earth populated by humans who only differ from us by size. Although there are satirical elements, this world within is treated as another planet, with its own geography and history, a mildly exotic fauna and flora, and nations with different politics and religions. *Voyage to the Center of the Earth* differs from its predecessors not merely because of its careful depiction of a society that has preserved happiness by rejecting progress, but because its heroes find it is too tedious to remain there.

Writing as "Horace Saint-Aubin", Honoré de Balzac penned *La Dernière Fée* [The Last Fay] (1823),[89] in which an alchemist, his family and his valet, Caliban, settle in an isolated village. After their deaths, their young son, Abel, who has read only fairy tales, falls in love with a local girl, Catherine,

---

[88] *Journey to the Center of the Earth*, Black Coat Press, ISBN 978-1-61227-487-4.

[89] Black Coat Press, ISBN 978-1-61227-547-5.

whom he mistakes for the legendary Pearl Fairy. But the scheming Lady Sommerset, infatuated with Abel, uses his delusions to her advantage. In it, the author tried to capitalize on the then-popular fantasy genre, and yet twist it in a new direction and use it in a novel way, more advanced in both literary and philosophical terms than the sophistications already added by generations of French writers over the past century.

Théodore Hersart, Vicomte de La Villemarqué, was a native of Brittany and intensely interested in its history and folklore. He caused some controversy when he published a collection entitled *Barzaz Breiz* [Breton Ballads, in Breton] in 1839, which ostensibly rendered many traditional Breton ballads into modern French, tacitly claiming much of French folklore for his native province. He was widely accused of falsifying the material, at least in the translation process, and probably by some outright fakery, but the collection nevertheless proved very popular. He followed it up with a two-volume collection of *Contes populaires des Ancient Bretons* [Popular Tales of the Ancient Bretons] (1842), which was an anthology of four Medieval romances adapted into modern prose, beginning with *Perceval*, in a version that includes one of the several long continuations of Chrétien de Troyes' original *Conte du Graal*—one of the most important Arthurian tales of the period. The collection is prefaced by a long essay examining the key elements of the Arthurian mythos, with separate essays on Arthur, Merlin and Lancelot, treating them as inventions that had arrived in Britain from continental Britanny, and had been initially developed there in a specifically Cambrian context before being reimported to France.

Hersart apparently began working on a much more elaborate version of that essay almost immediately, and, to all appearances, on his own prose epic summarizing the entire "tradition," but it took him too long, and by the time his *Myrdhinn, ou l'enchanteur Merlin: son histoire, ses oeuvres, son influence* [Myrdhinn, or the Enchanter Merlin: His History, His Works and His Influence] was ready for publication, it was 1862, and he had been comprehensively upstaged, as he wryly noted in his introduction.

We are now so accustomed to the popularity and familiarity of Arthurian fiction that it is difficult to imagine a time when it seemed so extraordinary as to be bizarre, but that was the case when Quinet conceived the project of writing his fictional "biography" of Merlin, *Merlin l'enchanteur* [The Enchanter Merlin] (1860).[90] How well the author knew Hersart is unclear, and such similarities as there are between their two versions of Merlin's biography—and the differences are much more obvious—are probably due almost entirely to the common sources on which they drew. Robert de Boron, who produced three significant Arthurian texts in verse in the 1190s, *Joseph d'Arimathie, Merlin* and *Perceval*, became an important source, not merely for Quinet but many other writers who helped popularize the character.

Paul Féval also turned the folklore of mist-shrouded, storm-beaten Ancient Brittany into fantasies of color and flamboyance, with stories such as *"Anne des Iles"* [Anne of the Isles] and *"La Femme Blanche des Marais"* [The White Lady of the Marshes] (1842), *"Le Joli Château"* [The Lovely Chateau] (1844) and *"Les Belles-de-Nuit"* (1862),[91] featuring the last priestess of the Celtic Gods, the vengeful White Lady of the Marshes and the last fairies of mythical Lyonesse.... These are tales that have the Devil and Death for their main characters, with graveyards and wind-swept, demon-haunted hills for their settings. The whistling of the tempest and the distant chimes of a tolling bell is always audible within them. The fabled White Lady avenges herself cruelly against the incredulous, who are well-advised never to entrust their boats to the current of the Oust once the north star had risen over the black trees of the Forêt-Neuve... Two men dressed in long shrouds, as white as snow pass in front of the Steward of

---

[90] Black Coat Press, ISBN 978-1-61227-303-7.
[91] In *Anne of the Isles*, Black Coat Press, ISBN 978-1-932983-92-0.

Plougaz; when the Moon lit their pale faces and hollow cheeks, he saw that there were no eyes in their orbits...

Antoine-Louis Duclaux, Comte de L'Estoille wrote several fantasy stories such as "*L'Edredon de Mademoiselle Marie*" [Mademoiselle Marie's Eiderdown] (1865), a didactic visionary fantasy in which a girl dreams of traveling to North Cape with an eiderdown, experiencing several educational encounters on the way; and "*Le Meunier de Carnac*" [The Miller of Carnac] (1866), a Breton fantasy similar to much of S. Henry Berthoud's early work. He then wrote a suite of *Arabian Tales, Haïcks et burnooses, chants arabes* (1865); the prose poems of *Symphony* (1867); the defiantly experimental. *Fusains* (1868); the epic drama *Vercingerorix* (1868), in which he attempts to reconfigure episodes reported in Julius Caesar's *Commentarii de Bellio Gallico* into a pseudohistory and imaginary prehistory of Gaul, one that includes an idiosyncratic theory of serial reincarnation; *La Chanson de l'alouette* [The Song of the Skylark] (1880), which similarly attempts to fuse a transfiguration of the author's own life-story with a fakeloristic pseudohistory of France; and the more upbeat "*Argentine*" and "*Lemmi Kainen*" (both 1892), reflective of a burst of interest in Scandinavian mythology, borrowing motifs from Hans Christian Andersen.[92]

A few modern critics have allotted L'Estoille a significant role in the development of the prose poem, between Aloysius Bertrand and Charles Baudelaire, but have often neglected his significant contribution to the development of French fantasy. His works are especially important in mapping the gradual elaboration and transfiguration of the idea of fays from being seemingly human enchantresses to immaterial beings of symbolic significance. A genuinely innovative writer, the author was a precursor of the experimentation subsequent-

---

[92] All collected in *The Miller of Carnac*, Black Coat Press, ISBN 978-1-64932-007-0; *The Song of the Skylark*, Black Coat Press, ISBN 978-1-64932-017-9; and *Argentine*, Black Coat Press, ISBN 978-1-64932022-3.

ly carried out by writers of the Symbolist Movement of the 1890s. His contribution to French fantasy was drastically underestimated, and he was almost forgotten until his recent rediscovery. However puzzling his work might be in its strangeness and unorthodoxy, it is not lacking in sanity, and its pathos is highly effective. It is a pity that it was so neglected at its time of publication, and it is fully deserving of a modern reappraisal.

In 1858, Gustave Flaubert produced what may very well be the first work of pure modern heroic-fantasy in the French language, *Salammbo*. It was a brash, colorful and exotic novel about ancient Carthage, the North-African city-state which challenged Roman domination during the Punic Wars in the 2nd century BC and was loosely based on an incident reported by Roman historian Polybius. In it, the author created the fictional character of Salammbo, the daughter of Carthaginian general Hamilcar, and told of her doomed love story with Matho, the leader of the rebel mercenaries who were besieging Carthage. While the supernatural was, at best, understated, *Salammbo* was a worthy precursor of the opulent, colorful, savage fantasies of Robert E. Howard and Matho was a true proto-*Conan*.

In *Paris Avant le Déluge* [Paris Before the Deluge] (1866),[93] Hippolyte Mettais displayed his imaginative reach, creating a novel that incorporates the lost city of Atlantis, the biblical story of the Flood, and the founding of Paris. Set more than four thousand years in the past, the book is a lesson about the rise and fall of civilizations with its credible mixture of exotic locales, spurned lovers, power grabs, lost dynasties and the constant quest for the favor of ancient gods. Within this mythological antediluvian world, the author unfolds a tale of religious and revolutionary sentiments that remains an important document in the history of French fantasy as well as the modern development of the Atlantis legend.

---

[93] Black Coat Press, ISBN 978-1-61227-328-0.

The most widely-read children's writer in France in the latter half of the 19th century was the Russian-born Sophie Rostopchine, Comtesse de Ségur. One of her earliest literary endeavors was a volume of *Nouveaux contes de fées pour les petits enfants* [New Tales of the Fays for Little Children] (1856).

One of the most prolific "collectors" of such tales was a famous man of law, Édouard-René de Laboulaye, who published three volumes of *contes bleus* allegedly collected in his travels, as well as a second-hand adaptation of an Oriental fantasy, *Abdallah, ou Le Tréfle à quatre feuilles* [Abdallah; or, The Four-Leafed Shamrock] (1859), which proved very popular.

This led to a reinvention of the subgenre of the *contes de fées*, although they were substantially different from the classic works of Madame d'Aulnoy, Comtesse de Murat, etc.

Fairy tales by Théodore de Banville were originally published in the daily newspaper *Gil Blas* between November 1880 and October 1881.[94] The tone of his stories covered a wide spectrum, ranging from farce to horror and wry moralistic tales, occasionally featuring demons, figures from Classical mythology, vampires, witches and even the Wandering Jew. The author can be seen a significant precursor of Surrealism, having influenced such writers as Alfred Jarry. Most of his stories have a definite panache, and the best of them are highly effective. More importantly, the whole is greater than the sum of its parts, a peculiar masterpiece, which fully entitles his *oeuvre* to be considered as a classic of fantastic literature.

The fays featured in Catulle Mendès' *contes merveilleux* also bear little resemblance to those from Madame d'Aulnoy's or the Comtesse de Murat's works. They have a much closer resemblance to English fairies, and Shakespeare's Puck. There is no evidence in Mendès' work that he ever read any of the

---

[94] In *Magical Tales*, Black Coat Press, ISBN 978-1-64932-061-2.

original *contes de fées* produced in the 1690s, or the pastiches produced in the mid-eighteenth century. One of his earliest tales in that vein was "*La Belle au bois rêvant*" [The Dreaming Beauty] (1882), which is an ironic gloss on the vulgarized abridgement of Perrault's "Sleeping Beauty". One fantastic tale produced toward the end of his career, "*L'Azure, l'or et le purple*" [Azure, Gold and Crimson] (1904), contains echoes of the initiating incident of Madame d'Aulnoy's "*La Princesse Belle-Étoile et le prince Chéri*" that might not be coincidental, but the author's story is an allegory that does not feature fays. There is, therefore, a certain irony in the fact that if one simply tabulates titles, Mendès wrote more tales featuring fays than any other French writer—more than forty—although a purist might judge that he wrote no "authentic" *contes de fées* at all.

Seventeen stories featuring fays of a sort were included in Mendès' first collection consisting almost entirely of fantastic tales, *Les Contes du rouet* [Spinning-Wheel Tales] (1885; revised in 1888 as *Les Oiseaux bleus*; tr. as *Bluebirds*). His other collection, *Pour lire au convent* (1887) contains four stories explicitly featuring fays, and several associational items, and there are more than twenty further stories in which they play a significant part scattered through his many other story collections. Fays only play a marginal role in Mendès' masterpiece, the novella *Luscignole* (1892); the character featured therein who is called *le roi fée* is a fake, all his "enchantments" being contrived by artificial and mechanical means, and he is clearly a transfiguration of Ludwig II of Bavaria, who was nicknamed the *märchenkönig*, of which *le roi fée* is an approximate translation. *Luscignole* is, in essence, an "anti-fairy tale," in which the fay king's attempt to play the *deus ex machina* role traditionally attributed to good fays goes awry, thus allowing the story to become a graphic horror story, but it retains a strong affinity with the tradition of fairy tales, in terms of its tone and the narrative structure that it reproduces in order to undermine its conventions. It has something in common with Balzac's tragic requiem for the genre, *La dernière fée* (see above).[95]

Mendès' belated contributions to the genre have closer affinities with it than he may have suspected. He was a deliberately subversive writer, not only employing the narrative dynamic of his fantasies to insist that amour is far from perfect, but frequently applauding certain aspects of that imperfection.

Judith Gautier was the daughter of the great Romantic writer, Théophile Gautier. Her *Isoline et la Fleur-Serpent* [Isoline and the Serpent-Flower] (1882)[96] features an extraordinary heroine and recycles the legend of Sleeping Beauty with a sharp ironic edge. The story deals with guilt and vengeance from beyond the grave. Her Oriental stories, collected in *Le Paravent de soie et d'or* [The Silk and Gold Screen] (1904)[97] are flamboyant reinterpretations of myths and legends. The author's works deal with the painful isolation of the individual and the destructive power of love. They commanded a considerable degree of critical respect and represented a refinement of the primitive Orientalism pioneered by early members of the French Romantic Movement. Judith Gautiermade a highly significant contribution to the development of a literary Orient that was subsequently exploited by many later writers.

Anatole France won the 1921 Nobel Prize for literature. Some of his earlier works, like "*L'Abeille*" [The Honey Bee] (1883); "*Balthazar et la Reine Balkis*" [Balthazar & Queen Balkis] (1889); and "*Histoire de la Duchesse de Cicogne et de M. de Boulingrin qui dormiront cent ans en compagnie de la Belle-au-bois-dormant*" [The Story of the Duchesse de Cicogne and Monsieur de Boulingrin Who Sleprt A Hundred Years Alongside Sleeping Beauty], all classic fairy tales, were collected in *Les Sept femmes de Barbe-Bleue et autres contes*

---

[95] In *The Little Fays in the Air*, Black Coat Press, ISBN 978-1-61227-846-9.
[96] Black Coat Press, ISBN 978-1-61227-152-1.
[97] In *Isoline and the Serpent-Flower*, q.v.

merveilleux The Seven Wives of Bluebeard and Other Marvelous Tales (1909).

Jean Lorrain's "*Mélusine Enchantée*" [Melusine Enchanted], first appeared in the *Écho de Paris* in 1892 (which Catulle Mendès was the literary editor) before being reprinted in *Princesses d'ivoire et d'ivresse* [Princess of Ivory and Drunkenness] (1902).

J.-H. Rosny Aîné penned three bold and lurid mythological fantasies dealing with erotic obsessions and ancient civilizations, *La Flûte de Pan* [Pan's Flute] (1897), *Amour Étrusque* [Etruscan Amour] (1898) and *Les Femmes de Setnê* [*Setne's Women*] (1903).[98]

Finally, one should include here Frédéric Boutet with "*La Vallée nommée Solitude*" [The Valley Named Solitude], originally published in *Contes dans le nuit* [Tales in the Night] (1898)

Occult & Esoterism

More than ever before, the occult and esoteric philosophies continued to fire the imaginations of those opposing the currents of thoughts of Cartesian naturalist literature, especially during the latter part of the 19th century. Two dominant figures of the times became the guiding lights of this type of *fantastique*:

The first was Eliphas Lévi, who wrote *Histoire de la Magie* [The History of Magic] (1860), *La Clef des Grands Mystères* [The Key to the Great Mysteries] (1860), *Dogme et Rituel de la Haute Magie* [Dogma and Rituals of High Magic] (1861), *Fables et Symboles* [Fables & Symbols] (1862), *La Science des Esprits* [The Science of Spirits] (1865) and the posthumously-published *Le Livre des Splendeurs* [The Book of Splendors] (1894) and *Le Grand Arcane, ou l'Occultisme*

---

[98] All in *Pan's Flute*, Black Coat Press, ISBN 978-1-61227-755-4

Dévoilé [The Great Arcana, or Occultism Unveiled] (1898). The author was the first modern writer to combine various occult and previously secret branches of research, such as alchemy, kabbala, witchcraft, etc., into a coherent and modern system of thought. His influence on the genre was enormous; it is no exaggeration to say that the entire field of occult literature and occult books would not exist without him. Unlike the "old masters" of previous centuries, Lévi simplified, vulgarized, democratized and, in effect, made the occult accessible to one and all. He reassured the Christians by expelling the old concepts of the Devil and emphasized the word science. He was the first to propose a unified theory of the occult, in which the paranormal and the supernatural are nothing but an as-yet-undiscovered part of science.

Lévi became, directly or indirectly, the unavoidable reference in the field, the source which all subsequent writers using occult themes—whether they were believers or unbelievers—felt bound to use. He, himself, became a fictional character, appearing as the White Magician Unken in Josephin Péladan's *La Victoire du Mari* [The Husband's Victory] (1889) and as Gaston Leroux's mysterious magus, Eliphas de Saint-Elme de Taillebourg de la Nox, in *Le Fauteuil Hanté* [The Haunted Chair] (1910). Ironically, Lévi denounced all his works on his death bed!

The other major figure of occult fantasy was Allan Kardec, whose *Le Livre des Esprits* [The Book of Spirits] (1857), and its numerous sequels, such as *Le Livre des Mediums* [The Book of Mediums] (1861), launched the *spiritisme*, and virtually created the sub-set of the *roman spirite*, devoted to the theme of communication between the living and the dead. The aurthor's work influenced such renowned writers as Victor Hugo, Charles Baudelaire, Honoré de Balzac (with *Séraphita*), Théophile Gautier (with *Spirite*), Villiers de l'Isle-Adam (with *Tribulat Bonhomet*), Camille Flammarion, Oscar Wilde, etc.

In addition to these, two other notable authors of *roman spirites* included:

Clément de La Chave, with *La Magicienne des Alpes* [The Magician of the Alps] (1861).

Henri Rivière, with *La Main Coupée* [The Severed Hand] (1862) and *La Possédée, ou La Seconde Vie du Dr. Roger* [The Possessed Woman, or The Second Life of Dr. Roger] (1863), *Les Méprises du Coeur* [The Mistakes of the Heart] (1865) and *L'Envoûtement* [The Spell] (1870) *Les Méprises du Coeur* collected a number of notable genre tales including "*Les Voix Secrètes de Jacques Lambert*" [Jacques Lambert's Secret Voices], "*Le Rajeunissement*" [Growing Younger] and "*Les Visions du Lieutenant Féraud*" [Lt. Feraud's Visions]).

Jules Claretie, with *Jean Mornas* (1885) and *L'Obsession* [Obsession] (1908).[99] The novel deals with the psychological anomaly that would nowadays be called multiple personality syndrome in the tradition of the classic *Strange Case of Dr Jekyll and Mr Hyde* (1886). Although it remains an "evil twin" story, its representation of the personality of the inconvenient "double" is, however, unusual and striking. The novel also portrays the obsessive quality of scientific research, thus adding to the rich tradition of literary mad scientists.

Charles Richet (writing as "Charles Epheyre"), with *Possession* (1887).

Léon Hennique, with *Un Caractère* [A Character] (1889).

Édouard Schuré's *L'Ange et le Sphinx* [The Angel and the Sphinx] (1897)[100] is one of the most phantasmagorical and intense Romantic and Symbolist novels on the themes of *femmes fatales*, reincarnation and expiation. The author of *The Great Initiates* (1889) penned a book that appeals to fans of flamboyant fantasy fiction as well as connoisseurs of Symbolist fiction. Young knight Konrad de Felseneck, last descendant of a noble line, discovers that a curse hangs over his family: women are the curse of the Felseneck since the betrayal of his

---

[99] Black Coat Press, ISBN 978-1-61227-213-9.
[100] Black Coat Press, ISBN 978-1-61227-879-7.

ancestor during the first crusade. Then he falls into the hands of the beautiful and cruel Gertrude, a young widow whose previous husbands have killed themselves in despair.

Of all the many other occult-inspired writers of the late 19th century, such as Stanislas de Guaïta, Papus, Saint-Pol Roux, Pierre Puvis de Chavannes, etc., the most prominent was undoubtedly Josephin Péladan, also known for his numerous aliases such as the Sâr Merodack, Princess Dinska, Miss Sarah and the Marquis de Valognes! His first novel, *Le Vice Suprême* [The Supreme Vice] (1884), was prefaced and praised by Barbey d'Aurevilly. In 1890, with writer Élémir Bourges, the author spearheaded a split from the Kabbalistic Order of the Rosicrucians (established in 1988 by de Guaïta) and founded his own neo-Catholic Rosicrucian Order, thus starting a famous feud between the two orders dubbed the "war of the two roses". Borrowing from Lévi, Kardec and various Eastern (or pseudo-Eastern) mystic sources, Péladan embarked on the writing of a fourteen-volume saga entitled *La Décadence Latine* [The Latin Decadence], of which *Le Vice Suprême* was the first, which was meant to be an occult version of Balzac's *Human Comedy*.

In these novels, the author was more concerned with the development of his occult philosophies—such as the notion of androgyny explored in *L'Androgyne* (1891)—than he was with the construction of a classic dramatic structure. In *La Victoire du Mari* [The Husband's Victory] (1889), the evil sorcerer Sextenthal cast a spell on Izel, a newlywed French girl during the Wagner Festival at Bayreuth. Her husband, Adar, enlists the help of white magician Unken to defeat Sextenthal. His *La Torche Renversée* [The Spilled Torch] (1925) was a sequel to the Round Table Mythos. Péladan's alter ego, the magus Sâr Merodack, featured in some of the books.

Following in his wake was fellow occultist Jules Bois, a noted expert and author of numerous books on satanism and magic, whose *L'Ève Nouvelle* [*The New Eve*] (1896) and *Le Mystère et la Volupté* [The Mystery and the Voluptuousness] (1901) were novels about magical love.

"Willy" (a pseudonym of Henry Gauthier-Villars)'s *Amour Astral* [Astral Amour] (1900)[101] was originally published as an eight-part serial in the *Nouvelle Revue* and was never reprinted in book form. As an account of the social and psychological aspects of the occult revival in the 19th century, it does have the advantage of a unique originality. It is more a commentary on occult fantasy than an occult fantasy in its own right, although it is willing to use the *fantastique* as a casual literary device for the purpose of that examination. Neurocyme, the elemental woman given flesh by the novel's protagonists Enogat de Sothermès and Doctor Callidulus, is described by them as a mixture of illusion and irony—and the same alchemical combination applies to the text, which is simultaneously all illusion and all irony.

Other writers representative of this *fantastique fin de siècle* included Paul Adam, Jean Lorrain, Joris-Karl Huysmans, Catulle Mendès (with *Zo'Har* (1886)), and Rachilde, the pen name and preferred identity of novelist and playwright Marguerite Vallette-Eymery, with *Monsieur Vénus* (1889), *L'Animale* [The She-Beast] (1893), *Le Démon de l'Absurde* [The Demon of the Absurd] (1894) and *La Princesse des Ténèbres* [The Princess of Darkness] (1896).

Finally, before closing this section, there were three very unique and otherwise unclassifiable writers who must be added as a footnote to this incredibly prolific century:

Émile Deschamps was a writer seemingly gifted with Edgar Cayce-like extraordinary powers. Known as a literary critic and dabbler—he wrote some librettos for Berlioz and Meyerbeer—he penned a very strange autobiography entitled *Les Réalités Fantastiques* [Fantastic Realities] (1854) in which he casually detailed his heretofore unrevealed encounters with the supernatural, since his childhood: instances of divination, successful readings, encounters with spirits, and his dealings with a young Jewish woman who was his spiritual soulmate.

---

[101] Black Coat Press, ISBN 978-1-61227-563-5.

While Deschamps behaved, outwardly at least, as a normal person, Alexis-Vincent-Charles Berbiguier de Terre-Neuve du Thym was a man afflicted with an acute and unique form of mental sickness. Virtually all of his adult life, he genuinely believed himself to be persecuted by the *Farfadets* [Little People, or Goblins], and saw their agents in his every day's encounters with doctors, lawyers, neighbors and the rest of society. Berbiguier wrote a three-volume, amazing autobiography, *Les Farfadets, ou Tous les Démons ne sont pas de l'Autre Monde* [The Goblins, or Not All Demons Come From Another World] (1821), which was also a wildly imaginative treatise on the *Farfadets*, their nature, their powers, their modes of operation, their very society, and which contained *Ghostbusters*-like methods on how to fight them effectively.

Finally, Gabriel Antoine Jogand-Pagès, using the pseudonym of "Léo Taxil", wrote *Le Diable au XIXème Siècle ou Les Mystères du Spiritisme* [The Devil in the 19th Century] (1892-95), a pseudo-documentary book about the Freemasonry, which included some grotesque and unbelievable descriptions of secret underground rituals, the summoning and worship of demons, etc. Jogand-Pagès was also known under his other pseudonym of "Henry Bataille", not to be confused with the playwright Félix-Henri "Henry" Bataille.

Belgian Fantastique

Unlike in France, where the *fantastique* was either a marginal phenomenon existing on the edges of mainstream literature, or something relegated to the entertainment of the lower classes, in Belgium, the *fantastique* became a major literary current. One can legitimately speak of a Belgian "school" of the *fantastique*, both in terms of quantity and quality. Quantity because Belgium produced a disproportionately high number of first-rate authors; quality because, in spite of each writer's individuality, there was a certain commonality among Belgian-born writers in terms of themes and approach to the *fantastique*.

Some scholars have explained this richness and propensity for the *fantastique* in Belgian literature by pointing out the Flemish taste for the baroque and the bizarre, a long fascination for ghost stories and other supernatural phenomenon, a natural inclination towards the *fantastique* seen as a refuge, if not a rebellion, against a bleak life, history and surroundings.

As French-language Belgian literature began to mature in the late 1800s, it incorporated the traditional Flemish and French-language (i.e.: Wallon) folklore. Romanticized versions of folkloric tales were the subject of the works of:

Marcellin La Garde, with *Le Val de l'Amblève* [The Valley of Amblève] (1879) and *Légendes Ardennaises* [legends From the Ardennes] (1886).

Henri de Nimal, with *Légendes de la Meuse* [Legends of the Meuse] (1898).

Eugène Demolder, with *Contes d'Yperdamme* [Tales from Yperdamme] (1891) and *La Légende d'Yperdamme* [The Legend of Yperdamme] (1897) were

The Germanic influence of authors such as Hoffmann and H. H. Ewers combined with the folkloric material to give rise to a tradition of writers producing collections of fantastic tales which eventually became known as the "Belgian School of the fantastique". What characterized these stories were their initial firm rooting in everyday reality, a reality of Brueghelian proportions, followed by an abrupt transition into, or eruption from, the supernatural, the latter presented not in vaporous terms but as another, equally tangible, always terrifying, form of reality.

Among the early proponents of this Belgian "school" were:

"Charle-Marie Flor O'Squar" (a pseudonym of Joseph-Charles Flor) with *Les Fantômes* [Phantoms] (1885)[102] with is a classic study of a haunting, in which the narrator refuses to

---

[102] Black Coat Press, ISBN 978-1-61227-586-4.

admit that the apparitions from which he suffers can be anything but hallucinations, but then ties himself in knots trying to explain them in terms of his own psychology, which he claims unconvincingly to be free from guilt. The story is one of the most interesting and elaborate 19th century developments of the theme of an ambiguous haunting, notable for its acidic artistry. The author's stories are darkly ironic *contes cruels*, remarkable for their relentless quest for originality, often striking in the unusual twists that give an extra turn of the screw to the psychological demolition of their protagonists.

Georges Eekhoud, with his collection *Kermesses* [Fiestas] (1884), *Cycle Patibulaire* [Evil-Looking Cycle] (1892), *L'Autre Vue* [The Other View] (1904) and *La Danse Macabre du Pont de Lucerne* [The Danse Macabre of the Lucerne Bridge] (1920).

Hubert Stiernet, with his *Contes au Perron* [Tales of the Balcony] (1893) and *Histoires Hantées* [Haunted Stories] (1907).

Pol Demade, with *Contes Inquiets* [Worried Tales] (1898), *Les Âmes qui Saignent* [The Bleeding Souls] (1910) and *Le Cortège des Ombres* [The Procession of Shadows] (1925).

Roland de Marès, with *En Barbarie* [Among the Barbarians] (1895).

Les Romans d'Aventure

NYCTALOPE CONTRE LUCIFER

PAR

JEAN LA...

LE VOLUME 1

0,95 centimes Select-Collection

CLAUDE FARRÈRE

La maison des hommes vivants

ROMAN

E. FLAMMARION, Éditeur, 26, rue Racine.

The Belle Époque

From a literary, if not historical, standpoint, it could be argued that the 19th century came to a crashing halt not in 1901, as per the calendar, but with the advent of World War I in 1914. The period between 1900-1914 is known as the *belle époque* [beautiful era]. As the 20th century began, old-fashioned gothic horror became less popular among the classical and mainstream writers, being increasingly relegated to the popular side of literature and the "Grand-Guignol" theater. Romanticism, too, fell out of fashion. The Naturalists were more interested in the sociological and psychological horrors inflicted by society upon its hapless victims rather than by vampires and werewolves and things that went bump in the night. A case could be made, for example, that Émile Zola's vivid descriptions of the sordid and loathsome underbelly of French society belonged to the horror genre.

The Symbolists and the Decadents fought against the growing popularity of the naturalist works of Zola, Gustave Flaubert and Edmond de Goncourt. They sought to tame the shadows, explore the darkness, map the horrors of hell and of the human soul, unveil the faces of evil and make them a subject of seduction. As we approached the year 1900, the notion of *fantastique décadent* became known as *fantastique fin de siècle* [*end of the century*]. And, as a reaction to the Naturalist school, it increasingly took refuge in subject matters whose roots lay deep in the Occult.

Meanwhile, with the advent of the *Belle Époque*, the *fantastique populaire* became increasingly modern. The haunted castles and historical sagas of Alexandre Dumas and Paul Féval made room for contemporary dramas. With the influence of Edgar Allan Poe and Jules Verne, the gothic and supernatural elements were assimilated and incorporated in adventures in which science and logic could no longer be ignored.

Fantastique Populaire

Many of the popular authors of the times happily straddled the line between *fantastique* and science fiction, Depending on the works. Gaston Leroux, Maurice Leblanc, Marcel Allain & Pierre Souvestre, Jean de La Hire, Gustave Le Rouge and Maurice Renard, to name but a few, were equally prominent in both genres, but arguably belonged to the *fantastique populaire* because their style and themes made them the literary successors of Eugène Sue, Alexandre Dumas and Paul Féval, rather than of Jules Verne and J.-H. Rosny Aîné.

The leading *feuilletoniste* of the *Belle Époque* was Gaston Leroux, a writer best known for his classic *Le Fantôme de l'Opéra* [The Phantom of the Opera] (1910),[103] about which little need be said. What few people know, however, is that the original novel, never faithfully adapted to the screen, contained memorable horrific moments, such as the exploration of the civilization beneath the Opera, with the mysterious creatures who lived there, and the heroes' grueling fight in the Phantom's mirrored chamber of horrors. Trained as a lawyer, the author was a renowned investigative journalist who even traveled to, and reported from, Russia just before the Bolshevik revolution. His journalistic skills helped the *fantastique* emerge from the gothic and romantic morass of the end of the 19th century, and, by making it more contemporary and real, gave it a new lease on life.

In *Le Fantôme de l'Opéra*, Leroux skillfully mixed fantastic events with real-life facts, such as the existence of an underground lake under the Opera. The same held true of *Le Fauteuil Hanté* [The Haunted Chair] (1909), a fantastic mystery novel in which a mad scientist used ingenious, murderous

---

[103] Black Coat Press, ISBN 978-1-932983-13-5.

devices to rid himself of applicants at the French Academy who have uncovered his dark secret. These novels read like sensational newspaper accounts of the surreal.

Leroux's eclectic curiosity conferred upon his *oeuvre* a wildly diverse nature. His first novel, *La Double Vie de Theophraste Longuet* [The Double Life of Theophraste Longuet] (1903), belonged squarely to the *fantastique*. In it, a retired merchant found himself possessed by the spirit of notorious 18th century French highwayman, Cartouche. He went on to discover a secret, underground society which had been living in vast caverns under Paris since the 14th century. Later, Leroux shied away from purely supernatural themes, a couple of exceptions being short stories such as the Hoffmannesque *L'Homme qui a Vu le Diable* [The Man Who Saw the Devil] (1908) and *Le Coeur Cambriolé* [The Stolen Heart] (1920).

When Leroux dealt with fantastic themes, it was in ways that were resolutely modern, and often derivative of the works of other popular writers. His classic *Balaoo* (1911) was about a murderous ape-man *à la* Poe's *Murder in the Rue Morgue*. *L'Épouse du Soleil* [The Bride of the Sun] (1912)[104] was a *Lost World* story with H. Rider Haggard elements. Finally, *La Poupée Sanglante* [The Bloody Puppet] (1923) and *La Machine à Assassiner* [The Killing Machine] (1924) were a strange combination of classic *fantastique* and science fiction. In the first volume, the brain of a man framed for murder and later guillotined is transplanted into the body of an android. In its sequel, the characters exposed a vampire cult—one without some of the more supernatural characteristics usually associated with vampirism—led by a depraved nobleman.

Leroux's literary idols being Dumas and Féval, it is no surprise that he was equally comfortable chronicling extravagant tales of murders, revenge, masked men, swooning women, mysterious dwarves and secret societies meeting in underground caverns, with or without fantastic elements. Like their American pulp counterparts of the 1930s, these sagas were

---

[104] Black Coat Press, ISBN 978-1-64932-038-4.

fantastic more in terms of their atmosphere than because of any specific supernatural concepts. In this vein, the author penned *Le Roi Mystère* [King Mystery] (1908), a *Monte-Cristo*-like story—a format he reused in several other novels, such as *La Reine du Sabbat* [The Queen of the Sabbath] (1910), *L'Homme de la Nuit* [The Night Man] (1911), *L'Homme qui Revient de Loin* [The Man Who Returned From Afar] (1916), *Le Sept de Trèfle* [The Seven of Clubs] (1921) and *Les Mohicans de Babel* [The Mohicans of Babel] (1926).

Finally, Leroux was also the author of a series of mystery novels, starring the character of dashing young journalist, *Joseph Rouletabille*, clearly an idealized projection of the author. The *Rouletabille* series included a few genre elements, and its gothic atmosphere justifies its inclusion. The series was comprised of seven novels, starting with the classic *Le Mystère de la Chambre Jaune* [The Mystery of the Yellow Room] (1907).[105]

Easily the equal of Leroux in fame, and arguably his superior in style, was Maurice Leblanc, the creator of the character of gentleman-burglar *Arsène Lupin* who has enjoyed a popularity as long-lasting and considerable as *Sherlock Holmes* or *Tarzan*. There are twenty-two volumes in the *Lupin* series. Several featured genre elements, such as a radioactive "god-stone" that has the power to cure people and cause mutations and becomes the object of a surreal gothic battle in *L'Île aux Trente Cercueils* [*The Island of the Thirty Coffins*] (1920);[106] a Fountain of Youth mineral water source hidden under a lake in the Auvergne, in *La Demoiselle aux Yeux Verts* [The Damsel With Green Eyes] (1927); and the mysterious and implacable Josephine Balsamo, the grand-daughter of Cagliostro, in La Comtesse de Cagliostro [*The Countess of Cagliostro*] (1924).[107]

---

[105] Black Coat Press, ISBN 978-1-934543-60-3.
[106] Black Coat Press, ISBN 978-1-61227-338-9.
[107] In *Arsène Lupin vs Countess Cagliostro*, ISBN 978-1-935558-32-3.

The character was introduced in a series of short stories serialized in the magazine *Je Sais Tout* in 1905. A literary descendent of Ponson du Terrail's *Rocambole*, *Lupin* was, like *Holmes*, an archetype. Although he was on the other side of the law, he was clearly a force for good, and those he defeated, always with characteristic gallic style and panache, were worse villains than he. Another thing that *Lupin* shared with *Holmes* was that its creator spared no effort in making him "real", including playing the part of John D. Watson and appearing as his biographer in several of the books. Also, like Doyle's hero, some of *Lupin*'s best adventures dealt with burning political issues of the times. And finally, Leblanc often alluded to other stories that had not yet been told.

The two characters were bound to meet and, in an unprecedented act of literary pastiche and cross-over, *Sherlock Holmes* himself appeared several times in the *Lupin* novels in the transparent guise of "Herlock Sholmes". In *"Herlock Sholmes arrive trop tard"* [Herlock Sholmes Arrives Too Late] (1907),[108] Sholmes meets a young Lupin for a brief time, unaware of who he is. Called in to solve an ancient riddle, Sholmes succeeds, but only to find that Lupin has gotten in the night before and stolen the treasure. However, having anticipated that the riddle would be easily solved by the Great Detective, Lupin, as a mark of respect and admiration, has left his car waiting for Sholmes at the exit of the secret tunnel.

This meeting marked the beginning of a stormy relationship between the two characters. As Lupin confides to Leblanc, when he first met Sholmes, he felt scrutinized to the core of his being and realized at once that, should they meet again, the Detective would recognize him, whatever the disguise.

And meet again they do in two more stories collected in *Arsène Lupin contre Herlock Sholmes* [Arsene Lupin vs. Her-

---

[108] In *The Hollow Needle*, Black Coat Press, ISBN 978-0-9740711-9-0.

lock Sholmes] (1908).[109] In the first story, Sholmes is called to Paris to help solve some mysterious robberies. The truth is that Lupin has been using secret passages built in houses designed by himself in the guise of an architect. Sholmes and his biographer (Dr. Wilson) have a chance meeting with Lupin and Leblanc. The two foes take each other's measure and the reader is led to the conclusion that, although the law made these two enemies, they could very well have been friends or allies under different circumstances.

In the second story, the same pattern is reenacted. This time, Lupin and Sholmes refuse to leave a sinking boat, each wanting the other to be the first to display a sign of weakness. Lupin pops up again on the ferry crossing the Channel and, this time, Sholmes lets him go rather than drag an innocent girl into the clutches of the Law.

Sholmes appeared twice more in the *Arsène Lupin* saga. Once at the end of the prodigious battle for the secret of *L'Aiguille Creuse* [The Hollow Needle] (1909),[110] the nickname for a huge natural rock formation off the Normandy Coast, which is hollow and houses the treasure of the Kings of France. (This is fiction, yet to this day, a large number of tourists, believe that the Needle is indeed hollow!) Unfortunately, Sholmes accidentally shoots Lupin's fiancée, Raymonde, when she throws herself in front of the Detective to save Lupin from a bullet fired by Sholmes.

The last time Sholmes is mentioned in the saga was in the Gentleman Burglar's greatest epic, *813* (1910).[111] In it, a formidable enigma may lead to the redrawing of the political map of Europe. Lupin is in jail in Paris when he learns that Sholmes has been called by the Kaiser, but has failed to solve the riddle. In this book, Lupin's adversary appears to be a

---

[109] *The Blonde Phantom*, Black Coat Press, ISBN 978-1-932983-14-2.
[110] Black Coat Press, q.v.
[111] Black Coat Press, ISBN 978-1-61227-412-6.

more-than-human, black-clad, merciless killer, whom the hero refers to as the "monster" or the "vampire".

Lupin was a villain, but one who fought on the side of good. Not so with *Fantômas*, another superior literary creation of the period, the brainchild of Marcel Allain and Pierre Souvestre. The character was created in 1911 and appeared in a total of thirty-two volumes written by the two collaborators, then a subsequent eleven volumes written by Allain alone after Souvestre's death in 1914. Allain went on to become the prolific author of well over 500 adventure, romance, detective novels and serials. His best-known achievement, however, remained the *Fantômas* series.

One should note here that *Fantômas*, however, had been narrowly preceded by Léon Sazie's *Zigomar* (1909).[112] Zigomar is a is an equally evil, nefarious character, a criminal genius, and was so popular at the time that his picture could be found on bags of bread, pipes and matchboxes. Masked, hooded, or in disguise, Zigomar constantly bedevils the law. The first of the masked super-criminals, he shares with Fantômas a taste for gratuitous, melodramatic crimes, imaginative atrocities (typhus-bearing mosquitoes being only one such example), murder, kidnapping, robbery, and torture. His inevitable escape from the clutches of the law, his perpetual evasion of justice, made him very popular with the public and he left his mark on the history of crime fiction.

Of Basque origin, the author was born in Algeria in 1862 and died in an accident in Suresne near Paris in 1939. When he was still a child, his father committed suicide after being ruined in a bank fraud. Sazie eventually became a journalist, before turning to theater and, eventually, to serial fiction. He created *Martin Numa, King of Detectives* in 1908, and *Zigomar* a year later. He was also a brilliant fencer who fought several duels.

But *Fantômas* soon eclipsed *Zigomar* and became one of the most popular characters in the history of French fantastic

---

[112] Black Coat Press, ISBN 978-1-61227-861-2.

literature. His adversaries were determined policeman Juve (who may be Fantômas' brother) and young journalist Jerôme Fandor, who eventually falls in love with Fantômas' daughter, Hélène. Another recurring character is the tragic figure of Fantômas' lover, Lady Beltham, who is constantly torn between her passion for the villain and her horror at his criminal schemes.

The character and the monstrously complicated plots designed by the authors were greatly admired by the Surrealists. The *Fantômas* novels were rich in gruesome scenes, such as Fantômas sending an innocent man made-up to look like him to the guillotine in *Fantômas* (1911)); Fantômas using gloves made of human skin to leave a deceased man's fingerprints on his victims in *Le Mort qui Tue* [The Dead Man Who Kills] (1911); Fantômas holding a King prisoner in a secret chamber under the Place de la Concorde in *Un Roi Prisonnier de Fantômas* [A King Prisoner of Fantômas] (1911); Fantômas risings from the grave (literally), having just escaped from the clutches of the Hangman of London, and leading his two nemeses on a wild chase that takes them from a plague-infested ocean liner to the deadly wastes of the South African Transvaal in *La Fille de Fantômas* [The Daughter of Fantômas] (1911);[113] Fantômas commandeering a hansom cab driven by a dead man to spread the plague through the streets of Paris in *Le Fiacre de Nuit* [*The Night Cab*] (1911); all the way to a cataclysmic conclusion that takes the heroes from the deadly streets of St. Petersburg to the Palaces of India, from the back alleys of Paris to the deck of the *Gigantic*, where Fantômas, and his arch-nemesis, Detective Juve, perish at last when the ship sinks in the frigid waters of the North Atlantic in *La Fin de Fantômas* [The Death of Fantômas] (1913).[114]

The first *Fantômas* book cover, showing a contemplative masked man dressed in a dinner jacket and holding a dagger, boldly stepping over Paris, is so well known that it has almost

---

[113] Black Coat Press, ISBN 978-1-932983-56-2.
[114] Black Coat Press, ISBN 978-1-61227-621-2.

become a cliché today. Just as *Sherlock Holmes* is the archetypal modern detective, *Fantômas* is the archetypal modern arch-villain. Among his better-known (and even more horrific) literary descendants are the Italian super-villains such as *Diabolik*, *Satanik*, *Killing* and *Kriminal*.

A lesser hero was the *Nyctalope* by Jean de La Hire, a prolific writer of numerous popular adventure series, many of which included fantastic elements.

The Nyctalope was Léo Saint-Claire, a crime-fighter who can see in the dark and sports an artificial heart. He made his first appearance in *Le Mystère des XV* [The Mystery of the XV] (1911),[115] even though his father, Jean, had previously appeared in *L'Homme Qui Peut Vivre dans l'Eau* [The Man Who Could Live Underwater] (1908). Both are science fiction sagas, the former about the conquest of the Red Planet, involving fighting a cabal of mad scientists and Wells' Martians; the latter, featuring the same mad scientists having created a water-breathing man to help them rule the world. The Nyctalope's adventures comprised twenty, volumes, most depicting Saint-Clair fighting power-mad supervillains gifted with powers that often owed more to magic than science, and rescuing and marrying chaste damsels in distress, making him the first, full-fledged super-hero in the history of pulp literature.

In *Lucifer* (1920),[116] his second appearance and possibly his greatest battle, the Nyctalope faces Baron Glô von Warteck, a.k.a. Lucifer, whose hypnotic powers, amplified by his "teledyname", threatens to enslave the world. In *L'Antéchrist* [The Antichrist] (1927) and its sequel, *Titania* (1929), Léo battles Leonid Zattan, evil incarnate, with the help of Mathias Lumen, a powerful Jewish mage. In *Le Maître de la Vie* [The Master of Life] (1938),[117] the Nyctalope faces a mysterious foe who has the power to kill remotely by the sim-

---

[115] *The Nyctalope on Mars*, Black Coat Press, ISBN 978-1-934543-46-7.
[116] Black Coat Press, ISBN 978-1-932983-98-2.
[117] Black Coat Press, ISBN 978-1-64932-116-9.

ple exercise of his will and eventually travels to a forbidden lamasery in the heart of Tibet to find his secretive adversary.

The Nyctalope's allies included his fiancée (later, wife and mother of his son, Pierre) Sylvie Mac Dhul, the Japanese Gnô Mitang, and the international C.I.D. (Committee of Information and Defense which he had created. His adventures took place on Earth, under water, in Tibet, on Rhea, an unknown satellite of Earth, on Mars, and even in the future.

It was at the start of the new century that the modern literary archetype of the mad doctor made its first appearance, first in the science fiction novels of André Couvreur, himself a medical doctor, reviewed in our companion volume, *The Handbook of French science fiction*. The characters of *Dr. Caresco*, introduced in 1899, was undoubtedly one of the first mad surgeons in popular literature. Caresco returned in *Caresco Surhomme* [Caresco, Superman] (1904),[118] in which the brilliant but mad scientist rules the body-shaped island of Eucrasia whose inhabitants have been transformed, or "improved", by a variety of advanced surgical techniques. The natives are addicted to sensual pleasures, and subservient to the will of Caresco, whom they call the "Superman" for fear that he will castrate them. By comparison, Sax Rohmer's *Fu Manchu* was first published in 1913.

Maurice Renard, far more important in the field of science fiction than fantasy, was the author of two archetypal "mad doctor" novels: *Le Docteur Lerne* [Doctor Lerne] (1908),[119] in which a Dr. Moreau-like mad scientist transplants not only organs between men and animals, but also between plants, and even machines; and the classic *Les Mains d'Orlac* [*The Hands of Orlac*] (1920), in which a virtuoso pianist receives the transplanted hands of a murderer and turns into a killer himself.

A worthy and more famous literary successor of *Caresco* and *Lerne* was *Dr. Cornelius Kramm*, the star of *Le Mysté-*

---

[118] Black Coat Press, ISBN 978-1-61227-254-2.
[119] Black Coat Press, ISBN 978-1-935558-15-6.

rieux Dr. Cornelius [The Mysterious Dr. Cornelius] (1912-13),[120] a sprawling saga serialized in eighteen volumes written by another prolific writer, Gustave Le Rouge. In it, Dr. Cornelius Kramm and his brother, Fritz, rule an international criminal empire called the Red Hand. Cornelius is a brilliant surgeon who can alter people's likenesses through the science of "carnoplasty". One of Cornelius' top agents is the evil Baruch Jorgell, the son of millionaire Fred Jorgell and a sadistic sociopath. Cornelius uses his surgical prowess to change Baruch's face, making him unrecognizable. The Red Hand's growing, global, evil web eventually causes the creation of an alliance of heroes, who band together to fight him and, ultimately, defeat it. These heroes are Dr. Prosper Bondonnat, an equally brilliant French scientist, American billionaire William Dorgan and his son, Harry, who is in love with the beautiful Isadora Jorgell, Baruch's kind-hearted sister, and British Lord Burydan, a colorful, freebooting adventurer. The villain's ultimate fate remains ambiguous... Does he die by his own hand, or does he live to fight another day?

Of all the pulp serials launched in France during the Belle Époque, the *Sâr Dubnotal* series, published by Eichler in 1909-1910 generally credited to the prolific adventure writer Norbert Sévestre.[121] Like William Hope Hodgson's *Carnacki*, published at the same time, the series liked to mix modern science, such as a camera capable of photographing astral bodies, or a telegraph capable of communicating with the dead, with more traditional occult spells and recipes. Despite its beautiful covers, the series, which was probably ahead of its

---

[120] In three volumes, *The Sculptor of Human Flesh*, Black Coat Press, ISBN 978-1-61227-243-6; *The Island of Hanged Men*, Black Coat Press, ISBN 978-1-61227-244-3; and *The Rochester Bridge Catastrophe*, Black Coat Press, ISBN 978-1-61227-245-0.

[121] *Sâr Dubnotal vs Jack the Ripper*, Black Coat Press, ISBN 978-1-934543-94-8; and *Sâr Dubnotal: The Astral Trail*, Black Coat Press, ISBN 978-1-61227-436-2.

time, lasted only twenty issues. The Sâr was the Master of Psychognosis, the Conqueror of the Invisible. He also used the aliases of El Tebib, meaning Doctor in Arabic, implying that he was a learned master of the occult. In spite of his stylish oriental guise, Dubnotal was, in fact, a western man, who had grown up in the Rosicrucian tradition, and then had learned the ancient secrets of the Hindu yogis. Through this, he had mastered their fantastic paranormal abilities. He was capable of telepathy, levitation and hypnosis. He also put into practice the theories of physician Cesare Lombrosi, who wrote *The Criminal Man* (1876), and believed that certain physical traits could indicate a born, atavistic criminal. Dubnotal lived in a comfortable apartment located beneath his sophisticated laboratory. His regular companion and assistant was the Italian medium, Gianetti Annunciata, his disciple Rudolph, his medium Gianetti Annunciata, and his trio of assistants, Frank, Fréjus and Otto. Dubnotal investigated mysteries of the occult, involving ghosts, astral bodies and poltergeists. He also thwarted the nefarious goals of recurring supervillains Tserpchikopf the Hypnotist, who was later revealed to be Jack the Ripper, and Russian terrorist mastermind Azzef.

Norbert Sévestre also wrote several Jules Verne-inspired novels and *La Révolte des Monstres* [The Revolt of the Monsters] (1928) which had mankind fighting giant insects.

Deserving of a footnote in this sub-genre is Guillaume Livet, whose creation was *Miramar, L'Homme aux Yeux de Chat* [Miramar, The Man with Cat Eyes] (1913), another arch-villainous mad scientist out to conquer the world. *Miramar* never gained the recognition of *Fantômas*, or even the *Nyctalope*, but could see in the dark and perform strange organ grafts on his victims.

Another product of the more bloodthirsty aspirations of the *Belle Époque* was the notorious "Grand-Guignol" theater. It was a theater specializing in gory horror plays and dark comedies, located on Impasse Chaptal in the 9th arrondissement of Paris, and it operated from April, 1897 to June, 1962.

Its sole competition was the Theatre des Deux Masques, which opened in February, 1921, but three years later, chose to concentrate instead of more conventional murder mysteries. The Grand-Guignol derived its name from Guignol, a character from a *Punch & Judy*-like show created in Lyons by Laurent Mourguet. Before it became a theater, the Grand-Guignol premises were first a chapel, then the atelier of the painter Rochegrosse, who was justifiably famous for his gory, realistic depictions of massacres and tortures of the saints.

Its first director and founder was playwright Oscar Méténier. Prior to establishing the theater, he had worked for the Paris police; his duties included assisting condemned men on their way to the guillotine. He started the theater as a place to produce his own plays, a combination of crime stories and naturalistic, social studies. One of the first plays he produced, *Mademoiselle Fifi* (1896), was based on an 1896 story by Guy de Maupassant) and portrayed materials that had never before been displayed on stage: a prostitute plunging a knife in the throat of an officer who had insulted her. The play's considerable success indicated that gore would sell seats, and the Grand-Guignol was born. Subsequently, Méténier had recurring problems with censorship which, on several occasions, closed him down, but that did not stop the theater from creating the first, modern representation of horror.

The next director of the theater was Max Maurey, who also wrote numerous comedies, and who, from 1899 to 1914, increasingly shifted the emphasis of naturalistic dramas to gore. It was him who had the idea of advertising that the theater had hired a doctor to assist fainting spectators. Maurey discovered playwright André de Lorde.

The Grand-Guignol produced short plays of one or two acts with no mood-breaking intermission between the acts. It offered four to six plays a night, alternating vaudeville, boulevard comedies and gore. Its adaptation of Egar Allan Poe's *Dr. Tarr and Prof. Feather* became hugely popular and gory, with a scene showing a madman scooping an eyeball out of his victim's socket. The stories featured few ghosts, vampires, devils and monsters. Instead, they relied on "real-life" monsters, madmen, serial killers, mad surgeons, insane alienists, freaks, and murderers with uncontrollable urges, twisted psychoses, weird erotic obsessions and dubious heredity. The Grand-Guignol plays successfully dramatized these then-new to the stage concepts. The writing displayed a surgical-like sense of brevity and effectiveness. Overcome by fear or horror, many people did faint. Some spectators, outraged by what they beheld, loudly summoned the police. Finally, women were said to attend the Monday matinées with their lovers often as a prelude to their illicit affairs.

Another branch of the *fantastique populaire* of the Belle Époque which straddled the line between science fiction and *fantastique* was the Extraordinary Voyage/Lost World exotic adventure, featuring hidden lands, secret civilizations, dastardly villains, and other melodramatic elements inherited from gothic literature, blending the formats of traditional adventures *à la* Jack London with crime fiction (with or without fantastic elements), science fiction and *fantastique*. These novels borrowed just as much from Jules Verne as they did from H. Rider Haggard, whose *King Solomon's Mines* had been published in 1885 and *She* in 1886.

The best example of this was Gaston Leroux's *L'Épouse du Soleil* [The Bride of the Sun] (1912),[122] mentioned above, in which young engineer Raymond Ozoux, accompanied by his uncle, arrives in Peru to meet his fiancée, Marie-Thérèse. Meanwhile, descendants of the Incas are preparing a great feast during which a virgin will be sacrificed to the Sun, walled up alive in a secret temple. At the same time, a mysterious Inca bracelet is sent to Marie-Thérèse purporting to be a gift of the Sun to his future bride. The girl is then kidnapped by the Incas and Raymond, his uncle and Marie-Thérèse's father set out on a trek across Peru to free her while a revolution shakes the country.

---

[122] Black Coat Press, q.v.

Other authors who mined this rich vein with novels often serialized in the magazines of the times, such as *Le Journal des Voyages* [*The Journal of Voyages*] (1877-1947), *Lectures Pour Tous* [Readings for All] (1898-1940), *Je Sais Tout* [*I Know Everything*] (1905-1921) and *L'Intrépide* [The Fearless], as well pulpish paperback imprints by publishers such as Ollendorff, Méricant, Férenczi, Lafitte, Baudinière, etc., included:

Maurice Maindron, with *La Gardienne de l'Idole Noire* [The Guardian of the Black Idol] (1910), an *Indiana Jones*-like novel taking place in India in the 1500s, featuring the efforts of a brave Spanish Captain to rescue a young princess from the unspeakable clutches of the evil worshippers of Kali.

Louis Boussenard, with *Les Étrangleurs du Bengale* [The Stranglers of Bengal] (1899).

René Thévenin, with *La Cité des Tortures* [The City of Tortures] (1906).

Georges Le Faure, with *Le Secret du Glacier* [*The Secret of the Ice Flow*] (1907) and *Un Descendant de Robinson* [*A Descendent of Robinson*] (1910).

Albert Bonneau, a.k.a. "Maurice Champagne", with *Les Reclus de la Mer* [The Recluse of the Sea] (1907) and *Les Sondeurs d'Abîmes* [The Probers of the Abyss] (1911).

Pierre Giffard, with *Le Tombeau de Glace* [The Tomb of Ice] (1908).

Octave Béliard, with *Les Merveilles de l'Île Mystérieuse* [The Wonders of Mysterious Island] (1911).

René-Marcel de Nizerolles, with his 1800-page serial *Les Voyages Aériens d'un Petit Parisien à travers le Monde* [The Aerial Voyages of a Little Parisian Across the World] (1910-12).

These authors, and more, continued to enrich the field after World War I, but because of the increasing blending of genres, these types of works began to lack supernatural and gothic elements and shifted fully into the science fiction genre.

Fantastique Littéraire

An increasing number of so-called literary or "mainstream" writers crossed the literary boundaries between Realism and the *fantastique*.

Octave Mirbeau penned a series of truly sadistic and mean-spirited tales of murders, cannibalism and ghostly revenge in *Le Jardin des Supplices* [The Torture Garden] (1899) and *Les Vingt et un Jours d'un Neurasthénique* [The 21 Days of a Neurasthenic] (1901).

Victor-Émile Michelet, with *Contes Surhumains* [*Superhuman Tales*] (1900).[123] The author's stories reveal his determined and constant ambition to push various envelopes in horror, fantasy and supernatural. He makes considerable efforts to distance his work from the conventional formulas. His tales draw energy and charm from the earnest esotericism of their central motifs, and poignantly exploit the author's fascination with death. Filled with the ironic spirit of the *contes cruels*, which dominated upmarket short fiction during the *fin-de-siècle*, they are visionary fantasies with a peculiar obliquity that is the hallmark of his work. Michelet took his fantasy and symbolism seriously, especially when their extrapolation led him by convoluted paths to the strange conclusions displayed in his work.

Pierre Louÿs' stories, collected in *Sanguines* [*Bloody Tales*] (1903), used the familiar themes of the decadent school, but gave them a refreshingly ironical twist: in one tale, an ancient Egyptian princess was spooked by the sight of a modern cigarette; in another, a madman climbed a mountain to hear a goddess sing; in yet another, a woman portrayed very differently from what she really was in a Balzac novel failed to convince the great writer than she was herself, and not a fictional character!

Gabriel Legué's *La Messe Noire* [*The Black Mass*] (1903) is a well-documented historical account of complex

---

[123] Black Coat Press, ISBN 978-1-61227-795-0.

cases of poisoning and demonic possession with dire legal consequences, such as torture and other various grisly punishments.

Gabriel de Lautrec's *Le Feu Sacré* [The Sacred Fire] (1904),[124] opens with a description of a secret ritual practiced by one of the cults of the French Occult Revival, and much of the discussion featured in the story deals with the nature and philosophy of magic. Despite its ground-breaking nature, it never achieved publication in volume form. His prose poems, published in *Poèmes en prose* (1898), *Histoires de Tom Joë* (1920) and *La Vengeance du portrait ovale* (1922) (a title borrowed from Poe),[125] are among the most important precursors of Surrealism, contemporary with the most significant contributions that Alfred Jarry made to the preliminary foundations of that movement. They are among the most extreme examples of the Decadent Movement and provide a fascinating commentary on its psychology and esthetics, at the crossroads of horror, fantasy and science fiction. Its singular inspiration owes as much to the author's predilection for dark humor, Grand Guignol and the mixing of genres, as it does to the influence of alcohol and hashish, which he used regularly.

Edmond Haraucourt, whose notable science fiction works were reviewed in *The Handbook of French Science fiction*, penned a collection of equally remarkable horror stories, *La Peur* [*The Fear*] (1907).

Maurice Level was Marcel Schwob's cousin, and he, too, contributed several notable genre works including *Les Portes de l'Enfer* [The Gates of Hell] (1910).[126] The tales, in the tradition of the *contes cruels*, range in subject from a man who keeps a secret with devastating effects, to a maniac who finds thrills in witnessing violent accidents, to a blind peasant who purposely loses his eyesight, to a prostitute who sleeps with the person who executed her husband. These rich and careful-

---

[124] Black Coat Press, ISBN 978-1-61227-876-6
[125] Black Coat Press, ISBN 978-1-61227-009-8.
[126] Black Coat Press, ISBN 978-1-61227-598-7 .

ly plotted stories ratchet up suspense, sentence by bewitching sentence. Their horror is based on human behavior and psychological drama, rather than supernatural elements, and the subtle beauty of their descriptions only further intensifies the turn of the knife when it inevitably comes—a truly decadent pleasure. The author's macabre stories were printed in Parisian newspapers and staged by the Grand-Guignol theater. Other works of note include *On?* [They?] (1908), *Lady Harrington* (1908), *L'Épouvante* [The Horror] (1908) and *Contes de l'Heure Présente* [Tales of the Present Times] (1914), co-written with Charles Robert-Dumas.

Anatole France, who went on to win the 1921 Nobel Prize for literature, wrote *Sur La Pierre Blanche* [The White Stone] (1905) and *L'Île des Pingouins* [Penguin Island] (1908), which are often classified as science fiction, but are better described as allegorical philosophical tales which use fantastic elements for satirical purposes. France did pen a major work of the *fantastique*, however, one which is truly revolutionary and represents a thematic bridge between John Milton's *Paradise Lost* (1667) and more modern renditions of the Prince of Darkness, *La Révolte des Anges* [The Revolt of the Angels] (1914). This is a startling tale in which the fallen angel Arcade organizes a new revolt among the fallen angels who are living on Earth, generally posing as artists; but Lucifer, who lives as a peaceful gardener, stops him by convincing him that the next battle needs to be won not on a celestial battlefield but in the hearts and minds of men.

Claude Farrère, the first recipient of the French Goncourt Award,[127] wrote *La Maison des Hommes Vivants* [The House of Living Men] (1911). In it, the author describes a sect of secret immortals, founded by Count Saint-Germain, who steal others' life-forces in order to preserve their own immortality. It was later adapted into a Grand-Guignol play by Pierre-Louis Rehm.

---

[127] The French equivalent of the British Booker Prize or the American Pulitzer Prize.

Satirical writer Alfred Jarry, creator of the grotesque and wildly amusing *Ubu Roi* (1896), He displayed a biting sense of satire when dealing with human evil and irrationality. He was a forerunner of the Theatre of the Absurd; his *Gestes et Opinions du Docteur Faustroll* [Deeds & Opinions of Dr. Faustroll] (1911) contained a so-called treatise of "pataphysics", a logic of the absurd and was later embraced by the Dadaists and the Surrealists.

Guillaume Apollinaire. was an *avant-garde* poet who penned a series of vivid, sometimes whimsical, often wildly fantastic, stories, always exhibiting a daring sense of the outrageous. In order to shock his readers, he liked to experiment with the form of the text; he also liked to defeat expectations, challenge dogmas and question matters of faith, always with a sense of the bizarre. *L'Enchanteur Pourrissant* [The Rotting Enchanter] (1909) was a poetic dialog between Merlin and Viviane. *L'Hérésiarque et Cie.* (1910) was a collection of short stories written between 1899 and 1910, which dealt with a variety of fantasy themes such as magic, invisibility, etc. The story *"Le Passant de Prague"* [The Pedestrian from Prague] featured the Wandering Jew telling his own story, making references to those who previously wrote about him, such as Goethe, Sue, Quinet and Richepin. The twist was that, far from being a cursed, unhappy figure, Ahasverus was a contented, even festive man. Because of his somewhat anarchistic outlook, and his love for typographical experimentation, Apollinaire was one of the first, true heralds of Surrealism.

Finally, Raymond Roussel was also a precursor of Surrealism with his elaborate word games in *Impressions d'Afrique* [Impressions of Africa] (1910) and the bizarre *Locus Solus* (1914), a book comprised of surreal scenes in which corpses replay their lives in a store window, a woman assembles a mosaic made of human teeth, a girl is seen swimming inside a diamond, etc.

Fantasy

Although it did not attract much attention at the time of its release, the publication of *Les Atlantes, Aventures des temps légendaires* [The Atlanteans: Adventures in Legendary Times] (1905)[128] can be seen in hindsight as a significant benchmark in the history of imaginative fiction, for it is the first great epic fantasy novel of the 20th century—and arguably, the first ever penned. Its authors were Charles Lomon et Pierre-Barthélemy. Gheusi, the proprietor and editor-in-chief of *La Nouvelle Revue*; he and his friend Lomon were both successful novelists, playwrights and operatic librettists, who had also collaborated on a script for a new dramatized version of Charles Nodier's *Trilby* produced in 1904. *Les Atlantes* provides, in many ways, an archetype of what the essence of late 20th century fantasy would be, filling the gap between the highly stylized heroic fantasies of William Morris, James Branch Cabell, Lord Dunsany and E. R. Eddison, and the more modern "sword and sorcery" subgenre, the prototype of which was created by Robert E. Howard, and further developed by such writers as Catherine L. Moore, Fritz Leiber, Clark Ashton Smith and Jack Vance.

It is not a coincidence that *Les Atlantes* was the work of two librettists, whose first and foremost love was the opera, for prose fiction is not where modern epic fantasy tropes began. Opera, with its melodramatic structure, is not only highly conducive to the exaggerations of fantasy, but also accommodates very well its epic conceptual scale. Although there do not appear to be any 19th century French operas set in Atlantis, Lomon & Gheusi would have been familiar with *Le Roi d'Ys* [The King of Ys] (1888) by Edouard Lalo, with a libretto by Édouard Blau, based on the Breton legend of a land catastrophically sunk as a result of the hellish fury of a woman scorned.

---

[128] *The Last Days of Atlantis*, Black Coart Press, ISBN 978-1-61227-456-0.

Gheusi's dramatic works also include a three-act "idyll" based on Breton legend, *Kermaria* (1897), and a "lyric tragedy" written in collaboration with Victorien Sardou with music by Camille Saint-Saëns, *Les Barbares* [The Barbarians]. Lomon's first significant production, *Le Marquis de Kenilis* (1879), was also set in Brittany, and his most famous libretto was for Charles Lefebvre's opera *Djelma* (1894).

Given all these pre-existing works, it was not surprising that the authors decided to write a libretto for an opera set against the background of the sinking of Atlantis. The fact that they had been unable to bring their own *Thekla*, a lyrical drama set in Byzantium, to the stage, might well have encouraged them to think in terms of a *feuilleton* serial instead. Indeed, *Les Atlantes* is rather stagey, built around a series of melodramatic confrontations, and might well have been drafted initially as a play. At any rate, it certainly seems to have been imagined in the authors' minds as a sequence of overwrought theatrical scenes. It owes its epic quality to the extravagant elaboration of its *dramatis personae*, which permit the evolution of the disaster that overwhelms Atlantis to be seen from multiple viewpoints, the only way to do justice to its complexity and scale.

Its formulation as prose fiction, however, allows its more expansive scenes—the conflict of the Bloody Day, the Battle of Lamb'ha and the sacking of the Temple of Light by the riotous mob—to be detailed in a fashion impossible to achieve on stage

Modern lovers of heroic fantasy might feel disappointed by the fact that Argall, the blond barbarian giant, initially established as the central character of the main narrative, has no sooner acquired the magic sword that gives him his superheroic status than he is sidelined by the wicked queen Yerra's amorous sorcery, leaving less capable characters with inferior weapons to occupy center stage by turns, until he is finally able to bring his own personal narrative to a conclusion. This narrative move is not inappropriate, however, given that the real heart and soul of the story is the moral conflict between the wicked queen and Soroe, the chaste martyr, with the "hero" as their pawn and prize. Some of the other plot-elements thrown into the mix, including the monstrous Guardian of the Threshold, the evil priesthood avid for human sacrifices, and the Fountain of Youth, now seem like standard props of generic fantasy, but it is worth remembering that, long before that genre became a marketing category, it had no standard tropes, and the fact that so many aspects of *Les Atlantes* have become clichés today is a tribute to the selective process by which its two authors fitted their legendary raw materials together to produce their ground-breaking work.

It is also notable that, although the novel was published as a single long narrative, it does foreshadow the three-phase structure whose standardization resulted in the trilogy becoming the most common form of modern generic fantasy: the "N-shaped plot" in which an initial phase of success is followed by a catastrophic series of disasters, prior to a challenging struggle for recovery.

Maurice Magre was one of the most far-ranging and extravagant French writers of fantasy in the first half of the 20th century, and perhaps the finest of them, because of the fertility and versatility of his imagination and the manner and purpose for which he deployed it. Between 1900 and 1905, he wrote several stories that could be called called *contes merveilleux*, often inadequately translated as "fairy tales," but that would be more accurately rendered as "tales of enchantment," or, in this case, disenchantment. Among these were "*Marcelle*" (1901), "*Le Premier amour du docteur Faust*" [Dr. Faust's First Love] (1902), "*Marinette et le Vieil Ondin*" [Marinette and the Old Water-Sprite] (1902), "*Histoire merveilleuse de Claire d'Amour*" [The Marvelous Story of Claire d'Amour] (1903), "*La Fleur de jeunesse*" [The Flower of Youth] (1903), "*Histoire d'un Grenadier qui n'avait pas de chance*" [The Story of an Unlucky Grenadier] (1903), "*Le Marchand de jouets*" [The Toy Merchant] (1903), "*Le Pauvre musicien et le Petit Genie*" [The Poor Musician and the Little Genie] (1903), "*La Poupée*" [The Doll] (1903), "*La Dernière Sirène*" [The

Last Siren] (1905) and "*Le Berger roi*" [The Goatherd King] (1905).[129] Although these stories might be considered atypical of Magre's works, which will be reviewed in our next chapter, variants of the symbolic figure of Claire d'Amour continued to recur in his *oeuvre*. The flower of youth was replaced in the fullness of time by other blooms, but that motif remained perennial in numerous variations.

Edmond Haraucourt's *Dieudonat* (1906, exp. 1912)[130] fits in the rich French tradition of the *contes merveilleux* by endowing its eponymous hero at birth with the supernatural ability to produce miracles. Upon adulthood, Prince Dieudonat is forced to leave his kingdom and embarks on a quixotic, picaresque, and ultimately tragic, journey. The novel is a work of such tremendous verve and ambition that it inevitably provokes admiration, and if the nutritive value of some of the food for thought that it contains is a trifle suspect, it is nevertheless a phenomenal feast.

Published in 1908, the same year as Gustave Le Rouge's *The Vampires of Mars* (reviewed in *The Handbook of French science fiction*), *Les Aventures Merveilleuses de Serge Myrandhal sur la Planete Mars* [The Marvelous Adventures of Serge Myrandhal on Mars][131] is a pioneering planetary romance, the third Martian epic after Arnould Galopin's more scientifically slanted *Doctor Omega* (1906) and Jean de La Hire's *The Nyctalope on Mars* (1911), three years before Burroughs began work on *A Princess of Mars*. In it, the bold French Engineer Serge Myrandhal travels to Mars in a ship propelled by the power of thought, followed by his fiancée, the brave American novelist Miss Annabella Carpenter, and her guardian, the eccentric British millionaire Sir Washington Pickman. There, they make numerous wondrous discoveries including that of a race of small, red-furred anthropoids living

---

[129] All in *The Marvelous Story of Claire d'Amour*, Black Coat Press, ISBN 978-1-61227-652-6.
[130] Black Coat Press, ISBN 978-1-61227-777-6.
[131] Black Coat Press, ISBN 978-1-61227-265-8.

underground, and beautiful winged humanoids. As a specimen of early planetary romance, is of considerable historical interest and remains very readable today, amusing and even thought-provoking.

Han Ryner's *Le Fils du Silence* [The Son of Silence] (1911)[132] tells of the quest of the legendary philosopher Pythagoras looking for a vision of utopia in the philosophical and religious doctrines of the Samothracian and Eleusianian Mysteries, and the teachings of Ancient Egypt and Zarathustra. The author's construction of his fictional Pythagoras is both intriguing and ingenious, and telling his story represented a challenging literary experiment as well constituting one of the most original adventures in the field of anarchist utopianism. His *Paraboles Cyniques* [Cynic Parables] (1913)[133] is a highly unusual and remarkable experiment in the development and use of the parable as an art-form and exemplifies his commitment to individualistic anarchism and pacifism.

Henri de Régnier was the most prolific and the most popular of the Symbolist writers to turn to high fantasy with his collection *La Canne de Jaspe* [The Stick of Jaspe] (1897), followed by *Histoires Incertaines* [Uncertain Tales] (1919).[134] His stories read like updated fairy tales of ghosts and monsters set against the cold palaces and forests of past centuries. A Byronesque man born out of his time, spiritually anchored in the 18th century, De Régnier updated classic fairy tales and told stories of ghosts, monsters and creatures from Faerie— untold tales of Bluebeard and Scheherazade, the legends of the Lady of the Seven Mirrors and the Knight Who Fell Asleep in the Snow, the adventures of Hermagore the Fisherman and Monsieur d'Amercoeur, who frequented the beds of princesses and the courts of kings, who bore the sword and wore the mask.

---

[132] Black Coat Press, ISBN 978-1-61227-549-9.
[133] In *The Son of Silence*, q.v.
[134] In *A Surfeit of Mirrors*, Black Coat Press, ISBN 978-1-61227-076-0

N° 3. CHAQUE RÉCIT EST COMPLET EN UN VOLUME 25 Cent.

GUSTAVE LE ROUGE
LE MYSTÉRIEUX DOCTEUR CORNÉLIUS

Le Sculpteur de Chair Humaine

LA MAISON DU LIVRE 28 R. MONSIEUR LE PRINCE PARIS.

Harry Dickson

LE SHERLOCK HOLMES AMERICAIN

No. 118 — Le Mystère de Bantam-House. — Prix fr. 1.-

Between the Wars
(1918-1945)

The confidence displayed by French Society in the early 1900s was sapped by the slaughter of World War I in which, out of 8 million Frenchmen drafted, 1.3 million were killed and 1 million severely crippled. Large sections of France were devastated and industrial production fell by 60%. Even deeper and longer-lasting, however, were the psychological wounds left by the war, and the awareness that such a fate could never be endured again.

It was, therefore, not surprising that French culture between the wars gave rise to an abundance of new ideas intending to break with the past: cubism, the music of Erik Satie, the search for a sense of spiritual exaltation as demonstrated in the films of Jean Cocteau, Marcel L'Herbier, Luis Buñuel and René Clair.

In French literature, the Dadaist and Surrealist movements exemplified that desire to break violently with the past, but the more conventional forms of the novel remained otherwise less innovative. The period was dominated by family saga novels (or *romans fleuve*), working-class novels in the tradition of Émile Zola, and regional novels advocating a return to the old-fashioned values of peasant life. This began to change only in the mid-1930s with the popularity of writers like André Malraux, Albert Camus and Louis-Ferdinand Céline), and the influences of American writers such as William Faulkner, John Dos Passos and James Joyce.

In the *fantastique*, the split between *fantastique populaire* and *fantastique littéraire* was definitively formed. The former was written by popular writers, walking in the footsteps of the *roman noir*, Alexandre Dumas, Eugène Sue and Paul Féval; the latter was written by literary-minded writers, and followed a tradition that had begun with E. T. A. Hoffmann, Edgar Allan Poe, the romantics and the symbolists.

Fantastique Populaire

Between the wars, the *fantastique populaire* continued to cater to the masses by providing cheap entertainment in the form of the *romans feuilletons* published in pulp-like magazines and cheap paperback imprints.

To the names of Gaston Leroux, Maurice Leblanc, Jean de La Hire, and Gustave Le Rouge, who all continued to write their unique blend of science fiction, fantasy, mystery and adventure. Must now be added the prolific Arthur Bernède, who wrote in the tradition of Paul Féval. The author was the creator of the dark-clad crime fighter, *Judex* (1917),[135] immediately adapted into serial form by Louis Feuillade and remade as a film in 1234 by Maurice Champreux and in 1963 by Georges Franju. Judex appears and disappears like a living shadow. Trained by the vindictive Woman in Black, he is a master of disguise and an excellent fighter. His loyal followers include a female athlete, a reformed ex-convict and a pack of vicious bloodhounds. Beneath the ruins of a castle is his secret lair, where he interrogates his prisoners through a "television" screen. His nemesis is Favraux, a corrupt banker who has left a trail of ruin and misery in his wake. Judex not only challenges Favraux, but also the evil Diana Monti, Favraux's fiancée who is as ruthless and powerful as he is. But as our hero struggles against the villains, he falls in love with Favraux's daughter, the beautiful, innocent Jacqueline.

Judex returned in *La Nouvelle Mission de Judex* [Judex's New Mission] (1919).[136] On the eve of World War I, the Paris underworld is dominated by the Secret Raiders, a vicious gang

---

[135] Black Coat Press, ISBN 978-1-61227-085-2.
[136] *The Return of Judex*, Black Coat Press, ISBN 978-1-61227-159-0.

of spies and extortionists. Their leader is a one-eyed mystic who meticulously records all the crimes that he intends to commit in the future. This mastermind has hypnotic powers that allow him to telepathically force honest citizens to commit crimes. Assisting this diabolical mesmerist is a seductive baroness. Besides being an expert cat burglar, she is also a superb pugilist capable of beating a man to a pulp. Only one man can stop these criminals: the shadowy vigilante known as Judex! However, the Secret Raiders discover that Judex is really the wealthy Jacques de Trémeuse. They strike at him through his family! Worse yet, Judex finds his efforts to protect his loved ones constantly sabotaged by the incompetence of one of his own agents! This exciting adventure foreshadows Fritz Lang's classic film trilogy about Dr. Mabuse.

After writing two more sequels, *Les Nouveaux Exploits de Judex* [Judex's New Adventures] (1925) and *La Dernière Incarnation de Judex* [Judex's Last Incarnation] (1925), Bernède created the ghostly figure of *Belphégor* (1927).[137] The sinister, ghostly presence of the mysterious Belphegor is haunting the Louvre, seeking the Treasure of the Kings of France. Against him are pitted the indomitable Chantecoq, the King of the Detectives, another of the author's recurring heroes, and the fearless journalist Jacques Bellegarde. A duel to the death begins between the murderous Phantom of the Louvre and his enemies throughout the City of Lights. This classic of French fantastic literature spawned no less than three motion pictures, one popular 1965 television series with Juliette Greco, and one animated show. Other notable genre novels included *La Devineresse* [The Seeress] (1930), *Le Sorcier de la Reine* [*The Queen's Wizard*] (1930), *Mephisto* (1931), *La Fille du Diable* [The Devil's Daughter] (1932) and *Vampiria* (1932).

Fascinax was a lesser known, yet colorful, French crime fighter created anonymously and published in 22 issues by the

---

[137] *Belphegor, The Phantom of the Louvre*, Black Coat Press, ISBN 978-1-61227-110-1.

Librairie des Romans Choisis in 1921. It is generally assumed that the series was written by different authors: some scholars have credited Gustave Le Rouge, since No. 3 is reminiscent of Dr. Cornelius No. 7, and No. 6 of Dr. Cornelius No. 14, but this theory is far from accepted.

Fascinax followed in the footsteps of *Sâr Dubnotal* (see previous chapter). Both characters are detectives of the occult, investigators of the supernatural, in the tradition of William Hope Hodgson's Carnacki. Fascinax is George Leicester, a British MD residing in the Philipines, who helps Hindu yogi Nadir Kritchna come back to life after having been put to death for a crime he did not commit. To thank him, the resurrected yogi takes George into the jungle and, in a mysterious temple, has him undergo various mystic rituals which confer upon him supernatural powers. George then uses the alias of Fascinax to fight evil, starting with Kritchna's green-eyed nemesis, the superhuman Numa Pergyll and his henchman, Franz Krypfer.

The battle with Pergyll continues in No. 2–turning into a deadly contest of wills and mind powers. Pergyll returns in No. 4, using a phony Mummy to spread evil. Another super-villain is the Queen of Sirens, a mysterious, water-breathing female supervillain, who fights both underwater and in the air (Nos. 10-11), and Croquignolle the deadly gnome (Nos. 10, 19). Other stories feature a cursed emerald (No. 6), a fake Martian invasion (Nos. 13-14) and a phony ghost (No. 18). Fascinax' vehicle is the "fascine" (introduced in No. 5), a car that can turn into an aeroplane. Nos. 13-22 were less imaginative, with fantasy elements more likely to be revealed as fake.

Marcel Allain tried to recreate the success of *Fantômas* with several other new characters in the same vein: *Tigris* (26 issues, 1928-30), a super-criminal and master of disguise. His nemesis is a police inspector named Rude and his son, Léon, who is in love with the same woman as Tigris; *Fatala* (22 issues, 1930-31), a female Fantômas, who, in the end, redeems herself; *Miss Teria* (12 issues, 1931), the codename of one of

Her Majesty's top secret agents on a quest to locate secret documents; and *Férocias* (20 issues, 1933), a master-criminal who infiltrates the ranks of the police, blackmails the French Government for a billion francs and uses his alias as a reference to his predecessor *Fantômas* (who has a cameo).

Jean Joseph-Renaud wrote popular *fantastique* serial novels for magazines, but in a more supernatural vein. He was one of the first French writers to credit Ambrose Bierce as an influence in his collection of tales *Le Clavecin Hanté* [The Haunted Harpsichord] (1920). His novel *La Vivante Épingle* [The Living Needle] (1922) used the then-popular myths of Ancient Egypt in the tradition of Théophile Gautier. Among his best genre novels or collections were *Les Doigts qui Parlent* [The Talking Fingers] (1917), *Lumières dans la Nuit* [Lights in the Night] (1923), *La Vasque d'Or* [The Golden Basin] (1925), *Le Seigneur Mystère* [Lord Mystery] (1929), *Au-Delà* [Beyond] (1932) and *Les Deux Idoles* [The Two Idols] (1932). The author also contributed a play, *La Visionnaire* [The Visionary] (1936), to the Grand-Guignol theater.

The Grand-Guignol theater reached its pinnacle between the wars and continued to reign supreme in the sub-genre of pure horror fiction. Camille Choisy managed it from 1914 to 1930. Unlike his predecessors, he was not a writer but a former set decorator. He was responsible for the development of the many, spectacular, gory special effects which became associated with the theater. He also discovered lead actress Paula Maxa and even bought a fully-equipped and functional surgical theater to serve as a prop for the plays. After Choisy came Jack Jouvin, who managed it from 1930 to 1938. Under his stewardship, some psychology was added to gore and the characters became more fleshed out. However, he lacked in other managerial areas and, with changing times and fashions, decline began to set in.

The greatest writing discovery of the Grand-Guignol was André de Lorde, nicknamed the "Prince of Terror", who became the Stephen King of the times. A small and polished man, the author was a prolific playwright who also wrote fashionable comedies as well as social novels. He penned over one hundred and fifty plays, often in collaboration with other writers, such as Pierre Chaine, Henri Bauche, Alfred Binet, Georges Montignac, and Charles Foleÿ. His celebrity during the period easily rivaled that of any other writers and he became the Grand-Guignol author *par excellence*, and probably the first best-selling gore writer in the genre's history. De Lorde's brand of horror relied on medicine and psychiatry rather than the supernatural. For him, a man who saw ghosts or conversed with spirits was a dangerous lunatic, possibly a potential murderer, not someone who communicated with the Beyond. His works were collected in several volumes, including *Théâtre d'Épouvante* [Theater of Horror] (1909), *Cauchemars* [Nightmares] (1912), *Théâtre Rouge* [Red Theater] (1922), *Les Drames Célèbres du Grand-Guignol* [Famous Tragedies of the Grand-Guignol] (1924), *Théâtre de la Peur* [Theater of Fear] (1924), *Théâtre de la Mort* [Theater of Death] (1928) and *La Galerie des Monstres* [The Gallery of Monsters] (1928).

One of the most distinctive genre writers of the 1930s, who also blended genres with deceptive facility, was Pierre Véry, whose mystery novels almost always incorporated surreal, almost supernatural, elements, explained away at the end, but not necessarily in an entirely rational manner. Some of his works belonged squarely in the *fantastique*, such as *Le Pays sans Étoiles* [The Starless Country] (1945), adapted into an eponymous 1945 feature film, and *Tout Doit Disparaître le 5 Mai* [Everything Must Go pn May 5th] (1961), his last book, a collection of fantastic tales. His first novel, the brilliant *Pont Égaré* [Lost Bridge] (1929), was clearly inspired by the Surrealists, as were *Les Métamorphoses de Jean Sucre* [The Metamorphoses of Jean Sucre] (1931) and *Le Meneur de Jeu* [The Game Master] (1934), which displayed his great talent for crafting quirky, odd little mysteries.

After winning an award for *Le Testament de Basil Crookes* [The Testament of Basil Crookes] (1930), (published under the pseudonym of "Toussaint-Juge"), Véry created the character of *Prosper Lepic*, a lawyer and poet whose face resembled that of an owl, who solves mysteries that almost, but never quite, fall into the supernatural. *Le Gentleman des Antipodes* [The Gentleman from the Other Side of the World] (1936), fort example, features a club of individuals whose faces look like animals. *Le Thé des Vieilles Dames* [The Tea of the Old Ladies] (1937) takes place in an odd village with a dream-like quality. In *L'Assassinat du Père Noël* [The Murder of Santa Claus] (1934), the inhabitants of a snowbound mountain village discover the corpse of a mysterious man dressed as Santa Claus. *Les Disparus de Saint-Agil* [The Saint-Agil Disappearances] (1935) has students vanishing at a boys' school.

Claude Aveline also straddled the line between the *fantastique* and detective fiction. He was the author of several collections of strange and fantastic stories, such as *Trois Histoires de la Nuit* [Three Stories of Night] (1931), *C'est Vrai mais il ne faut pas le croire* [It's True But You Can't Believe It] (1939), *Les Plus Belles Histoires de Peur* [The Most Beautiful Tales of Fear] (1942) and *Temps Mort* [Dead Time] (1945). The author became justly famous for creating the character of detective Frédéric Belot.

In 1934, Édouard Letailleur penned three notable horror thrillers, *Le Cimetière des Lépreux* [The Graveyard of Lepers], *La Demeure de Satan* [The House of Satan] and *Perkane, le Démon de la Nuit* [Perkane, The Night Demon].

Finally, Léo Gestelys contributed several adventure novels with gothic or exotic genre elements. Among these were *Le Trésor des Derviches* [The Treasure of the Derviches] (1937) and *La Maison de la Mort* [The House of Death] (1938).

Fantastique Littéraire

The *fantastique littéraire* between the wars reflected the dichotomy mentioned above, torn between the extremes of Surrealism and Dadaism on the one hand, and more traditional modes of expression, relying on old-fashioned supernatural devices on the other. The only notable foreign influence was that of Henry James and Sigmund Freud, whose theories were used by numerous writers as keys to unlock closed doors in their explorations of the attics of the human soul.

The Surréalists

The desire of both the Dadaists and their literary successors, the Surrealists, was to destroy both existing social structures and the notion of ordered text. Dadaism began as a nihilistic artistic movement that paralleled the political anarchist movements of the times. In France, it was heralded in literary form by writers Alfred Jarry and Guillaume Apollinaire. By the time of the latter's death, in 1918, he had made it possible for the never-ending search for the bizarre in literature to be viewed not just as an amusing but pointless game, but as a true method, a metaphysical quest, reflecting more profound concerns and higher literary ambitions.

It was no coincidence that, in 1918, poet Tristan Tzara published the first Dadaist Manifesto, displaying the desire to submit the content and the form of poetry to an uncontrolled eruption of social violence: "I want to destroy the compartments of the brain as well as those of social order; I want to throw the hand of heaven into hell and the eyes of hell into heaven."

After 1922, the Dadaist movement began to lose its force as its participants turned towards Surrealism. By emphasizing the subconscious and using devices such as automatic writing, the Surrealists also sought to destroy the "rationalistic" culture that had led France into the horror of World War I. But unlike the Dadaists, whose emphasis was on negation, the Surrealists embraced a mutated form of the earlier romanticism: they praised Baudelaire, Nerval, Sade, Lautréamont, Rimbaud and Mallarmé. They glorified pulp heroes such as *Fantômas* and *Doctor Cornélius*.

Surrealism was a means of reuniting the conscious and the unconscious, reality and fantasy, and let dreams loose on the day-time world. Its major spokesman was André Breton, a former medical student who had worked as a neuro-psychiatrist, and was well acquainted with the writings of Freud, whom he met in 1921. In 1919, he joined forces with writer Louis Aragon (also a medical doctor) and Philippe Soupault to launch the magazine *Litérature* which published the first surrealist texts.

In 1924, Breton published his first Surrealist Manifesto which defined Surrealism as "pure psychic automatism through which one can express verbally, through writing or any other medium, the real process of thought, transcribing it without any control exercised by reason, and free of any aesthetic and moral concern." In 1930, he published a second Manifesto, but by then, various internecine quarrels, splinters and political problems arising from the cohabitation with Communism, had brought the disintegration of the movement.

As mentioned above, surrealism embraced fantasy. "The *merveilleux* is always beautiful," wrote Breton. "Anything marvelous is beautiful; indeed only the marvelous is beautiful." He showed the way with *Nadja* (1928), a novel which mixed everyday occurrences with surreal and psychological aberrations.

Blaise Cendrars, writer, poet and journalist, openly declared his admiration for Gustave Le Rouge's *Doctor Cornelius*. His *La Fin du Monde Filmée par l'Ange* [The End of the World Filmed by an Angel] (1919) and *Moravagine* (1926) were surrealist novels. The latter was named after, and told the story of, an evil madman who escapes from a lunatic asylum and causes a spree of terror and destruction that rivaled those of *Cornelius* and *Fantômas*. But unlike its popular predecessors, *Moravagine* transforms its pulpish protagonists and situations through the use of vivid poetry and surreal imagery. It was an ode to sheer violence, evil and chaos unleashed, a foreboding herald of the events that would come during World War II.

Other major writers who stood out among the current of *fantastique surréaliste* that arose in the 1920s and 1930s included:

Playwright Jean Giraudoux created an impressionistic form of drama by emphasizing dialogue and style rather than realism, combining tragedy, humor and fantasy in a heretofore unknown and brilliant manner. In *Intermezzo* (1937), a timid ghost revolutionizes a small provincial town. *Ondine* (1939) was about a water sprite who falls in love with a mortal.

Julien Gracq's first novel, *Au Château d'Argol* [At the Castle of Argol] (1938), was immediately hailed by the Surrealists because it combined the literary effects of the *roman noir* with the poetry of Rimbaud. The book takes place in a *Gormenghast*-like castle where the young owner, his friend and the beautiful Heide spend their time playing morbid and decadent games.

The *fantastique surréaliste* contributed, in an almost logical fashion, to the development of some truly unique and remarkable fantastic poetry.

In *Les Nouvelles Révélations de l'Être* [The New Revelations of Being] (1938), poet Antonin Artaud crafted a tapestry of surreal prophecies inspired by the Tarot imagery. His *Les Tarahumaras* (1945) was a collection of magical texts written under the influence of peyote.

Jean Cocteau produced such acclaimed works as the poems of *L'Ange Heurtebise* [The Angel Heurtebise] (1925), the plays *Orphée* [Orpheus] (1926) and *Les Chevaliers de la Table Ronde* [The Knights of the Round Table] (1937), and the hauntingly beautiful and surreal 1945 film version of *La Belle et la Bête* [*Beauty and the Beast*].

Finally, Jules Supervielle, a writer of Basque descent, incorporated Hispanic vistas and themes in *L'Homme de la Pampa* [The Man from the Pampa] (1923), *Le Survivant* [The Survivor] (1928), *L'Enfant de la Haute Mer* [The Child from the High Sea] (1931) and his plays *La Belle au Bois* [The Beauty in the Wood] (1932) and *Robinson* (1949).

Other Surrealist writers used fantastic elements such as dreams, alternate realities, and exotic or initiatic journeys to surreal lands and places, in their works. Among the most notable were:

Non-conformist Benjamin Péret, who wrote several fantastical tales in the 1920s and 1930s, collected a decade later in *Main Forte* [Strong Hand] (1946) and *Dernier Malheur, Dernière Chance* [Last Woe, Last Chance] (1946).

Ethnologist Michel Leiris, whose novel *Aurora* (1928) owed its title to a pun on the word "horror" and harked back to the influences of the *roman noir*.

Georges Limbour, whose fantastical stories were collected in *L'Illustre Cheval Blanc* [The Illustrious White Horse] (1930).

René Crevel (who committed suicide at 35), with the wildly surreal *Mon Corps et Moi* [My Body And I] (1925), *La Mort Difficile* [The Difficult Death] (1926), *Babylone* (1927) and *Êtes-Vous Fou?* [Are You Mad?] (1929).

Robert Desnos, with *La Liberté ou l'Amour!* [Liberty or Love!] (1927).

Some other mainstream writers who also dabbled with Surrealist themes included Paul Éluard, Max Jacob and Pierre Reverdy.

Other Mainstream Authors

Outside of the more extravagant arena of Surrealism, the presence of the *fantastique* continued to grace the pages of mainstream literature, often through a discrete intrusion of the supernatural into a novel, especially among the more "high brow" authors. It was not intended to shock or surprise the reader, as it did in Surrealist works, but simply to cohabit in parallel with our more mundane reality. This approach to the *fantastique* was a precursor of today's magical realism.

For example, Henri-Alban Fournier, who used the pseudonym of "Alain-Fournier" wrote *Le Grand Meaulnes* (1913), a classic romantic novel in which a runaway boy encounters a strange, other-worldly girl. It was adapted in an eponymous 1967 film directed by Jean-Gabriel Albicocco, which sadly ignored the underlying fantasy elements of the novel.

The same theme was carried over in the Faustian variation, *Marguerite de la Nuit* [*Marguerite of the Night*] (1922), by Pierre Mac Orlan, which was also made into a film.). The author's other novels showed a wide variety of influences, ranging from Nerval and Schwob to Stevenson, In *Le Rire Jaune* [The Yellow Laugh] (1914), mankind perishes from irrepressible laughter. *La Bête Conquérante* [The Conquering Beast] (1920) is an *Animal Farm*-like parable. *Le Nègre Léonard et Maître Jean Mullin* (1920) depicts the catastrophic consequences of the disappearance of all evil from Earth. In *La Cavalière Elsa* (1921), Russia invades Europe. Finally, *Malice* (1923) was the morbid yet erotic tale of the Devil's progressive corruption of a man through lascivious sex and money.

The Devil was also very much the focus of Georges Bernanos's *Sous le Soleil de Satan* [Under the Sun of Satan] (1926), a much-celebrated religious novel in which the Devil appears to tempt a country priest.

The *fantastique* of Pierre Benoît was equally unobtrusive: it discreetly seeped through his many, colorful novels, rightly famous for their exotic locales, eccentric characters and steamy plots. His classic *L'Atlantide* (1919) takes place place in 1896 in the French Sahara. Officer André de Saint-Avit has been asked to investigate the mysterious disappearances of other officers and explorers in the desert. During one of his desert missions, Saint-Avit and his fellow trappist monk/officer Jean Morhange save the life of a Targui warrior Cegheir-ben-Cheikh, who is secretly Queen Antinea's procurer. They are drugged and awaken in Atlantis—a royal palace hidden inside a mountain, overlooking a beautiful palm oasis, itself surrounded by the unbreachable Hoggar mountains. Queen Antinea is the granddaughter of Neptune and Clito, the last Kings of Atlantis, and through Cleopatra Selene, also a descendent of the Ptolemies of Egypt. Antinea keeps an underground mausoleum of red marble with 120 alcoves, or niches, carved in the wall—so far, 53 are filled with the numbered and labeled bodies of her former lovers, the lost soldiers and explorers. The bodies have been preserved forever by being dipped into a metallic bath of sulfate of orichalcum, the famous, legendary metal of the Atlanteans. At the center of the room is an orichalcum throne where Antinea will eventually sit and rest for eternity once all the holes have been filled. Saint-Avit succumbs to Antinea's charms, but Morhange resists her. A spurned Antinea then incite Saint-Avit to kill Morhange with a silver hammer, which he does. When Saint-Avit discovers his friend's body, now No. 54 in the red marble room, he recovers his senses. With the help of Antinea's black slave, Tanit-Zerga, he escapes—she dies in the desert, but Saint-Avit is rescued.

In October 1919, an article by Henry Magden in a French quarterly literary magazine accused the author of having plagiarized H. Rider Haggard's *She* (1887). Benoît decided to sue. In the following months, much literary controversy erupted, on both sides of the channel, mostly filled with chauvinism, but little scholarly research. Benoît eventually lost the case the following year, due to the superficial resemblances between the two works, and the Court's interpretation of the laws of libel. Since then, Haggard scholars have also put forth the notion that Benoit may also have plagiarized one of Haggard's lesser-known novel, *The Yellow God* (1908), which includes a magic mask and other weird fetish objects, a lost race, reincarnation, and a sort of vampirism by an immortal woman whose many husbands she has preserved as mummies.

Even though that thesis is still widely propagated among English-speaking reviewers of *L'Atlantide*, it is in fact less than convincing. The "case against", as it were, is as follows:

In his pleadings, Benoit noted that he did not speak, nor read, English, a fact never challenged during his lifetime. No one has yet come up with a satisfactory explanation of how he could have read either *She* or *The Yellow God*. The renowned publisher Pierre-Jules Hetzel, had put out a French edition of *King Solomon's Mines* in 1888, but in its postface, he had stated that he would not publish its sequel (*Allan Quatermain*) because it featured a ridiculous and obnoxious Frenchman named Alphonse, and because, while still of some interest, it was not, in his opinion, as good as the first volume. Hetzel's judgment carried a lot of weight in French literary circles, and as a result, none of Haggard's subsequent works were translated, at least not until much later. *She* was eventually serialized in 1898 in a newspaper, *La Vie Moderne*, in a severely abridged translation which had removed any passages that could be deemed prurient. There was therefore no French edition of *She* when *L'Atlantide* was written. As to *The Yellow God*, it was not translated until... 1985! There was no French edition of any kind which Benoit could have consulted.

Benoit's sources for *L'Atlantide* are neither hard to find, nor hard to document, and they certainly are more obvious than any elements found in Haggard's novels. They are:

Benoit had lived in French North Africa from 1892 to 1907 and did his military service there. His father was a military intendent, first in Tunis, then in Algiers. He was familiar with the notorious theories of French geographer E. F. Berlioux first published in 1874, and expanded in 1883 in *L'Atlas primitif et l'Atlantis*, of the Saharan Sea, and his locating Atlantis in the Hoggar mountains of the Saharan Atlas.

He knew from life experience that parts of the Hoggar were still totally unexplored, and were guarded by the fierce Targuis, or Tuaregs, or Blue Men of Sahara (because of the color of their robes). He likely had heard of a popular Targui legend about a sorceress who lived in sumptuous gardens in Mount Garet-el-Djenoun (The Mountain of the Spirits of Solitude). A feature of the legend was that no man who had ever gone looking for the sorceress had ever returned. (Similar legends can be found in other cultures as well.)

Benoît's father, or his research, would have told him of the then-famous case of two French lieutenants, Quiquerez and Segonzac, who had gone out on a mission into the desert, from which only Quiquerez had returned, under suspicious circumstances. Had he killed his fellow officer? Had they been ambushed? Had Quiquerez abandoned his companion? The truth was never discovered. Benoît also knew of the ill-fated 1880 Flatters Expedition into the Hoggar which had been massacred by the natives.

Finally, historical research informed the author of the existence of the legendary Tuareg Queen Tin Himan from the 4th Century AD, who claimed to be a descendent of Cleopatra Selene, the daughter of Cleopatra and Marc Antony.

All of these are clearly the foundation upon which *L'Atlantide* was built, and none of this bear any resemblance to either *She* or *The Yellow God*.

Anyone who actually reads the three novels in question will soon realize that there are in fact few real similarities beyond superficial, thematic ones. Unlike Ayesha, Antinea is full of pride and without any shred of conscience or decency; she devours men for breakfast and uses her wiles to compel Saint-Avit to kill his friend. Antinea is a female sphinx, an avenging fury, a vampire of sorts, the ultimate femme fatale. Unlike Ayesha, Antinea lives in, and enjoys luxury, her servants, and the best the modern outside world can bring her. Unlike Ayesha, Antinea is not a victim of the gods, she is the gods. Interestingly, H. P. Lovecraft wrote to Clark Ashton Smith: "*Atlantideer*, by Pierre Benoît, has excellent style but is more adventurous than fantastic,"[138] not bothering to point at any real or imagined similarities with Haggard, which he would likely have done, had he felt it justified.

Haggard himself remained conspicuously silent during the lawsuit; after the affair was over, a French publisher decided to publish a new edition of *She* for the first time in book form (1920), to which Benoît wrote a very informative and courteous foreword, wishing Haggard's novel much success.

L'Atlantide was the subject of several film and television adaptations, and even an unauthorized sequel, *La Nouvelle*

---

[138] H. P. Lovecraft, *Selected Letters* II.298, 1 October 1927.

Atlantide [The New Atlantis] by Georges Grandjean (1922) (Benoît sued and the book was destroyed).

Other Benoît novels worthy of mention included *La Chaussée des Géants* [The Giants' Path] (1922), *Le Puit de Jacob* [Jacob's Well] (1925), *Le Roi Lépreux* [The Leper King] (1927) and *Le Soleil de Minuit* [The Midnight Sun] (1930).

In the second tiers of literary (or mainstream) writers, the *fantastique*, when present, was more deliberate, often relying more fully on the true and tested supernatural elements crafted in past centuries. By far, the most remarkable author in this category was Claude Farrère, who had become famous first through his exotic novels of Indochina and then his character studies. In parallel with his mainstream production, Farrère penned several outstanding genre works such as *La Maison des Hommes Vivants* [The House of Living Men] (1911), mentioned in our previous chapter. He continued his production between the wars with collections of fantastic tales such as *Contes d'Outre et d'Autres Mondes* [Tales from Beyond and Other Worlds] (1921), *Histoire de Très Loin ou d'Assez Près* [Tales of Very Far or Near Enough] (1923), which included his classic "*Où?*" [Where?], *L'Autre Côté* [The Other Side] (1928), *La Marche Funèbre* [The Funeral March] (1929) and *La Porte Dérobée* [The Hidden Door] (1930). His works clearly owed their inspiration from Maupassant, and easily crossed into the domain of science fiction. *Où?* was a remarkable exploration of the "out there", a fourth dimension which followed different laws of time and space. Surprisingly, *L'Autre Côté* won the prestigious Goncourt literary award in 1928, showing that the *fantastique* still carried its letters of nobility.

Fernand Mysor never achieved any great success and has been almost forgotten. In *La Ville Assassinée* [The Murdered City] (1925),[139] Blasius, an unknown and mocked scholar, manages to create a philosopher's stone which transforms eve-

---

[139] Black Coat Press, ISBN 978-1-61227-791-2.

rything it touches into gold. This diabolical man acquires an island, gathers other unfortunate people, builds a fantastic city and reigns over it. The novel has affinities with accounts of island utopias gone wrong and doomed super-scientific cities. Science enables the fulfillment of the ancient alchemical dream, but gold here functions as a symbol of modern civilization as an irresistible force of corruption. Other titles include *La Mort du Soleil* [The Death of the Sun] (1926) and *Par TSF* [By Wireless] (1927).

Pierre Frondaie, an author better known for his naturalistic novels, published several collections of fantastic tales such as *Contes Réels et Fantaisistes* [Real and Fantastic Tales] (1930), *Quand le Diable s'en mêle* [When The Devil Meddles] (1935) and *Les Fatidiques* [Fated Tales] (1946), many of which featured the character of *Jean Pharg*, a mysterious narrator in the tradition of William Hope Hodgson's *Carnacki*.

Frédéric Boutet, who wrote a famous *Dictionnaire des Sciences Occultes* [Dictionary of Occult Sciences] (1937), also penned a number of Poe-like novels such as *Le Reflet de Claude Mercoeur* [Claude Mercoeur's Reflection] (1921), *Le Spectre de M. Imberger* [The Ghost of Mr. Imberger] (1922) and *Les Aventuriers du Mystère: Tableau de l'Au-Delà* [The Adventurers of Mystery: Scene From Beyond] (1927).

In the midst of an abundant production of mainstream novels devoted to French farmers, Ernest Pérochon produced a true *roman spirite*, *Les Ombres* [The Shadows] (1923), as well as several of collections of fantastic tales such as *Huit Gouttes d'Opium* [Eight Drops of Opium] (1925) and *Contes des Cent Un Matins* [Tales of 101 Mornings] (1930).

Léon Daudet's *Un Jour d'Orage* [A Stormy Day] (1925) was also a provincial fantasy, taking place in Provence and featuring the famous seer Nostradamus. Another novel in the same vein was *Le Sang de la Nuit* [The Blood of the Night] (1926).

Maurice Level (see previous chapter) contributed to the Grand-Guignol and wrote *Les Morts Étranges* [*Strange Deaths*] (1921*), La Cité des Voleurs* [City of Thieves] (1924) and *L'Énigme de Bellavista* [The Mystery of Bellavista] (1929) (co-written with Jean Prudhomme).

Other notable authors of the period included:

Renée Dunan with *Baal* (1924), in which the great and seductive sorceress Madame Palmyre teaches her assistant Renée the secret of her magic, including her ability to interact with creatures from other worlds, such as the unspeakable Baal, whose octopus-like form is the three-dimensional projection of an unfathomable four-dimensional entity. The author's *Les Amantes du Diable* [The Devil's Lovers] (1929)[140] is a heroic saga about Satanism and Witchcraft that follows the adventures of a poacher and his daring wife in war-torn 16th century France. These two ground-breaking supernatural thrillers from an early feminist writer, also known for her crime fiction and erotic historical novels, depict witchcraft as having its psychological origins in sexuality, reflecting the repression of the sexual impulses by the social norms of the times.

Jean Cassou, who penned *La Clef des Songes* [The Key to Dreams] (1929), *De l'Étoile au Jardin des Plantes* [From the Étoile to the Botanical Gardens] (1935) and *Les Enfants Sans Âge* [The Ageless Children] (1946).

Laurence Albaret, whose collection *Le Grand Ventre* [The Great Belly] (1944) contained some very bizarre stories.

A special place must be allocated here to Marcel Aymé, novelist, playwright and master of social satire and modern fairy tales. His fantastic universe mixed broad country wit such as *La Jument Verte* [The Green Mare] (1933) with local folk legends such as *La Vouivre* (1943), a book about a snake woman who lives in a swamp. His later collections of short stories combined a lighter but nevertheless piercing wit with fantasy elements treated as disarmingly common place occurrences. *Le Passe-Muraille* [The Walker Through Walls] (1943) is a classic yarn about an obscure civil servant who turns into a daring super-criminal after acquiring the power to

---

[140] Both, Black Coat Press, ISBN 978-1-61227-046-3.

walk through solid objects. *Le Nain* [The Dwarf] (1934) is about a dwarf who finally begins to grow at age 30. Finally, his short animal fables, *Les Contes du Chat Perché* [The Tales of the Crouching Cat] (1931) and *Autres Contes du Chat Perché* [Other Tales of the Crouching Cat] (1954), easily made him an equal of Perrault.

Fantasy

As mentioned in our previous chapter, Maurice Magre was one of the most extravagant writers of fantasy because of the fertility and versatility of his imagination and the manner in which he deployed it. He was an ardent defender of Occitan cause and did much to publicize the martyrdom of the Cathars in the 13th century, often preferring legends and romantic epics to the historical truth.

Having tried sex and opium as roads to the ideal and found them wanting, the author found a further potential resource, in the occult underworld of Paris In three novellas, "*Les Colombes poignardées*" [Stabbed Doves] (1917), "*La Tendre camarade*" [The Tender Comrade] (1918) and "*L'Appel de la bête*" [The Call of the Beast] (1920),[141] the intrusion of the fantastic is limited, confined to opium dreams in the first two, and maintained in a strictly ambiguous fashion in the third. Thereafter, the fantastic was liberated in all of his fiction, initially mostly in a malign role, but eventually serving much more various functions, many of them life-enhancing.

In *Priscilla of Alexandria* (1925),[142] a contender for the Goncourt Literary Award, his shocking imagery, violence and amorality, make it a masterpiece of classic fantasy, and its perversity can now be seen as a virtue, as well as a remarkable achievement. It has retained its power to shock today, when

---

[141] All in *The Call of the Beast*, Black Coat Press, ISBN 978-1-61227-653-3
[142] Black Coat Press, ISBN 978-1-61227-667-0.

melodramatic inflation has raised the stakes in generic horror fiction.

In the novella "*La Vie amoureuse de Messaline*" [The Love Life of Messalina] (1925), the eponymous character is possessed by a version of the god Priapus and becomes an incarnation of lust; "*La Luxure de Grenade*" [The Vice of Granada] (1926),[143] is a violent melodrama about a great conflict between rival brotherhoods dedicated to good and evil. In it, Isabelle, the daughter of a Castilian nobleman once sold as a slave by the raiders of Granada, uses magic to seduce the scholar Almazan away from the studies that he has commenced with Rosenkreutz, despite the threat of assassins dispatched by Tomas de Torquemada to murder the freethinkers of Europe.

In *Le Mystère du Tigre* [The Mystery of the Tiger] (1927),[144] an obsessed zookeeper and animal tamer goes into the Indonesian jungle to experience a mystic transformation that highlights the relationship between humans and animals, and between humans and their own animality. The book offers one of the most obvious examples of Magre's stubborn defiance of convention. As its protagonist gradually slides from unrepentant unpleasantness into a kind of remorseful divine madness, it shows itself for the truly remarkable work it is.

Le Livre des lotus entr'ouverts [Lotus Blossoms] (1926) was a collection of prose poems; it was followed by the novel *Le Poison de Goa* [The Poison of Goa,] (1928).[145] In it, the unfortunate Rachel, who is in desperate straits and has to undergo a terrifying ordeal, realizes that she has just found an unexpected opportunity to avenge the death of her mother and brutal torture of her father during a pogrom. The action unfolds in the mid-19th century in the decadent Portuguese colo-

---

[143] In *The Angel of Lust*, Black Coat Press, ISBN 978-1-61227-668-7.

[144] Black Coat Press, ISBN 978-1-61227-673-1.

[145] In *The Poison of Goa*, Black Coat Press, ISBN 978-1-61227-674-8.

ny of Goa in India. The tense and dramatic plot, the graphic images of the city, as it is gradually consumed by the march of time, make the novel a remarkable work of fantasy in both strength and artistry.

Lucifer (1929)[146] reads as a kind of confession exploring a demonic possession resulting from a casually-made diabolical pact—which might or might not be entirely subjective and psychological. The Church is at best impotent, at worst in tacit alliance with the forces of evil and the narrator is forced to find his own way out of his predicament—if he can. As an account of metaphorical possession, it is detailed with a persuasive conviction, if one regards its essential purpose as that of sowing a discomfort in the reader's mind similar to one experienced by the author.

The novella "*La Nuit du Haschich et de l'Opium*" [The Night of Hashish and Opium] (1929)[147] is set in India. In it, a young, lovely, divorcée is caught in a magical trap by men who bet that they could force the beautiful woman who once turned them down to dance in the magical temple of Chillambaram.

In *Le Sang de Toulouse* [The Blood of Toulouse] (1931),[148] Dalmas Rochemaure, the son of a cathedral-builder, embarks on the sacred mission to preserve Occitania from the armies of French invaders hell-bent of exterminating the Cathar heresy. The young equerry of the count of Toulouse faces unending combats and carnage, saving the most precious treasure from the ashes of the tragic pyre of Montsegur. The novel is dramatic and poignant, full of verve and intensity, ending with a memorable flamboyant finish; it remains Magre's finest achievement, as well as his most celebrated.

In *Le Trésor des Albigeois* [The Albigensian Treasure] (1938),[149] we follow the adventures of Michel de Bramevaque,

---

[146] Black Coat Press, ISBN 978-1-61227-676-2.
[147] In *Lucifer*, q.v.
[148] Black Coat Press, ISBN 978-1-61227-677-9.
[149] Black Coat Press, ISBN 978-1-61227-686-1.

who launches himself in search of the Holy Grail after receiving a supernatural injunction. The author, with elegant simplicity, leads us through a series of adventures and trials on the quest for the sacred artifact hidden by his Albigensian ancestors in the Languedoc soil. Long considered as one of the best works of esoteric literature of 20th century, the book, rooted in the Cathar religion, is rich in spirituality, demonstrating that, behind the visible face of things, often hides another, much more subtle. This is a superb novel of fantastic realism, steeped in a dark and tormented atmosphere.

In *Jean de Fodoas* (1939),[150] the eponymous hero leaves his natal city of Toulouse, traveling to the heart of India in the heyday of the Mogul Empire, to the court of Emperor Akbar the Great. Adventure and mysticism are brought together in the novel, because Jean's cousin has recruited him to accomplish a mysterious task at Akbar's court, involving the treasure of Genghis Khan and the enigmatic Baphomet that was once allegedly worshipped by the Knights Templars. A picaresque and rambunctious adventure story, *Jean de Fodoas* is a stylish example of Magre's ability to bring together adventure and mysticism.

"*Le Côté d'ombre des âmes*" [The Dark Side of Souls] (1937) and "*Révélation des mondes invisibles*" [The Revelation of Invisible Worlds] (1937)[151] are prose-poems with a continuing first-person narrative that, although clearly fictitious and exceedingly rich in the fantastic, is proffered by an unnamed protagonist who is clearly an alter ego of the author.

Mélusine, ou le secret de solitude [Melusine, or The Secret of Solitude] (1941)[152] might be Magre's swan song, and its delicate imaginative flourishes the last gasps of his prolific and fecund imagination. His revision of the classic legend of Mélusine of Lusignan is ingenious and the visionary sequences depicting the protagonist's communications with nature are

---

[150] Black Coat Press, ISBN 978-1-61227-698-4.
[151] In *Melusine*, Black Coat Press, ISBN 978-1-61227-703-5.
[152] Black Coat Press, q.v.

vividly effective and demonstrate that the author's poetic gifts had not waned.

Joseph-Charles Mardrus continued the tradition of *Arabian Tales* with *La Reine de Saba* [The Queen of Sheba] (1919) and a rewritten, expanded version of the *Thousand and One Nights*, *Le Livre des Mille et Une Nuits* [The Book of the Thousand and One Nights] (1920-24).

The prolific Alexandre Arnoux liked to blend genres, easily crossing the lines between science fiction, fantasy and mainstream literature. A number of his novels and plays were modern retelling of classic legends, such as *Légende du Roi Arthur et des Chevaliers de la Table Ronde* [Legend of King Arthur & The Knights of the Round Table] (1920), *Huon de Bordeaux* (1922) and *Merlin l'Enchanteur* [Merlin the Enchanter] (1931); others were pure fantastical tales such as *Abisag, ou l'Église Transportée par la Foi* [The Church Transported by Faith] (1918), and the collections *Suite Variée* [Varied Suite] (1925) and *Sortilèges* [Spells] (1949).

Charles Guyon also relied on classic fairy tales and folk legends, with *Les Bons Petits Lutins* [The Good Little Goblins] (1923), *Les Contes de Grand'Maman* [Granny's Tales] (1926), *Les Petits Lutins de Carnac* [The Little Goblins of Carnac] (1926), *Récits Légendaires des Bords du Rhin* [Legendary Tales of the River Rhine] (1926), *La Caverne de la Fée Cocasse* [The Cavern of the Fairy Cocasse] (1927) and *Légendes du Roi de Thulé* [Legends of the King of Thule] (1931).

The writing team of Charles and Henri Omessa were notable for their *Anaïtis, Fille de Carthage* [*Anaitis, Daughter of Carthage*] (1922), a powerful heroic-fantasy in the vein of Gustave Flaubert's *Salammbo*. They also penned *Le Troisième Oeil de Civa* [The Third Eye of Shiva] (1932) and *Histoires de l'Autre Monde* [Tale from Another World] (1934).

Nicolas Ségur penned two interesting fantasies: *Le Secret de Penelope* [Penelope's Secret] (1922)[153] picks up where Homer's *Odyssey* ends, after the slaying of Penelope's suitors and the discovery that her stubborn virtue was somewhat exaggerated, which causes Ulysses to seek advice from Minerva, Menelaus and his old tutor, the centaur Chiron. *Le Paradis des Hommes* [The Human Paradise] (1930)[154] is a scathingly sarcastic satire in which God offers to grant wishes expressed unanimously by the entirety of humankind. The wishes voiced are carefully extrapolated in such a way as to suggest that, however effective individuals might be at screwing up their wishes, a committee composed of the whole human race could do a far more comprehensive job.

Jean Carrère with *La Fin d'Atlantis* [The End of Atlantis] (1926),[155] which extends a rich tradition of French literary fantasies redeploying the myth of Atlantis; it is a historical melodrama, an adventure story and a heroic fantasy depicting the fall of the great and marvelous Empire of Atlantis. The novel is more sophisticated than most Atlantean fantasies. Its account of the fall of Atlantis echoes that of the Roman Empire, and contains an elaborate criticism of contemporary European society, whose own crisis of degeneration is supposedly reflected therein.

In Félicien Champsaur's *La Pharaone* [Pharaoh's Wife] (1929),[156] the Mage Ormus, claiming to be the reincarnation of Tutankhamun, has gathered around him a coterie of disciples chosen amongst the world's wealthiest elite in order to relive the Mysteries of Ancient Egypt. One of them, the Duchess of Rutland, might be the reincarnation of Am-Phaoli, the Pharaoh's wife. But is it all star-crossed love over the chasm of centuries, or an elaborate scheme by two conniving conmen aiming to steal the Duchess' fortune? The novel is primarily a

---

[153] Black Coat Press, ISBN 978-1-61227-733-2.
[154] Black Coat Press, ISBN 978-1-61227-617-5.
[155] Black Coat Press, ISBN 978-1-61227-618-2.
[156] Black Coat Press, ISBN 978-1-61227-156-9.

love story wrapped in fantasy. Whether its heroine really is Tutankhamun's wife or not, what truly matters are the psychological effects that her belief in the notion of serial reincarnation might have on her attempt to find a purpose in life.

The traditional connection between the *fantastique littéraire* and the folk tales and legends of the French countryside was reactualized by the efforts of scholars such as "Pierre Saintyves" (a pseudonym of Émile Nourry) (1870-1975), who reprinted *Les Contes de Perrault et les Récits Parallèles* (1923) and *En Marge de la Légende Dorée* [On the Margins of the Golden Legend] (1930); Arnold Van Gennep, with his *Manuel de Folklore Français Contemporain* [Manual of Contemporary French Folklore] (1943); and Henri Pourrat, with his thirteen-volume collection, *Trésor des Contes* [Treasure of Folk Tales] (1948-62). In the late 1930s, publisher Fernand Nathan even started a popular imprint of folk tales retold in a modern style accessible to children and young adults, called *"Contes & Légendes"*.

Finally, a fantasy tale which defies classification and needs no introduction here is Antoine de Saint-Exupéry's world-famous *Le Petit Prince* [The Little Prince] (1943).

Belgian Fantastique

Jean Ray

The most famous author of Belgian fantastique was, without a doubt, Jean Ray, whose real name was Jean Raymond de Kremer. The author is generally regarded by genre scholars as the French-language equivalent of Poe or Lovecraft. He began his career as a pulp writer, writing anything and everything, using a variety of aliases, the most famous being that of "John Flanders". He even had several stories published under that name in *Weird Tales*.

The "Jean Ray" signature first appeared in 1912, with a few short stories published in French, followed in 1919 with two more short stories, *"La Vengeance"* [The Revenge] and *"Le Gardien du Cimetière"* [The Cemetery Keeper], this time belonging to the *fantastique*. From 1920, he participated in the *Journal de Gand*, then, from 1923, edited *L'Ami du Livre*, in which he published most of the stories that would constitute his first collection, published by La Renaissance du Livre in 1925, *Les Contes du whiskey* [Tales of Whiskey], In March 1926, however, he was arrested and charged with fraud. Bankrupted, he was sentenced to six years and six months in prison and was finally released in February 1929. In the meantime, the signature of "John Flanders" had appeared in the Dutch-language magazine *Ons Land* in June 1928, then in *La Revue Belge* in 1920 and 1930. At the end of 1931, his second collection, *La Croisière des ombres* [The Cruise of Shadows] was published by Éditions de Belgique under the name "Jean Ray" but to critical and commercial failure.

The author then wrote numerous stories for a variety of children's adventure magazines, using over 100 pseudonyms and, from 132 onward, embarked on the *Harry Dickson* series (see below). It was the most prolific period of his life in terms of publications: in 1936, he published 96 original stories and nearly 300 articles, while in 1937, there were 108 original fictions and still some 300 articles. Les Auteurs Associés published several of his collections: *Le Grand Nocturne* [The Grand Nocturnal] (1942), *Les Cercles de l'Épouvante* [The Circles of Terror] (1943), *Les Derniers Contes de Canterbury* [The Last Tales of Canterbury] (1944), as well as his two novels, the classic *Malpertuis* (1943) and *La Cité de l'Indicible Peur* [The City of Unspeakable Fear] (1943).

After World War II, the Éditions de la Sixaine published *Le Livre des Fantômes* [The Book of Ghosts] (1947). In 1961, Belgian publisher Marabout released *Les Vingt-cinq meilleures histoires noires et fantastiques* [Twenty-five best fantastic tales] and two unpublished collections *Le Carrousel des Malefices* [The Spellbound Merry-Go-Round] (1964) and

Les Contes Noirs du Golf [Dark Tales of Golf] (1964), as well as an unpublished novel *Saint-Judas-de-la-Nuit*. Jean Ray passed away in Ghent on September 17, 1964.

Malpertuis is about an ancient, terror-filled mansion where a dying warlock trapped the aging gods of Olympus inside the "skins" of ordinary Flemish citizens. It was immediately hailed as a classic of the genre and was made in 1972 into an eponymous film by Belgian film-maker Harry Kumel starring Orson Welles as the warlock Cassave.

La Cité de l'Indicible Peur is more of a horror thriller. In it, a series of ghastly deeds and creatures plague the small, isolated British village of Ingersham. Eventually, there was a rational explanation, except for a single ghost, who turned out to be harmless. It, too, was made into a 1964 film, unfortunately in a comedic vein.

The last part of Ray's prodigious literary output was, however, involved the *Harry Dickson* pulp series, sub-titled "the American Sherlock Holmes". Some pulps were translations of American series such as *Nick Carter*, but many others, like *Sâr Dubnotal*, *Fascinax* or *Fantômas*, were written by local authors. Among these, the best and the most famous of all was this unauthorized Holmesian pastiche, which had began as a German pulp in 1907. The original series was comprised of 230 issues in total. The name *Sherlock Holmes* was actually used for the first 10 issues, and replaced by that of *Harry Dickson*, or *Harry Taxon* (depending on the editions) after threats from Doyle's lawyers. Sixteen issues of the original German series were adapted into French in 1907-08 by Fernand Laven for the magazine *La Nouvelle Populaire* under the title *Les Dossiers Secrets du Roi des Détectives* [The Secret Files of the King of Detectives]. A Dutch/Flemish edition was later launched in 1929. In 1931, its publisher asked Jean Ray to translate the Dutch edition into French.

Quickly, the author became tired of translating the mediocre original stories. Using the titles and the colorful covers by noted German artist Alfred Roloff as starting points, he began to create his own stories. Out of 178 French-language *Harry*

Dicksons, most experts agree that Ray totally recreated 109, and approximately adapted maybe another dozen. It is no exaggeration to say that Roloff's covers greatly contributed to the series' success since, when they stopped, the series was cancelled. Because the covers generally depicted events taking place before World War I, although the stories themselves were supposed to take place in the 1930s, Ray had to draw on his fertile imagination to create an atmosphere of musty death and decadence, of small villages where time and fashions had stood still.

The adventures of Harry Dickson and his young assistant, Tom Wills have delighted several generations of readers. Because they were written by a master of the *fantastique*, they quickly became more fantasy-oriented than the Holmesian canon. The best and most fondly remembered *Harry Dickson* stories were not those where the Great Detective fought a spy or a blackmailer in true Holmesian fashion, but those that pit him against some monstrous fallen angel. What the intellect lost in logic and deduction, the readers gained in pure entertainment and fantasy.

Although a rational explanation—often itself leaning heavily towards science fantasy—was always provided at the end of each story, under Ray's pen, Dickson battled a series of villains that even Holmes would never have dreamed of: Euryale Ellis, a beautiful woman who had the power of turning her victims into stone and may have been a reincarnation of the legendary Gorgon, Medusa (No. 163); Gurrhu, a living Aztec god who hid in an underground temple located beneath the very heart of London, filled with scientifically-advanced devices (No. 93); the last, living Babylonian mummies who found refuge under a Scottish lake (No. 147); a nefarious blood-drinking serial killer dubbed the "Red-Eyed Vampire" (No. 81); the enigmatic, tuxedo-suited avenger known as "Kric-Kroc, the Walking Dead" (No. 146); a death-dealing android with a silver face (No. 151); the murderous spy codenamed the Blue Stork (No. 119), the super-villain Mysteras who relies on elaborate and deadly illusions (Nos. 103-104);

the blood-thirsty Hindu god Hanuman (No. 68), the killing sect of the Moon Knights; and many more. *Harry Dickson*'s fame in France rivals that of *Sherlock Holmes* and *Arsène Lupin.*, and the character thrives on today in two competing comic-book series.[157]

Loved by a growing number of fans, Jean Ray was sadly only "discovered" by the critics and the mainstream public just before his death, in the early 1960s. His fiction provided a transition between the purely supernatural horrors of past centuries and modern concepts such as parallel dimensions and alien entities *à la* Lovecraft. His protagonists, however, were resolute and more likely to face the forces of darkness than go mad or cringe away from them in terror. There is no way to overestimate Ray's importance in French-language horror fiction. He left a powerful mark not only upon French, but also Flemish, genre literature. Like Lovecraft, he became the forefather of a virtual school of modern horror writers.

Fantastique Populaire

As French-language Belgian literature began to mature in the late 1800s, the "Belgian School of the Strange" incorporated the traditional Flemish and French-language (i.e.: Wallon) folklore into romanticized versions. Among these were:

Albert Mockel, the author of *Clartés* [Lights] (1901) and *Contes pour Enfants d'Hier* [Tales for Yesterday's Children] (1908).

Charles Van Lerberghe, with *Selection Surnaturelle* [Supernatural Selection] (1905).

---

[157] In *Harry Dickson – The Heir of Dracula*, Black Coat Press, ISBN 978-1-934543-90-0; *Harry Dickson vs. The Spider*, ISBN 978-1-61227-304-4; *Harry Dickson vs Mysteras*, Black Coat Press, ISBN 978-1-64932-086-5; and *Harry Dickson – Krik-Krok, The Walking Dead*, Black Coat Press, ISBN 978-1-64932-157-2.

Jehan Maillart, with *Contes Chimériques* [Chimerical Tales] (1905).

This tradition continued after World War I with Jean de Bosschère, the author of numerous fantastic tales collected posthumously in *Contes de la Neige et de la Nuit* [Tales of Snow and Night] (1954). His novel *Satan l'Obscur* [*Satan the Obscure*] (1933) dealt with the Devil in terms similar to Bernanos.

Another popular author was Horace Van Offel, who penned several commercial genre novels such as *Le Tatouage Bleu* [The Blue Tattoo] (1917), *La Terreur Fauve* [The Fawn Terror] (1922), *Le Jongleur d'Épées* [The Sword Juggler] (1930), *La Flûte Corsaire* [The Corsair Flute] (1933) and *Le Capitaine du Vaisseau-Fantôme* [The Captain of the Ghost-Ship] (1943).

Fantastique Littéraire

Parallel to this popular current, Belgian fantastic literature was also influenced by the Symbolists, the best example being poet Maurice Maeterlinck. Already known in the 1890s, the author consolidated his literary reputation by winning the Nobel Prize for Literature in 1911. The author of the classic *Pelléas et Mélisande* (1892) also wrote the perennial classic *L'Oiseau Bleu* [*The Blue Bird*] (1908), an allegorical fantasy conceived as a play for children.

The Devil was very much at the center of the works of one of the greatest literary figures in Belgian history. the eccentric playwright Michel de Ghelderode. He was a true visionary whose folkish morality plays and stories resonated with violence, demonism, holy madness and typically Belgian, Hyeronimus Bosch-like humor and fantasy. His plays, such as *Fastes d'Enfer* [Feasts of Hell] (1929), *Magie Rouge* [Red Magic] (1934) and *La Ballade du Grand Macabre* [The Ballad of the Great Macabre] (1935), brought to life the macabre tradition of Flemish culture. They were eventually embraced by the *avant-garde* theater and exerted a powerful influence on the art. His collection *Sortilèges* [Spells] (1941) contained twelve dark, anguish-ridden stories, all told in the first-person narrative, which contributed to a claustrophobic sense of inescapable doom. Together, these stories formed a uniquely beautiful panorama of horrors.

One author who contributed the most to the creation and embellishment of the notion of "fantastic realism was Franz Hellens. A precursor of the Surrealists, he displayed from his earliest collections of tales a lyrical, romantic approach to fantasy. *Les Hors-le-Vent* [The Out-Wind] (1909), *Les Clartés Latentes* [The Latent Clarities] (1912) and *Nocturnal* (1919) were his first explorations into the land of dreams, which he later dubbed his "second life". His novel *Mélusine* (1920) was generally considered a proto-surrealist novel. A friend of Maeterlinck and Supervielle, the author published the magazine *Le Disque Vert* [The Green Disk] in 1922, which he co-edited with Henri Michaux. A prolific writer, Hellens always returned to the *fantastique*, contributing several milestone collections such as *Réalités Fantastiques* [Fantastic Realities] (1923), *Nouvelles Réalités Fantastiques* [New Fantastic Realities] (1941) and *Fantômes Vivants* [Living Ghosts] (1944).

His co-editor, Henri Michaux penned a series of fantasy novels that real like Jack Vance: *Un Barbare en Asie* [A Barbarian in Asia] (1932), *Voyage en Grande Garabagne* [Voyage in Great Garabagnia] (1936), *Au Pays de la Magie* [In the Land of Magic] (1941) and *Ici, Poddema* [Here, Poddema] (1946), The author loved creating imaginary lands, peopled with colorful inhabitants who followed strange customs. One of his imaginary societies lived in perpetual anxiety; another refused to acknowledge the past and the future; in the land of magic, physical laws were subject to psychic rules, etc.

Lastly, one should mention Robert Poulet, whose entire fiction challenged the very notion of "being", such as in *Handji* (1930), where two soldiers create a human avatar to rescue them from oblivion; *Le Trottoir* [The Sidewalk] (1931);

Ténèbres [Darkness] (1934); and *Prélude à l'Apocalypse* [Prelude to the Apocalypse] (1944).

JEAN RAY
MALPERTUIS

Le seul roman du maître de la littérature fantastique !

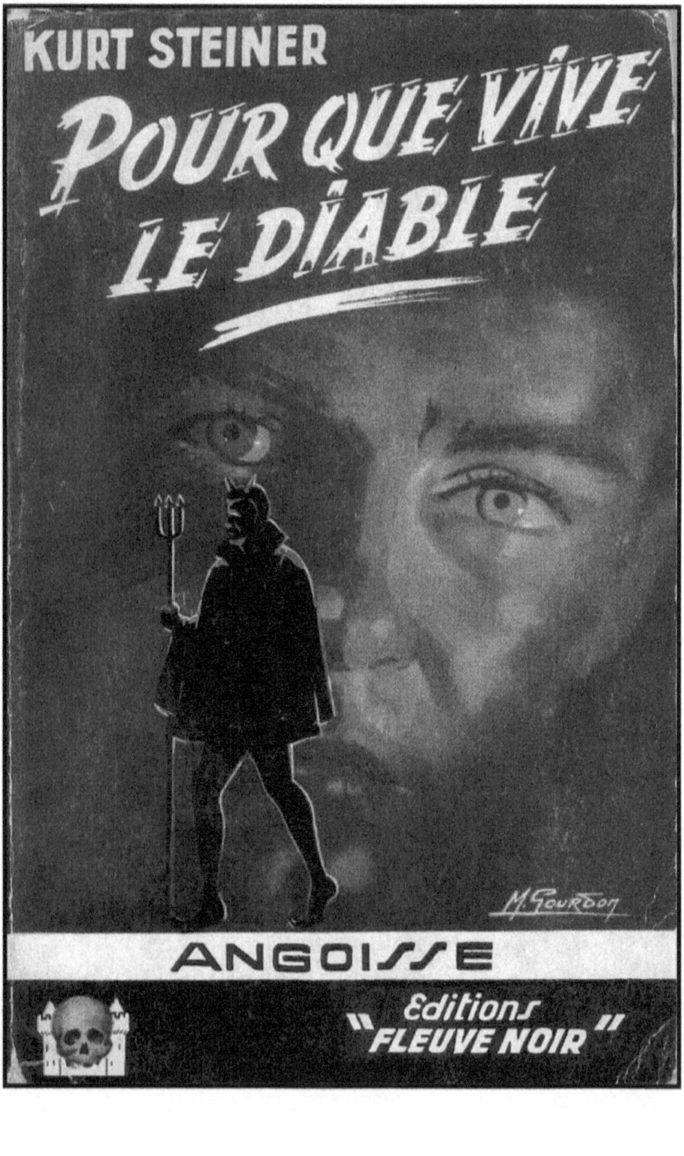
KURT STEINER
POUR QUE VIVE LE DIABLE
M. GOURDON
ANGOISSE
Editions "FLEUVE NOIR"

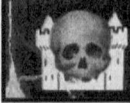

The 1950s & 1960s

World War II exacted both a huge physical and a devastating psychological toll on French culture. France's defeat in 1940, followed by four years of occupation and, in some cases, of collaboration or resistance, confronted writers with choices they had never had to face before. The ensuing discovery of the atom bomb, and the polarization of the political conflict between East and West, introduced sharp new fears into the cauldron of the collective unconscious.

After World War II, mainstream French culture increasingly frowned upon works of unbridled imagination and preferred instead to embrace the more naturalistic and political concerns of the Existentialists, embodied by writers such as Jean-Paul Sartre, Albert Camus, Simone de Beauvoir and Boris Vian. The Existentialists depicted man as being alone in a bleak, godless universe. In the 1950s, the *Nouveau Roman*, pioneered by Françoise Sagan, continued the literary experiments of the surrealists by rejecting the traditional framework of fiction. Some of its most notorious contributors included Marguerite Duras, Alain Robbe-Grillet, Jean Cayrol, Michel Butor and Nathalie Sarraute.

Yet, paradoxically, despite being deliberately marginalized by literary critics and the literary establishment, the *fantastique* thrived as it never had before. Both in terms of quality and quantity, the modern period is the richest, and some of its authors among the best, in the history of the genre.

For this chapter, we have divided the last fifty years into three chronological sub-divisions: the first, dubbed the "1950s & 1960s", starts in the immediate post-war period of the late 1940s, continues through the 1950s and the early 1960s, when France shed its colonial past. experienced a post-war economic boom and a period of unprecedented stability, and ends approximately in 1969, with the political and sociological upheavals caused by the notorious "events" of May 1968, which created a virtual cultural revolution and a sharp shift to the left in France's cultural scene.

The second sub-division, dubbed the "1970s", reflects this period of transformation and ends in the early 1980s, after the full impact of the Left's election to power in 1981, a factor which paradoxically broke its stranglehold on culture.

The third and last sub-division, dubbed the "1980s & 1990s", runs from the early 1980s to the end of the 1990s and of the 20th century.

We have also retained our previous division between the *fantastique littéraire* on the one hand, comprised of works with literary ambition and generally published by mainstream houses, and the *fantastique populaire*, on the other hand, written for entertainment and/or shock value and generally published in specialized paperback imprints. This division, however, more so than at any other previous time in history, becomes increasingly arbitrary and difficult to maintain as we approach the 1980s. In the 1960s, authors such as Roger Blondel a.k.a. B.-R. Bruss and Michel Bernanos a.k.a. Michel Talbert used different pseudonyms depending on which sides of the literary fence they wrote. But in the 1980s, even popular authors such as Claude Klotz, Georges-Olivier Châteaureynaud or René Réouven were also published by mainstream literary houses.

Finally, within our chronological outline, we have attempted to regroup some authors by sub-genres, but that is also a difficult and often debatable notion. The proliferation of styles and the explosion of approaches to the *fantastique* during the last half of the century is nothing short of remarkable. French modern *fantastique* does not speak with one voice, or even a few, but with many. The sources of inspiration range from the traditional *fantastique* based on classic supernatural concepts, to new surrealism, regional *fantastique* rooted in country folk legends, symbolism and esoterism.

Major foreign influences on French modern *fantastique* include Franz Kafka (whose *The Trial* was translated into French in 1933 and *The Castle* and *Metamorphosis* in 1938), Jorge Luis Borges, H. P. Lovecraft, whose works were greatly admired by Jean Cocteau, by then a member of the French Academy, Dino Buzzati, Julio Cortazar, Vladimir Nabokov, Gabriel Garcia-Marquez and Richard Matheson. These writers virtually redefined modern *fantastique* by showing that it could embrace much more than mere ghost stories.

Later, more recent, influences included the American and Italian "gore" movies, the unavoidable duo of Stephen King and Robert E. Howard (whose *Conan* did not become a household name in France until the early 1980s), role-playing games such as *Dungeons & Dragons*, and R. L. Stine's *Goosebumps* series, etc. The growth of gore fiction and sword & sorcery during the last decade of the century can be seen as a dubious tribute to the Americanization of world culture.

Still, when considered in its entirety, French modern *fantastique* looks like a gigantic melting pot, or a huge orchestra in which all the instruments have successfully blended their music together in order to achieve a wholly new vision of the world, a vision that could only be created through the unique medium of the *fantastique*.

Fantastique Populaire

After a brief economic and artistic lull caused by the war, the *fantastique populaire* thrived again in the post-war period, following in the footsteps of the now-classic tradition established by the Grand-Guignol theater.

Among the celebrities who were seen attending the Grand-Guignol during World War II were Hermann Goering, Ho Chi Minh and General Patton. Eventually, piling horror upon horror led to auto-parody and a general lack of believability. World War II, with its parade of true-life horrors, could be said to have contributed to the decline and fall of the

Grand-Guignol. Reality appeared to have, temporarily at least, overtaken fiction. The theater's last manager, Charles Nonon, declared in an interview granted to *Time* magazine: "We could not compete with Buchenwald."[158]

For the record, the last directors of the theater were: Éva Berkson, Marcel Maurey (the son of Max), Raymonde Machard, Christiane Wiegant, and, finally, Nonon.

In the literary field, the *fantastique populaire* was more than ever synonymous with horror, and was primarily meant to thrill, entertain and shock the readers, not offer them a subtle, sophisticated, literary experience. Its niche existed between the thriller genre, especially when it involved gory or surreal crimes, and the popular adventure/science fiction literature developed in the 1920s and 1930s. Many of the authors easily crossed from one genre into another, but a few, more specialized writers nevertheless emerged.

By far the most distinguished among them was Jean-Louis Bouquet, whose early works included film novelizations and film scripts, such as Luitz-Morat's *La Cité Foudroyée* [The Thunderstruck Town] (1924) and Germaine Dulac's *Le Diable dans la Ville* [*The Devil in the City*] (1924). Under the pseudonym of "Nevers-Severin", the author went on to pen several somewhat surreal, popular murder mysteries such as *Doum* (1943), *Les Mystères de Montmartre* [The Mysteries of Montmartre] (1944) and *L'Homme des Antipodes* [The Man from the Other Side of the World] (1944). His best genre fiction, however, was published under his own name and collected in *Le Visage de Feu* [The Face of Fire] (1951) and *Les Filles de la Nuit* [The Daughters of Night] (1951, retitled *Aux Portes des Ténèbres* [At the Gates of Darkness] by his publisher). In his works, Bouquet gave a new lease on life to such classic themes as witches' curses, reincarnation and spells enabling men to enter occult realms.

The notorious writing team of Pierre Boileau and Pierre Ayraud, a.k.a. "Thomas Narcejac", better known as Boileau-

---

[158] 30 November 1962.

Narcejac, acquired justified world-wide fame for their famous thriller *Celle qui n'était plus* [She Who Was No More] (1952), which was filmed in 1956 by Henri-Georges Clouzot as *Les Diaboliques*. They also wrote the screenplay adaptation of Georges Franju's 1960 classic *Les Yeux Sans Visage* [Eyes Without a Face], based on Jean Redon's novel. Finally, their novel *D'Entre les Morts* [From the Dead] (1956) provided the story for Alfred Hitchcock's *Vertigo*. While their thrillers were always resolved with rational explanations, they succeeded in creating an unforgettable atmosphere of fear, relying on seemingly surreal events. *Le Mauvais Oeil* [The Evil Eye] (1956) and *Au Bois Dormant* [The Sleeping Woods] (1956) made use of classic folk legends and fairy tales. *Les Magiciennes* [The Magicians] (1957) and *Maléfices* [Spells] (1961) explored the darkest recesses of the human soul. ...*Et mon tout est un Homme* [...And What Is Left Is A Man] (1965) was a variation on the Frankenstein myth. Lastly, Boileau-Narcejac were chosen to continue Maurice Leblanc's popular *Arsène Lupin* series, for which they produced five successful novels.

Frédéric Dard is better known as a prolific mystery writer, and the author of a popular series of detective novels noted for their creative use of French slang, written under the byline of and featuring the character of Police Commissioner San-Antonio. Using the pseudonym of "Frédéric Charles", the author also wrote two grand-guignolesques horror novels, *La Maison de l'Horreur* [The House of Horror] (1952) and *N'ouvrez pas ce Cercueil* [Don't Open This Coffin] (1954). Under the pseudonym of "Marcel G. Prêtre", he wrote *La Cinquièrme Dimension* [The Fifth Dimension] (1968) for *Angoisse*. Under his own name, he wrote sevedral brilliant hard-boiled thrillers, some of which included genre elements, such as *Coma* (1959) and *Puisque les Oiseaux Meurent* [Since the Birds Die] (1960). He also penned a number of fantastic stories, which were later collected as *Histoires Déconcertantes* [Unsettling Tales] (1977).

The novels of Raoul de Warren belonged to the traditional *fantastique*, making use of such time-tested concepts as specters, ghouls, demons, etc. *L'Énigme du Mort Vivant* [The Mystery of the Living Dead] (1950) and *La Bête de l'Apocalypse* [The Beast of the Apocalypse] (1956) were among this popular author's best genre works. Several of his works, written in the late 1940s and early 1950s, were reprinted by the publisher L'Herne in the 1980s, including *L'Insolite Aventure de Marina Sloty* [Marina Sloty's Strange Adventure] (1981), *Rue du Mort-qui-Trompe* [Street of the Dead Who Cheats] (1984), *Et le Glas Tinta Trois Fois* [And the Bell Tolled Three Times] (1989) and *Les Portes de l'Enfer* [The Gates of Hell] (1991)

The 1950s saw the emergence of popular paperback imprints entirely devoted to horror novels, following a pattern previously established with adventure and science fiction by publishers such as Tallandier and Ferenczi. Most of these imprints, however, were short-lived. Among these were: *Épouvante* [Terror], with seven volumes published in 1954-55 by La Corne d'Or; another *Épouvante*, with a single volume published in 1954 by Édica; *Frayeurs* [Fears], with five volumes published in 1954-55 by L'Arabesque; and *L'Étrange* [Strange], with four volumes published in 1956 by Robert Laffont.

Some notable authors published by these imprints included Léo Gestelys with *Nuit d'Épouvante* [Night of Terror] (1946), *Le Fluide d'Or* [The Golden Fluid] (1949) and *L'Île des Malédictions* [The Island of Curses] (1955); and Robert Georges-Méra with *Que le Diable l'Emporte!* [Let The Devil Take It!] (1952), *L'Inhumaine Création du Professeur Lynk* [Prof. Lynk's Inhuman Creation] (1954), *La Mort aux Vifs* [Death to the Living] (1954) and *Le Monstrueux Professeur Lynk* [The Monstrous Prof. Lynk] (1960).

The major genre imprint that dominated the 1950s and 1960s, however, was publisher Fleuve Noir's *Angoisse* [Anguish], which was started in 1954 in the wake of their successful science fiction imprint, *Anticipation*, and continued monthly until 1974, publishing a total of 261 volumes, a feat probably unique in the annals of horror literature. *Angoisse* relied heavily on its sister imprint *Anticipation* for its stable of authors, and therefore published only French authors, with five exceptions: American writers David H. Keller, Evangeline Walton and Donald Wandrei, British author Virginia Lord and German author Roger Sattler and Walter Mauckner (under the pseudonym of "Georges Gauthier").

Among the best authors published by *Angoisse*, first and foremost was André Ruellan, a medical doctor who used the pseudonym of "Kurt Steiner" for his popular works. Whether writing as Ruellan or Steiner, he was also one of France's best science fiction authors of the period. For *Angoisse*, he penned twenty-two horror novels, mastering all the classic themes and creating some new ones as well. Zombies appeared in *Le Bruit du Silence* [The Sound of Silence] (1955); ghastly other dimensions in *Fenêtres sur l'Obscur* [Windows into Darkness] (1956) and *Les Pourvoyeurs* [The Purveyors] (1957); modern vampires in *Le Seuil du Vide* [The Threshold of the Void] (1956) and *Syncope Blanche* [White Faint] (1958); witchcraft in *La Marque du Démon* [The Mark of the Demon] (1958); haunted castles in *Lumière de Sang* [Blood Light] (1958); and pacts with the Devil in *Pour Que Vive Le Diable* [For The Devil To Live] (1956). Other notable titles included: *De Flamme et d'Ombre* [Of Flame and Shadows] (1956), *Je Suis Un Autre* [I Am Other] (1957), *Les Dents Froides* [The Cold Teeth] (1957), *L'Envers du Masque* [The Other Side of the Mask] (1957), *La Marque du Démon* [The Mark of the Demon] (1958), *Dans un Manteau de Brume* [In a Cloak of Mist] (1959) and *Glace Sanglante* [Bloody Ice] (1960)

Perhaps because of his medical background, the strength of his novels lied in their detailed, almost clinical, atmosphere of heavy, oppressive, bludgeoning horror, which anticipated the stronger, gorier, books of the next decades. In 1979, Ruellan signed the script and novelization of Alain Jessua's remarkable 1979 modern horror movie, *Les Chiens* [The Dogs], in which an attack dog trainer, played by Gérard Depardieu, uses people's fears to slowly take over a town.

René Bonnefoy used the pseudonyms of "René Blondel" and "B.-R. Bruss" to separate his literary and popular works. He, too, was one of France's best popular science fiction authors of the period. For *Angoisse*, he penned nine novels, including *L'Oeil était dans la Tombe* [The Eye Was in the Tomb] (1955); *Maléfices* [Spells] (1956), about a local bridge cursed by two Egyptian talismans incorporated into its metal; *Nous Avons Tous Peur* [We Are All Afraid] (1956), about a nightmarish creature who stalks an isolated village; *Terreur en Plein Soleil* [Terror Under a Full Sun] (1958), about a telepath who sadistically drives people to commit suicide; *Le Tambour d'Angoisse* [The Drum of Terror] (1962), about the members of an Australian ethnological expedition who are driven insane by the drumbeats of invisible natives; *Le Bourg Envoûté* [The Spellbound Village] (1964), about evil forces which return to plague a village every two centuries; *La Figurine de Plomb* [The Lead Statuette] (1965), about a mystical object which enables its owner to change the course of his fate; and finally, *Le Mort qu'il faut Tuer* [The Dead Man Who Must Be Killed] (1971), a variation on the theme of *Donovan's Brain*.

Bruss liked to depict strange and pathetic characters, moving in a mundane, yet suffocating, environment. The horrific elements were introduced slowly, but implacably, in a clear and colorful style. In his novels, men were usually the predestined victims of unspeakable Lovecraftian-like forces. His horror novels have few equals in their spellbinding atmosphere of oppressive horror.

Adrien Sobra, a former English teacher, was already a mainstream, if little known, novelist who had published a few novels and thrillers (using the anagrammatic pseudonym of "Ange Arbos") before he turned to writing popular horror fiction under the pseudonym of "Marc Agapit". He wrote forty-three novels for *Angoisse* and was one of the best and most respected authors of the imprint. Unlike his colleagues, he used the supernatural sparsely, his catalog of horrors being somewhat more akin to Ruth Rendell rewritten by the Grand-Guignol. The author delighted in throwing a light on the perversity of the human soul, showing sordid, lonely, ordinary people ravaged by time, slowly sinking into madness. His heroes often came from cursed families. They exhibited an unhealthy sexuality and may even have had physical handicaps, like in *La Bête Immonde* [The Awful Beast] (1959),[159] whose hero is blind, and *École des Monstres* [Monster School] (1963). His protagonists were often young boys who became natural prey for decrepit, evil females, or innocently trafficked with the most monstrous, unnatural creatures, as in the classic *Greffe Mortelle* [Mortal Transplant] (1958), which was praised by Jean Cocteau, and *Le Miroir Truqué* [The Trick Mirror] (1973).

Agapit's supernatural elements, when he chose to use any, were more likely to be Hell and the Devil, as in *Agence Tous Crimes* [All-Crime Agency] (1958) and *L'Héritage du Diable* [The Devil's Inheritance] (1971), or borrowed from classical mythology, such as the Minotaur in *La Nuit du Minotaure* [The Night of the Minotaur] (1965), the Furies in *Les Ciseaux d'Atropos* [The Scissors of Atropos] (1973), Oedipus in *Piège Infernal* [Infernal Trap] (1960), Shakespeare's *Tempest* in *L'Île Magique* [The Magical Island] (1967) and the Wandering Jew in *Monsieur Personne* [Mister Nobody] (1967). Other notable titles included: *Puzzle Macabre* [Macabre Puzzle] (1959), *Opéra de la Mort* [Death Opera] (1960), *Phantasmes* (1962), *Le Voyage en Rond* [The Circular Journey] (1964), *Les Yeux Braqués* [The Staring Eyes] (1965), *La Guivre* (1966), *La Goule* [The Ghoul] (1968), *La Dame à l'Os* [The Lady with a Bone] (1969), *Une Sorcière m'a dit* [A Witch Told Me] (1970) and *Le Poids du Monde* [The Weight of the World] (1970).

Another writer of note who contributed to *Angoisse* was renowned film writer Jean-Claude Carrière, who penned six *Frankenstein* pastiches (with plotting assistance from Guy Bechtel for the first one), continuing the adventures of Mary Shelley's immortal creature: *La Tour de Frankenstein* [The

---

[159] *Despair*, Black Coat Press, ISBN 978-1-932983-06-7.

Tower of Frankenstein] (1957), *Le Pas de Frankenstein* [The Step of Frankenstein] (1957), *La Nuit de Frankenstein* [The Night of Frankenstein] (1957), *Le Sceau de Frankenstein* [The Seal of Frankenstein] (1957), *Frankenstein Rôde* [Frankenstein Prowls] (1958) and *La Cave de Frankenstein* [The Cellar of Frankenstein] (1959). The author's approach was startingly different from both the Universal and Hammer versions. In his novels, he followed the footsteps of the Monster, christened "Gouroull", as he made his way back from Iceland, to Scotland, and then Germany and Switzerland, from the late 1800s to the 1920s. Unlike its predecessors, Gouroull was a ruthless, demoniacal thing, the very incarnation of evil. His yellow, unblinking eyes hid a cunning, inhuman intelligence. The Monster barely spoke, but used his razor-sharp teeth to slit his victims' throats. Carrière insisted on the physical inhumanity of the creature: the Monster did not breathe, its skin was white as chalk but strangely impervious to flames, its strength and speed were prodigious, what ran in is veins was not blood, and it had no normal heartbeat; even its thought process was shown to be alien. The plots have the Monster pursuing his own, evil agenda, generally unafraid of the weaker humanity, and woe to anyone standing in his way. Even people who tried to help or reason with him were just as likely to be killed by the inhuman fiend.[160]

The *Frankenstein* novels were released under the pseudonym of "Benoît Becker", a house name created by the publisher and also used by writer/journalist José-André Lacour, who wrote six other *Angoisse* novels, without the character of *Frankenstein*.

"André Caroff" (a pseudonym of André Carpouzis) wrote seventeen science fiction horror thrillers for *Angoisse* novels, starting in 1964, with an 18th novel being published

---

[160] Three sequels were written by Frank Schildiner and published by Black Coat Press in 2015-19.

much later in the *Anticipation* imprint.[161] These starred the *Sinistre Mme Atomos* [The Sinister Mrs. Atomos], a deadly, brilliant, but twisted female Japanese scientist out to revenge herself against the United States for the bombings of Hiroshima and Nagasaki. A sample plot had the evil title character unleash a deadly new threat, such as radioactive zombies, only to be stopped in the nick of time by the heroes, Smith Beffort of the FBI, Dr. Alan Soblen and Yosho Akamatsu of the Japanese Secret Police. With the help of former criminal Owen Bernitz, Beffort also organized the "Green Dragon" squad to fight Madame Atomos. An interesting development was the creation by Madame Atomos of a younger version of herself, Mie Azusa, dubbed "Miss Atomos", groomed to continue the fight should she die. Mie eventually fell in love with Beffort, married him and joined forces with him to fight her evil progenitrix. Madame Atomos herself regenerated into a younger self in the thirteenth novel, but remained as revenge-bent as ever. Starting in 1968, the series was adapted into black and white, digest-sized comics by French publisher Aredit. [162]

---

[161] Three authorized sequels, written by Michel and Sylvie Stéphan, were published in 2013-15.
[162] The *Madame Atomos* series in available from Black Coat Press in 11 volumes: 1. *The Terror of Madame Atomos* (includes *La Sinistre Mme Atomos* (1964) & *Mme Atomos Sème la Terreur* (1965)), ISBN 978-1-935558-41-5; 2. *Miss Atomos* (includes *Mme Atomos Frappe à la Tête* (1965) & *Miss Atomos* (1965)), ISBN 978-1-61227-018-0; 3. *The Return of Madame Atomos* (includes *Miss Atomos contre KKK* (1966) & *Le Retour de Mme Atomos* (1966)), ISBN 978-1-61227-030-2; 4. *The Mistake of Madame Atomos* (includes *L'Erreur de Mme Atomos* (1966) & *Mme Atomos Prolonge la Vie* (1967)), ISBN 978-1-61227-069-2; 5. *The Monsters of Madame Atomos* (includes *Les Monstres de Mme Atomos* (1967) & *Madame Atomos Crache des Flammes* (1967)), ISBN 978-1-61227-087-6; 6. *The Revenge of Madame Atomos* (includes *Mme Atomos Croque le Marmot* (1967) & *La Ténébreuse Mme Atomos*

Prior to creating *Madame Atomos*, Caroff had penned the adventures of *Dr. François Petit*, a sociopath *à la* Hannibal Lecter, visibly inspired by the real-life French serial killer, Dr. Petiot. In the 1970s, after the cancellation of *Angoisse*, the author continued his prolific writing career in the *Anticipation* imprint.

Leading *Anticipation* writer Richard Bessière contributed five novels to *Angoisse* under the pseudonym of "Dominique H. Keller", created especially to not lose the benefit of the name recognition that came from having published American writer David H. Keller.

Other *Anticipation* writers who contributed to *Angoisse* during the 1950s and 1960s included:

Veteran writer Maurice Limat, with thirty-three novels, most of which were devoted to two interconnected series, the first following the adventures of *Teddy Verano*, a ghostbuster and detective of the supernatural mysteries, reintroduced in *Mandragore* (1963), and the second dedicated to *Mephista*, a spin-off of the *Verano* series, introduced in *Mephista* (1969).[163] Is Mephista a fictional character born of the minds of screenwriters? Or is she a demon from the bowels of Hell?

(1968)), ISBN 978-1-61227-119-4; 7. *The Resurrection of Madame Atomos* (includes *Mme Atomos Change de Peau* (1968) & *Mme Atomos Fait Du Charme* (1969)), ISBN 978-1-61227-157-6; 8. *The Mark of Madame Atomos* (includes *L'Empreinte de Mme Atomos* (1969) & *Mme Atomos Jette Un Froid* (1969)), ISBN 978-1-61227-223-8; 9. *The Spheres of Madame Atomos* (includes *Mme Atomos Cherche la Petite Bête* (1970) & *Les Sphères de Mme Atomos* (1979)), ISBN 978-1-61227-259-7 ; as well as the Stéphan authorized sequels: 10. *The Wrath of Madame Atomos* (includes *Mme Atomos Sème la Tempête* (2013) & *Mme Atomos Parie sur la Mort* (2014)), ISBN 978-1-61227-330-3 ; and 11. *The Sins of Madame Atomos* [*Mme Atomos joue sur les maux*] (2015), ISBN 978-1-61227-672-4.

[163] Black Coat Press, ISBN 978-1-61227-434-8.

Is she Edwige Hossegor, the beautiful and kind-hearted actress, whose evil alter ego kills mercilessly; or the equally stunning Olga Mervil, who is ready to sign a pact with Satan in order to replace Edwige? A movie studio is plagued by mysterious murders; a cult of devil worshippers in the catacombs of Paris; and a deadly circus of freaks... At the center of it all is Teddy Verano, the P.I. whose mission in life is to expose monsters and defeat evil. The Mephista character proved popular with the readers and went on to appear in twelve more titles.

Peter Randa (a pseudonym of André Duquesne) with five novels, including *Parodie à la Mort* [Death Parody] (1960), which was adapted into a Grand-Guignol play; and

Jimmy Guieu with *Oniria* (1962).

Writers who wrote exclusively for *Angoisse* included:

Michel Bernanos, the son of Georges Bernanos (see above), who contributed three novels under the pseudonym of "Michel Talbert" and whose *Les Nuits de Rochemaure* [The Nights of Rochemaure] (1963) has since become a cult classic.

"Dominique Arly" (a pseudonym of Constant Pettex), who penned nineteen supernatural thrillers (1965-74) with mildly erotic elements, a number of which starred the attractive *Rosamond Lew*, introduced in *Les Pistes Maudites* [The Accursed Trails] (1970).

"José Michel" (André Caroff's mother), with six novels (1966-70), including *La Dernière Fuite* [The Last Flight] (1966).

Jean Murelli, with twelve titles (1958-69), including *Ce Mur Qui Regardait* [That Staring Wall] (1959) and *Ma Peau de Fantôme* [My Ghostly Skin] (1969).

Patrick Svenn, with three novels, including *L'Heure Funèbre* [The Funereal Hour] (1954).

Belgian author Jean David, with *Une Chose dans la Nuit* [A Thing in the Night] (1956) and *Les Griffes de l'Oubli* [The Claws of Oblivion] (1957).

"Erik J. Certon" (a pseudonym of Frédéric Certoncini) with *Un Drame de l'au-delà* [A Tragedy from Beyond] (1960); and

Franc Puig with *L'Étrange Monsieur Borman* [The Strange Mr. Borman] (1960).

Last but not least, thriller writer Jean Redon published only one *Angoisse*, the classic *Les Yeux Sans Visage* [Eyes Without a Face] (1959). This novel about a brilliant but crazed surgeon who killed women to transplant their faces on his disfigured daughter was adapted into a Grand-Guignol play and into the 1959 horror film mentioned above. It also helped inspire a whole series of other horror films.

Fantastique Littéraire

The New Surrealists

Even though the surrealists lost some of their appeal because of the War and were no longer at the forefront of the literary scene after it, a number of writers continued to produce genre works.

In 1951, Julien Gracq wrote the brilliant *Le Rivage des Syrtes* [The Shores of the Syrtes] (1951) which was awarded the Goncourt literary prize. It took place in the imaginary land of Farghestan, which had been at war with its neighbor for three hundred years.

More reflective of the times was Boris Vian, a literary descendent of Alfred Jarry and a fine dramatist of the absurd. Many of his plays and novels contained elements borrowed from Surrealism as well as from traditional *fantastique* and even science fiction: *L'Écume des Jours* [Froth on the Daydream] (1947) was a surreal narrative; *L'Arrache-Coeur* [Heartsnatcher] (1953) was a fable about metamorphosis. His stories collected in *Les Fourmis* [The Ants] (1949) blended surrealism and fantasy.

Filmmaker and dramatist Alain Robbe-Grillet is justifiably famous for the minute precision with which he describes situations that are totally strange and surreal. In *Le Labyrinthe* (1959), he showed us a soldier lost in a mysterious, maze-like city, buried under everlasting snow, carrying a package under his arm. We never learn who the soldier is, what the package contains, or to whom he is to deliver it. *Instantanés* [Snap Shots] (1962) is a collection of tales loaded with surreal imagery: a living mannikin, an escalator going nowhere, a secret chamber that cannot be accessed, the paintings of Chirico, etc. Other significant works included *La Maison de Rendez-Vous* [The House of Rendezvous] (1965), *Topologie pour une Cité Fantôme* [Topology for a Phantom City] (1976) and *Djinn* (1981).

Robbe-Grillet's special brand of Kafkaesque, metaphysical, oneiric *fantastique* was also very much in evidence in the films that he wrote and/or directed such as *L'Année Dernière à Marienbad* [Last Year In Marienbad] (1961), directed by Alain Resnais, *L'Éden et Après* [Eden and Afterwards] (1971), *Glissements Progressifs du Plaisir* [Progressive Slidings Into Pleasure] (1974) and *La Belle Captive* [The Beautiful Prisoner] (1983).

Jacques Sternberg is a Belgian writer, but he deserves to be profiled in this section. He, too, wrote for film director Alain Resnais, penning the script of his 1968 surreal time travel feature, *Je t'aime, Je t'aime*. He wrote just as much science fiction as *fantastique*. once stating that he considered science fiction to be only a branch of the *fantastique*. His approach was complex and resolutely modern. In his works, the causes of terror are not ghosts or vampires, but the present-day city, often depicted as a giant, evil entity, ready to crush the hapless humans who dare live within its body. This theme reappears in novels such as *L'Employé* [The Employee] (1958), *L'Architecte* [The Architect] (1960) and *La Banlieue* [The Suburb] (1976). Sternberg's short fiction, collected in *La*

Géométrie dans l'Impossible [The Impossible Geometry] (1953), *La Géométrie dans la Terreur* [The Terror Geometry] (1958), *Contes Glacés* [Icy Tales] (1974) and *Contes Griffus* [Clawed Tales] (1993), to name but a few, successfully mixed several diverse elements: a very dark sense of humor, an almost British knack for pure nonsense, a Kafkaesque notion of the absurd, a definite taste for the macabre, and finally, a somber, pessimistic vision of the world and the future. In his fiction, love is never a source of redemption, but something impossible, almost alien, as in *Sophie, la Mer, la Nuit* [Sophie, The Sea, The Night] (1976) or *Le Navigateur* [The Navigator] (1977).

Roland Topor began his career in the *fantastique* as a renowned artist and cartoonist—he designed René Laloux's animated feature, *La Planète Sauvage* [Fantastic Planet] (1973)—but was soon recognized as a talented writer as well. He became associated with film-makers Fernando Arrabal and Alexandro Jodorowsky in the 1960 neo-surrealist movement dubbed "Panique", about which he later wrote *Café Panique* [*Panic Café*] (1982). Topor published some of his first short stories in the pages of *Fiction*, crafting brilliantly sarcastic, horribly mocking, sadistic little vignettes, collected in titles such as *Quatre Roses pour Lucienne* [Four Roses for Lucienne] (1967). He quickly became known as a writer of unbound imagination, gifted with a uniquely dark sense of humor. His *La Cuisine Cannibale* [Cannibal Cooking] (1970) remains a masterpiece in that vein. His novel *Le Locataire Chimérique* [The Imaginary Tenant] (1964) was adapted into the 1976 film *The Tenant* by Roman Polanski.

Other notable, modern Surrealist writers of the 1950s and 1960s included:

André Frédérique wrote numerous short stories collected in *Histoires Blanches* [*White Tales*] (1945) and *Aigremort* [*Bitterdeath*] (1947), displaying a flair for the macabre and the ability to evoke fear with soft, paranoid touches.

Pierre Bettencourt, the author of several collections of short, surreal, absurd little tales, such as *La Folie Gagne*

[Madness Is Winning] (1950), *Fragments d'Os pour un Squelette* [Bone Fragments for a Skeleton] (1950), *Histoires à Pendre ou à Laisser* [Stories to Take or Leave] (1951) and *Histoires comme il faut* [Stories As They Are] (1955). His fiction is remarkable for its humor, comparable to that of American writer Fredric Brown.

Maurice Blanchot, with Kafkaesque utopias such as *Le Très-Haut* [The Most High] (1948), *Le Ressassement Éternel* [The Eternal Repetition] (1951) and *Le Dernier Homme* [The Last Man] (1957).

Jean Marie Amédée Paroutaud, with *La Ville Incertaine* [The Uncertain City] (1950), the story of a man who is condemned to death for murder and manages to flee to another country. But that country is subject to total chaos and anarchy. Eventually, the murderer prefers to return to his homeland, finding the certain death that awaits him preferable to pure, insane irrationality. Another notable work was *La Descente Infinie* [The Infinite Descent] (1977).

François Valorbe, whose works, such as *Soleil Intime* [Intimate Sun] (1949), *La Vierge aux Chimères* [The Virgin of Chimeras] (1957) and *L'Apparition Tangible* [The Tangible Apparition] (1969), also featured surrealistic elements. His later novel, *Voulez-Vous Vivre en Eps?* [Do You Want To Live In Eps?] (1969), was notable for its wonderful blend of fantasy and surrealism.

René Bonnefoy, already mentioned, wrote popular horror and science fiction novels under the pseudonym of "B.-R. Bruss". As "Roger Blondel", he penned several beautifully crafted, surreal novels such as *Le Mouton Enragé* [The Rabid Sheep] (1956), *L'Archange* [The Archangel] (1963), the literary tale of a man about to embark on a cosmic journey, and *Le Boeuf* [The Ox] (1965), a bitterly acid and surreal tale about teaching. His best work was *Bradfer et l'Éternel* [Bradfer and the Eternal] (1964), a picaresque, satirical novel about a simple man who travels through imaginary lands with his words and a stubborn desire to "get to the bottom of things" as his only weapons.

One writer who defied any attempt at classification was Pierre Gripari, who broke onto the literary scene with several truculent, colorful genre novels, such as *Pierrot la Lune* [Pierrot-Of-The-Moon] (1963) and *La Vie, la Mort et la Resurrection de Socrate-Marie Gripotard* [Life, Death and Resurrection of Socrate-Marie Gripotard] (1968), a novel about a Candide-like superman. His *L'Incroyable Equipée de Phosphore Noloc* [The Incredible Voyage of Phosphore Noloc] (1964) was a homage to Jules Verne in which the hero, Phosphore Noloc ("Colon" spelled backwards), discovers that our cosmos is really inside a woman's womb during some form of incomprehensible act of cosmic copulation. Earth is a female egg moving inside the placenta of a giant uterus (the stars are the small dots lining the uterus' inner walls) and every day, each "new" sun is but a dying sperm, but one day, one of these sperm will hit Earth and fertilize it. Gripari's novels could just as easily be classified as science fiction, fantasy, satire or surrealism. His works reflect a dazzling variety of influences, ranging from the Occult to Dickens, Rabelais, Voltaire and Russian literature. He also published two collections of genre stories, *Diable, Dieu et autres Contes* [The Devil, God and Other Tales] (1965) and *Contes de la Rue Broca* [Tales of Broca Street] (1967), a collection of modern fairy tales, which became very popular in the late 1970s and were eventually adapted for animation.

Other Mainstream Authors

Marcel Béalu was one of the leading writers of the *fantastique littéraire* of the immediate post-war period. His tales were half-way between prose and poetry, and his fantasy followed the classic path of Hoffmann, Poe and Gérard de Nerval. In his fiction, hapless souls became slowly trapped in dream-like realities where inhuman forces held sway. *L'Expérience de la Nuit* [The Experience of Night] (1945) dealt with the power to see into other dimensions. His classic

L'Araignée d'Eau [The Water Spider] (1948) was about an impossible love between a man and a watery creature who slowly turned into a girl. Rejected by her human lover, she drowned him. (It was adapted into an eponymous 1968 feature film.) Béalu's shorter stories, collected in *Mémoires de l'Ombre* [Memoirs of Shadow] (1941; rev. 1959) and *L'Aventure Impersonelle* [The Unpersonal Adventure] (1954; rev. 1964), were a series of sometimes poetic, often morbid, vignettes in terror, all built around the theme of trafficking with the darkness. A later novel, *La Poudre des Songes* [The Dust of Dreams] (1977), followed the same pattern.

Marcel Brion was the other major writer of the *fantastique* of the immediate post-war period Unlike Béalu, his approach of the supernatural almost always referred to the romantic tradition and the search for a mystical absolute, being at heart a dreamer. *De l'Autre Côté de la Forêt* [On the Other Side of the Forest] (1966), *Les Miroirs et les Gouffres* [Mirrors and Abysses] (1968) and *Nous Avons Traversé la Montagne* [We Have Crossed the Mountain] (1972) were all about esoteric journeys where love enabled the protagonists to go behind the surface of things and find the true reality. *L'Ombre de l'Arbre Mort* [The Shadow of the Dead Tree] (1970) and *Le Journal du Visiteur* [The Diary of a Traveler] (1980) were about love defying death; in the latter, a man fell in love with a woman who had been dead for three hundred years and succeeded in bringing her back to life for a brief moment. Brion's most famous collection were *Les Escales de la Haute Nuit* [The Shore Leaves of the Deepest Night] (1942) and *La Chanson de l'Oiseau Étranger* [The Song of a Strange Bird] (1958).

André Pieyre de Mandiargues loved fairy tales, and everything that was baroque and fabulous. This elegant, stylistic author wrote numerous short stories, collected in *Le Musée Noir* [The Black Museum] (1946; rev. 1974), *Soleil des Loups* [The Sun of the Wolves] (1951) and *Feu de Braise* [Ember Fire] (1959). His tales owed their inspiration to sources as varied as Sade, the *roman noir*, Nodier, Mérimée and Bierce. The author's gift was to make the invisible visible with an implacable sense of logic and an almost maniacal precision. His stories did not try to terrify as much as they attempted to convey a sense of "wrongness". Erotic love and death were easily intertwined in his nightmarish visions, such as in his later novel *La Motocyclette* [The Motorbike] (1963).

André Dhôtel was an explorer of the *fantastique*, a cartographer who wandered through strange lands where the rules of logic rarely seemed to apply. Influenced by the folk legends of his native Ardennes—a forest-covered mountain range located between France and Belgium—the author used adolescents as his protagonists to make us experience weird and wondrous events, which were always presented in a disturbingly matter-of-fact way. His *La Chronique Fabuleuse* [The Fabulous Chronicle] (1955) and *Le Pays où l'on n'arrive Jamais* [The Unreachable Country] (1955) belonged to that vein. His classic *Les Voyages Fantastiques de Julien Grainebis* [The Fantastic Voyages of Julian Grainebis] (1958) featured a young man who first experienced life as a tree, then visited a robotic utopia and eventually brought his mother back from a village which suffered from the curse of invisibility.

Noël Devaulx was the last major author of the immediate post-war period. His own brand of *fantastique* relied of the intrusion of strange, subtle, mysterious, unexplained, and ultimately unexplainable, elements into everyday reality. His short stories were dubbed by critics "allegories without explanations, parables without keys". His best collections were *L'Auberge Parpillon* [The Parpillon Inn] (1945), *Le Pressoir Mystique* [The Mystic Press] (1948), *Bal chez Alféoni* [A Ball at the Alfeonis] (1956) and *Le Lézard d'Immortalité* [The Lizard of Immortality] (1977). Devaulx also wrote a novel, *Sainte Barbegrise* [Saint Greybeard] (1952).

Other genre writers of note who emerged during this period included:

André de Richaud who, like a French Richard Matheson, was one of the first authors to introduce the concepts of modern psychology into the *fantastique*. In *La Nuit Aveuglante*

[The Blinding Night] (1945), the protagonist could not remove a devil's face-shaped mask from his face because it reflected the evil contained within his soul. *Je ne suis pas mort* [I Am Not Dead] (1965) was another notable work in the same vein.

Marcel Schneider was the author of a remarkable *Histoire de la Littérature Fantastique en France* [History of Fantastic Literature in France] (1964), and also a talented writer who followed the traditions laid out by Nodier and Nerval. His novels mixed classic themes, such as impossible loves, ancient gods and goddesses, with images pulled from the subconscious mind. *La Première Île* [The First Island] (1951) was about the theme of the androgyne; *Le Guerrier de Pierre* [The Stone Warrior] (1969) featured a man turned into stone. His best collections, where the fantastic intrudes upon modern settings with disturbing consequences, included *Aux Couleurs de la Nuit* [In the Colors of Night] (1953) and *Opéra Massacre* [Opera Slaughter] (1965).

Roger Caillois was also an historian of the genre, the writer of *Approches de l'Imaginaire* [Approach of the Imaginary] (1970) and the editor of a deservedly famous *Anthologie du Fantastique* [Anthology of the Fantastique] (1977). But he was also the author of numerous genre works, such as *Méduse* (1960), *Trois Leçons des Ténèbres* [Three Lessons of Darkness] (1978) and *La Lumière des Songes* [The Light of Dreams] (1984), all traditional in inspiration.

Michel Bernanos was, as we mentioned above, the fourth son of renowned writer Georges Bernanos, the author of *Sous le Soleil de Satan*. He lived an adventurous life, including two stays in Brazil in 1938 and 1948, which inspired him to write the classic *La Montagne Morte de la Vie* [The Dead Mountain of Life] (1967), which was published only after his untimely death in 1964. The book tells the terrifying experiences encountered by two men, shipwrecked on a mysterious desert island, who eventually discover that the mountain which dominates the island is home to a mysterious entity. Bernanos also wrote the poetic *Le Murmure des Dieux* [The Whisper of the

Gods] (1964) under the pseudonym of "Michel Drowin", and several horror novels for *Angoisse* (see above).

Another notable author was André Beucler, whose strange short fictions were collected in *Trois Oiseaux* [Three Birds] (1957) and *Ténèbrus* (1968).

Even the renowned existentialist writer Simone de Beauvoir is to be credited for *Tous les Hommes sont Mortels* [All Men Are Mortals] (1946), in which a 13th century man becomes immortal and regrets it.

Playwright Maurice Toesca wrote several allegorical genre novels such as *Le Singe Bleu* [The Blue Monkey] (1948), *Le Bruit Lointain du Temps* [Time's Far-Away Sound] (1961) and *Les Loups-Garous* [The Werewolves] (1966).

One cannot write a panorama of the French *fantastique* of the 1950s and 1960s without mentioning the monthly magazine *Fiction*, created in 1953, which started as a French edition of *F & SF*, but also published many French authors of the *fantastique* until about 1968, after which it devoted itself entirely to science fiction. During its early period, *Fiction* published stories by such distinguished foreign authors as Borges, Matheson, Calvino and Buzzati, but also by French writers such as Jean Ray, Pierre Véry, André Maurois, Maurice Renard, Jean-Louis Bouquet, Jacques Sternberg, etc. Many noted French genre authors made their first appearance in its pages.

Among these were Alain Dorémieux, who eventually became its editor in 1957. His short stories were later collected in *Mondes Interdits* [Forbidden Worlds] (1967), *Promenades au bord du Gouffre* [Walks on the Edge of the Pit] (1978) and *Couloirs sans Issue* [No Exit Corridors] (1981) showed the influence of Richard Matheson, and were charmingly morbid in tone. A recurring theme was the presence of strange, almost always deadly, female creatures. Finally, Dorémieux became one of France's foremost anthologist of horror fiction, compiling several anthologies of various authors (including one devoted to Matheson) and editing the ten-volume series, *Territoires de l'Inquiétude* [Territories of Worry] (1991-96).

Another *Fiction* alumni of note was Fereydoun Hoveyda, an Iranian-born writer who also contributed articles and reviews to the magazine under the pseudonym of "F. Hoda". His short stories were classic little gems, collected in *Dans une Terre Étrange* [On a Strange Earth] (1968) and *Le Losange* (1968).

Other notable "alumni" included Jacques Sternberg, Roland Topor, Gabriel Deblander, Julia Verlanger and Christine Renard, all reviewed in other sections below.

Female Authors

While one would be hard-pressed to find any particular differences between the works of the women writers reviewed in this section and those of, say, Béalu or Brion, it nevertheless is a fact that the emergence of a new generation of women as major writers of the *fantastique* was one of the most interesting aspects of the immediate post-war.

As mentioned above, many of these women were first published in the pages of *Fiction* in the late 1950s and early 1960s. Some wrote both science fiction and *fantastique*. Those women whose works belonged squarely in the domain of the *fantastique* included:

Lise Deharme had previously collaborated with both André Breton and Julien Gracq. She was the "lady with a glove" featured in the former's *Nadja*. Her fantasy novel *La Porte à Côté* [The Next Door] (1949) featured a female succubus who cast her spell on the modern-day descendent of an 18th century nobleman she once cursed. The ending, in which the succubus turns into a movie star is resolutely modern and ironic. Her collections of short stories, such as *Cette Année-là* [That Year] (1945) and *Le Pot de Mousse* [The Pot of Moss] (1946), or heer later novels such as *Le Château de l'Horloge* [The Castle of the Clock] (1955), also mixed fantastic and surreal elements with a sense of finely tuned irony.

The fact that most of the collections of stories penned by female authors were often published ten or fifteen years after the original publication of the stories themselves is evidence that the publishing market of the 1950s and 1960s was not yet prepared to deal with the notion of women being just as good, or even better, than men as writers of *fantastique* and fantasy. The most notable names included:

Françoise d'Eaubonne, with *Démons et Merveilles* [Demons & Wonders] (1951).

Marianne Andrau, with *Lumière d'Épouvante* [Light of Terror] (1956).

Julia Verlanger, whose brilliant and ground-breaking fantasy tales were collected in *Les Portes Sans Retour* [The Gates of No Return] (1976) and *La Flûte de Verre Froid* [The Flute of Cold Glass] (1976). (More about her below.)

Christine Renard, whose intimate tales of the fantastic were collected in *La Mante au Fil des Jours* [The Mantis on the Flow of the Days] (1977).

Nathalie C. Henneberg, whose flamboyant and baroque fantasies were collected in *L'Opale Entydre* [The Entydre Opal] (1971). (More about her below.)

Other women writers of the post-war period were drawn to a more traditional, more literary, type of *fantastique*, and were published by mainstream houses. While they arguably never gained the fame of their male counterparts, together, they nevertheless represent an outstanding body of work that is simply impossible to ignore.

Yvonne Escoula's stories were romantic, full of poetic notions about lost youth, desires and dreams, reminiscences of past lives and evocations of parallel realities. Her most notable books included *Poursuite du Vent* [Pursuit of the Wind] (1947), *Promenade des Promesses* [Boulevard of Promises] (1948), *Contes de la Ventourlière* [Tales of the Ventourliere] (1965) and *La Peau de la Mer* [The Skin of the Sea] (1972).

Geneviève Gennari also liked to cross the border between reality and dream, causing the reader to lose his hold on physical existence. Her most notable works included *La Fon-*

taine Scellée [The Sealed Fountain] (1950), *Le Rideau de Sable* [The Curtain of Sand] (1957), *Nouvelles du Temps et de l'Espace* [Stories of Time and Space] (1964) and later, *Dieu et son Ombre* [God and his Shadow] (1981) and *Le Manuscrit* [The Manuscript] (1989).

Mainstream writer and film director Nelly Kaplan used the pseudonym of "Bélen" to pen a number of erotic short stories based on either fantastic or science fiction themes. These were collected in *Et Délivrez-nous du Mâle* [And Free Us from the Males] (1960), *La Géométrie dans les Spasmes* [Geometry in Spasms] (1961) and *La Reine des Sabbats* [The Queen of Sabbaths] (1962).

Simone Balazard, with the surreal *Le Château des Tortues* [The Castle of Turtles] (1962) and *Le Rocher Rouge* [The Red Rock] (1972).

The wonderful Marguerite Cassan, whose mischievous sense of humor shone in the stories gathered in *Histoires à Coté* [Sideway Stories] (1963), *Fil à Fil* [Thread to Thread] (1965) and *À Développer dans l'Obscurité* [To Develop in the Dark] (1967).

The gothic Martine Chevrier, with *La Fontaine de Sang* [The Fountain of Blood] (1966) and *La Fête des Morts* [The Festival of the Dead] (1974).

Finally, Marie-Thérèse de Brosses, whose *Assunrath* (1967) was a Matheson-like tale of a woman shrunk down to insect-size.

Fantasy

André Ruellan, writing as "Kurt Steiner", was arguably the first writer to introduce modern heroic-fantasy in the *Anticipation* imprint of Fleuve Noir with his *Aux Armes d'Ortog* [Under Ortog's Arms] (1960), and its sequel *Ortog et les Ténèbres* [Ortog and the Darkness] (1969).[164] The world of

---

[164] In *Ortog*, Black Coat Press, ISBN 978-1-935558-28-6.

Dal Ortog Dal of Galankar is a futuristic Earth where sophisticated science cohabits with a pseudo-medieval society. In the first novel, Ortog was sent by the ruling Sopharch, Karella, to find a cure for the slow death that is killing Earth and its inhabitants after a devastating interplanetary war. Ortog eventually returned with such a cure, but too late to save his love, Karella's daughter, Kalla. In the sequel, Ortog and his friend Zoltan, embarked on an Orpheus-like quest through the dimensions of Death to find Kalla's soul and bring her back to Earth. Ortog is armed with the devastating "Blue Weapon" in the form of a sword whose blade disintegrates everything it touches. He eventually found Kalla, lost her again and returned to Earth, cursed with immortality.

Another precursor of modern French heroic-fantasy was Nathalie C. Henneberg, the Russian-born wife of German-born science fiction writer, Charles Henneberg who, in the 1950s, penned a series of flamboyantly gothic space operas, featuring superhuman protagonists, often soldiers or mercenaries, victims of violent, romantic passions. After her husband's death in 1959, Nathalie pursued her late husband's writing career, but relied increasingly on fantasy rather than science fiction elements.

Les Dieux Verts [The Green Gods] (1961)[165] told the romance of Argo and Atlena during the Emerald Age of Earth, in the future, when Man's Empire is on the decline and the world is ruled by the eponymous "Green Gods", powerful entities from the vegetable kingdom. *Le Sang des Astres* [The Blood of the Stars] (1963) was a colorful gothic fantasy in which an astronaut from the year 2700 journeys to a medieval Earth-like world ruled by kabbala, where legends live, and where he eventually falls in love with a female salamander. Her masterpiece was *La Plaie* [The Plague] (1964), a sprawling 600-page novel that told of the desperate battle by a handful of humans and angel-like mutants against a wave of pure, malevolent evil sweeping the galaxy, and which incarnates

---

[165] Black Coat Press, ISBN 978-1-935558-47-7.

itself in the bodies of the "Nocturnes" [*Nocturnals*]. Henneberg's works stood alone in the literary landscape of the 1960s, even in the world of science fiction and the *fantastique*. Her use of the French language, betraying Germanic and Russian influences, was unusually well-suited to creating larger-than-life heroic characters and epic romances. Like the British and American masters of the genre, she knew how to build full-blown, intricately detailed baroque and colorful universes. Her fantasy short stories were later collected in *Démons et Chimères* [Demons and Chimeras] (1977) and *D'Or et de Nuit* [Of Gold and Night] (1977).

Folklore & Legends

The traditional connection between fantasy and the folk tales and legends of the French countryside in the tradition of S. Henry Berthoud, Georges Sand and Anatole Le Braz was upheld by the prodigious and prolific Claude Seignolle, who wrote numerous books collecting and preserving country legends, as well as many short stories and novels making use of the local folklore, including gruesome peasant witchcraft rituals, devil worship, werewolves, etc.

In the first category, we would include *En Sologne* (1945), the two-volumes *Contes Populaires de Guyenne* [Popular Tales of Guyenne] (1946), *Le Diable dans la Tradition Populaire* [The Devil in Popular Traditions] (1959), *Le Folklore du Languedoc* (1960), *Le Folklore de la Provence* (1963), *Les Évangiles du Diable* [The Devil's Gospel] (1964) (the Devil being a recurrent theme), collecting and annotating all of the popular beliefs on the subject in a 900page tome, *Le Berry Traditionnel* (1969), *Contes Fantastiques de Bretagne* (1969), etc.

Seignolle's own brand of fictional *fantastique* was influenced by his "sorcerous childhood"—the title of a 1994 collection—spent in the misty plains of his native Sologne, and a terrifying encounter with the Devil incarnated in a local warlock which he claimed to have experienced at age 15 in 1932. This conferred a real sense of authenticity to his books, which were almost devoid of any literary artifices. His major works included *La Malvenue* [The Illcome] (1952; rev. 1965), *Le Bahut Noir* [The Black Dresser] (1958), *Le Diable en Sabots* [The Devil in Clogs] (1959), *La Brume ne se lèvera plus* [The Mist Will No Longer Rise] (1959; rev. 1963), *Histoires Maléfiques* [Maleficent Tales] (1965), *Contes Macabres* [Macabre Stories] (1966), *Les Chevaux de la Nuit* [The Night Horses] (1967), *La Nuit des Halles* [The Night of the Halles] (1965), *Invitation au Château de l'Étrange* [Invitation to the Castle of the Weird] (1969), *Histoires Vénéneuses* [Poisonous Tales] (1970) and *Contes Sorciers* [Sorcerous Stories] (1974).

Other writers who used the rich French country folklore as a source of inspiration included:

Jean Blanzat, the author of stories often featuring the Devil, such as *L'Orage du Matin* [The Morning Storm] (1942), *La Gartempe* (1957), *L'Iguane* [The Iguana] (1966) and *Reflets dans un Ciel d'Or* [Reflections in a Golden Sky] (1973).

Eugène Bressy, the author of *Légendes de Provence* [Legends of Provence] (1963).

Jean-Loup Trassard, whose tales featured the western province called Mayenne, with *L'Érosion Intérieure* [The Inner Erosion] (1965), *L'Ancolie* [The Ancoly] (1975) and *Histoires Fraîches* [Fresh Tales] (1981).

Finally, two African authors from Benin chose to recount their native legends in French: Olympe Bhély-Quénum, with *Le Chant du Lac* [The Song of the Lake] (1965), in which a lake spirit interferes with the local villagers' lives, and other collections devoted to African tales such as *Un Piège sans Fin* [An Endless Trap] (1978), *L'Initié* [The Initiate] (1979) and *Les Appels du Vodou* [Call of the Voodoo] (1994); and Jean Pliya, the author of *L'Arbre Fétiche* [The Fetish Tree] (1963) and *Kondo le Requin* [Kondo the Shark] (1965)

Benjamin Matip, a writer from Cameroon, penned a collection of fairy tales, *À la Belle Étoile* [Under the Night Sky] (1962).

Algerian writer Mohammed Dib wrote *Baba Férane* (1959), a collection of Algerian folk tales, then *Qui se Souvient de la Mer?* [Who Remembers the Sea?] (1962), a dreamlike novel about a man trapped in a strange, living city. Other notable works included *Cours sur la Rive Sauvage* [Run on the Wild Shore] (1964), which dealt with the intersection between dimensions, and *Le Talisman* (1966).

Occult & Esoterism

The *fantastique ésoterique* is a category that can be split into two separate sub-sections. The first consists of novels which derive their inspiration from the Occult, following in the footsteps of the Symbolists and the *roman spirite*; the second is that of the "vulgarization" books intending to popularize occult concepts.

In the first category, we should mention:

Noël de La Houssaye's *L'Apparition d'Arsinoë* [The Apparition of Arsinoe] (1947), in which the author-narrator is a white magician who uses Cornelius Agrippa's secrets to invoke the ghost of Arsinoe, the first Queen of Egypt.

Marguerite Yourcenar's *L'Oeuvre au Noir* [The Dark Work] (1968), in which a Renaissance Italian warlock attempts to use alchemy to understand and, ultimately, control the universe.

Patrick Ravignant's *La Peau de l'Ombre* [The Skin of the Shadow] (1963), an initiatic novel about immortality.

The tradition of the *roman initiatique*, that is to say of a novel describing an initiation, an esoteric journey at the end of which the protagonist can access the true nature of reality, was upheld by André Hardellet. In his classic *Le Seuil du Jardin* [The Threshold of the Garden] (1958), the author's protagonist, painter Steve Masson, meets an inventor who has created a "magic lantern" that can give life to memories; but it is eventually destroyed by a mysterious organization. *Le Parc des Archers* [The Park of the Bowmen] (1962) featured a writer's rebellion against a totalitarian tyranny located in an alternate universe. Steve Masson made a return appearance in a cameo. *Lourdes, Lentes* [Heavy, Slow] (1969), a novel originally credited to "Steve Masson" and later republished under Hardellet's own name, also starred Masson, this time in a dreamlike quest for a lost love. In *Lady Long Solo* (1971), the author himself explored a long-dead Paris, meeting ghosts and fictional characters. *Les Chasseurs* [The Huntsmen] (1966) was a collection of fantastic tales. In Hardellet's works, the hero may be crushed by reality on our plane, but he ultimately triumphs on another plane. The recurring character of Steve Masson is the magus who unlocks the eternal mysteries of life and the universe.

While technically beyond the scope of our research, we feel that some of the Occult "vulgarization" books deserve to be mentioned here, for several reasons. First, their theories are often reflected in the fantastic fiction of the times, as was the case with the works of Éliphas Lévi, Allan Kardec, Helena Blavatsky, or the Occultists of the Golden Dawn. However, unlike the occultists and esoteric writers of previous eras, who were addressing a very limited audience, the modern authors reached a vast, uninformed, undiscriminating readership. Second, in the same fashion as Richard S. Shaver, Erich Von Daniken or Charles Berlitz, they often incorporated outlandish concepts in their historical (or pseudo-historical) research, blurring the line between fact and fiction, science and fantasy. In Gérard de Sède's *La Race Fabuleuse* [The Fabulous Race], for example, the Merovingian Kings were said to carry alien genes!

The popularity of these esoteric vulgarization books in France can be traced to the publication in 1960 of the best-selling *Le Matin des Magiciens* [The Morning of the Magicians] by Jacques Bergier and Louis Pauwels. In it, information about the Nazis' presumed connections with the Occult, the role of secret societies operating behind-the-scenes, the nature of alchemy, the practice of sorcery, ancient astronauts, pre-cataclysmic civilizations, etc. were all evoked in a modern, investigative documentary style *à la X-Files*. The considerable knowledge of Bergier in both the fantastic and esoteric fields combined with Pauwels' literary skills to create a unique best-seller. *Le Matin des Magiciens'* commercial success, as well as that of the magazine *Planète*, also edited by Pauwels, contributed to the creation of a full-blown industry of esoteric vulgarization books.

Among the authors who followed in those footsteps, the foremost was "Robert Charroux" (a pseudonym of Robert Joseph Grugeau), a French Von Daniken who specialized in the belief of ancient, technologically-advanced societies and extra-terrestrial visitations. His first best-seller was *Histoire Inconnue des Hommes depuis 100.000 Ans* [Unknown History of Man for the Last 100,000 Years] (1963), soon followed by *Le Livre des Maîtres du Monde* [The Book of the Masters of the World], *Le Livre du Mystérieux Inconnu* [The Book of the Mysterious Unknown], *Le Livre du Passé Mystérieux* [The Book of the Mysterious Past], and several more titles like it.

Gérard de Sède wrote a dozen of best-selling works about the Templars, the Cathars, the Holy Grail, Rennes-le-Château and the Merovingian Kings, which inspired *Holy Grail, Holy Blood* and *The Da Vinci Ciode*. His career began with *Les Templiers sont parmi nous* [The Templars Are Among Us] in 1962 and continued with *Le Trésor Maudit de Rennes-le-Château* [The Accursed Treasure of Rennes-Le-Château], *La Race Fabuleuse* [The Fabulous Race], *Le Secret des Cathares* [The Secret of the Cathars], *Le Sang des Cathares* [The Blood of the Cathars], etc.

Another specialist of the Templars was Louis Charpentier whose *Les Mystères Templiers* [The Templar Mysteries], published in 1967, exploited the same vein.

Other notable authors in the genre included:

Noted science fiction editor Jacques Sadoul, with *Le Trésor des Alchimistes* [The Alchemists' Treasure].

Guy Tarade, with *Les Dossiers de l'Étrange* [The Strange Files].

Denis Saurat, with *L'Atlantide et le Règne des Géants* [Atlantis & The Reign of the Giants].

ESP expert Jean Prieur, with *Les Témoins de l'Invisible* [The Witnesses of the Invisible] and *Les Visiteurs de l'Autre Monde* [The Visitors from Another World].

Science fiction writer Jimmy Guieu, with two tomes about UFOs, *Les Soucoupes Volantes viennent d'un Autre Monde* [The Flying Saucers Come from Another World] and *Black-Out sur les Soucoupes Volantes* [Black-Out on the Flying Saucers], the latter prefaced by Jean Cocteau.

The YAs

The post-war period saw a boom in specialized imprints aimed at children and young adults. Some of the most famous were Hachette's *Bibliothèque Rose* for children, which published Enid Blyton's *Fearless Five*; and the *Bibliothèque Verte* for young adults, which reprinted abridged versions of Dumas, Verne, etc.; G.P.'s *Bibliothèque Rouge & Or*; Delagrave's *Aventure & Jeunesse*; Gasnier's *Jeunesse de France*; Rageot's *Bibliothèque de l'Amitié* and Alsatia's *Signe de Piste*.

To the extent that French educators still believed that the *fantastique* (and even more so, science fiction) were harmful to young minds, children's books and young adult books were kept carefully free of genre elements, except of course for sanitized Fairy Tales, and Legends, such as Fernand Nathan's imprint *Contes & Légendes* already mentioned.

Nevertheless, there were a few authors who made original contributions to the field of YA *fantastique*:

Alice Coleno wrote a series of modern fairy tales, remarkable both for their style and imagination: *La Forêt de Cristal* [The Crystal Forest] (1946), *Contes de Diamant* [Diamond Tales] (1957), *Les Jardins de la Licorne* [The Gardens of the Unicorn] (1957) and *La Montagne des Démons* [The Mountains of Demons] (1963) were all fantasy classics for children, worthy of Perrault or d'Aulnoy.

Renée Aurembou's novels were young adult adventures which drew their inspiration from some of the most mysterious aspects of French history: *La Maison des Fonds Noirs* [The House of Dark Recesses] (1954), *Le Mystère de l'Abbaye Brûlée* [The Mystery of the Burned Abbey] (1966) and *Le Trésor de Montségur* [The Treasure of Montsegur] (1966) are among her most notable works.

Jacques Chabar penned two fantasy-oriented novels, *La Cité du Serpent à Plumes* [The City of the Feathered Serpent] (1954) and *Le Retour du Serpent à Plumes* [The Return of the Feathered Serpent] (1957).

Other writers of juvenile novels who occasionally included mild fantasy elements in their works included Henriette Robitaillie with *Le Château des Malices* [The Castle of Tricks] (1945), *Contes des Bois et de la Lande* [Tales of Woods and Moors] (1949), *Le Secret de l'Oeil Jaune* [The Secret of the Yellow Eye] (1949) and *Le Monstre des Abîmes* [The Monster from the Abyss] (1951). She was also the author of the juvenile series *Norr le Mystérieux* [Norr the Mysterious] (1957).

Mainstream romance novelist Guy des Cars penned the delightful *Mon Ami Touche-à-Tout* [My Friend Touches-Everything] (1946), a children's fantasy in which a boy invokes a pantheon of modern muses and fairies (for electricity, science, etc.).

Also worthy of note were:

Belgian writer Jean-Claude Alain, with his five-volume light fantasy series devoted to the exploits of *Mikhaïl*, Prince of Hallmark (1953-55).

Jean-François Pays, with his three-volume series, *Sous le Signe de Rome* [Under the Mark of Rome] (1961-63), featured a young Gaul boy named Loic and a young Roman boy named

Marcus (the future emperor Marcus-Aurelius) chase after a sacred bull called Toukaram.

Pierre Debresse, with *Samorix et le Rameau d'Or* [Samorix and the Golden Branch] (1965) and *Le Trésor de Carthage* [The Treasure of Carthage] (1967) were notable historical fantasies.

X. B. Leprince, with the medieval fantasy series, *La Quête Fantastique* [The Fantastic Quest] (1969). The author also penned several juvenile adventure novels, many with mild fantasy elements, such as *Le Tesbi de Nacre* [The Mother of Pearl Tesbi] (1958) and *Le Crapaud d'Ambre Jaune* [The Yellow Amber Toad] (1965).

Michel Peyramaure, with novels such as *La Vallée des Mammouths* [The Valley of the Mastodons] (1966), *Les Colosses de Carthage* [The Colossus of Carthage] (1967), *La Citadelle Ardente* [The Fiery Citadel] (1978), *La Tête du Dragon* [The Dragon's Head] (1978), *Quand Surgira l'Étoile Absinthe* [When the Absinthe Star Rises] (1980), *La Porte Noire* [The Black Gate] (1985) and *La Chair et le Bronze* [The Flesh and the Bronze] (1985).

Serge Dalens was one of the editors and most popular writers of the *Signe de Piste* imprint, for which he contributed collections of fantastic tales such as *Les Contes du Bourreau* [Tales of the Executioner] (1955) and *2 + 2 font... 5* [2+2 = 5] (1969), as well as two popular series, the medieval adventures of Prince Éric, starting in 1957 with *Le Bracelet de Vermeil* [The Vermillion Bracelet] (1937) and *Les Enquêtes du Chat-Tigre* [The Tiger-Cat Investigates], a series of juvenile investigations, co-written with Jean-Louis Foncine under the pseudonym of "Mik Fondal".

Finally, with *Les Exploits de Fantômette* [The Exploits of Fantômette] published in 1961 by the *Bibliothèque Rose*, Georges Chaulet created one of the most popular and endearing characters in modern juvenile fiction. Fantômette is a masked teenage girl whose real name is Françoise Dupont. With the help of her two goofy but well-intentioned friends, Boulotte and Ficelle, she thwarts criminals and evil-doers everywhere. Her adventures are liberally sprinkled throughout with fantasy and science fiction elements. The *Fantômette* series continued for over fifty volumes, the last one being published in the 2000s. It also spun off a popular television and animated series and a comic-book.

Belgian Fantastique

During the 1950s and 1960s, Belgian *fantastique* was dominated by the existence of the *Marabout* imprint of Belgian publisher Gérard. *Marabout* began in the late 1940s as a general literature and non-fiction paperback imprint. In 1953, they began publishing a line of juvenile adventure novels featuring the famous *Bob Morane* adventure series by Henri Vernes, and *Nick Jordan*, a spy series by André Fernez.

By 1960, *Marabout* was publishing new editions of classic stories by Alexandre Dumas, Edgar Allan Poe and, a year later, Jean Ray, the latter with his famous collection, *25 Histoires Noires et Fantastiques* [25 Dark and Fantastic Tales] (1961). Its considerable success led to more reprints of classic genre works by Eugène Sue, Paul Féval, Ponson du Terrail, Frédéric Soulié, Gérard de Nerval, Théophile Gautier, Erckmann-Chatrian, as well as translations of Bram Stoker, Mary Shelley, Hanns Heinz Ewers, Matthew Lewis and Charles-Robert Maturin, establishing *Marabout* as the first popular paperback *fantastique* imprint.

More Jean Ray titles followed, reprints as well as new collections such as *Le Carrousel des Malefices* [The Spellbound Merry-Go-Round] (1964) and *Les Contes Noirs du Golf* [Dark Tales of Golf] (1964). Between 1961 and 1966, *Marabout* published eight Ray volumes and then embarked on a reprinting of the *Harry Dickson* series that lasted for sixteen volumes.

They also published collections by Michel de Ghelderode, Franz Hellens, Marcel Béalu, André Pieyre de Mandiargues and several volumes of Claude Seignolle stories.

Another author reprinted by *Marabout* was poet Marcel Thiry who had published some genre poetry in the 1920s. His collection of fantastic tales, *Nouvelles du Grand Possible* [Tales of the Great Possible], was published by *Marabout* in 1949 and reprinted in 1967.

Marabout also published "Thomas Owen" (a pseudonym of Gérald Bertot) The name "Thomas Owen". The name first appeared as that of a policeman in *Ce Soir, Huit Heures* [Tonight At 8] (1941), a mystery thriller with some mild genre undertone, written by Bertot under the pseudonym of "Stéphane Rey". Bertot, now writing as "Owen", introduced his amateur detective character, *Madame Aurelia*, in *Destination Inconnue* [Destination Unknown] (1941). *Madame Aurelia* appeared in *Un Crime Swing* [A Swing Crime] (1942), L'Or Indigo [Indigo Gold] (written in 1942 but published only in 1995) and *Hôtel Meublé* [Furnished Hotel] (1943).

Owen's first true genre books were *Initiation à la Peur* [Initiation to Fear] (1942) and *Les Chemins Étranges* [The Strange Paths] (1943), the latter a collection of fantastic tales. All of his subsequent books, except one mainstream novel, *Les Grandes Personnes* [The Adults] (1954), were fantastic collections: *La Cave aux Crapauds* [The Toad Cave] (1945), *Pitié pour les Ombres* [Mercy for the Shadows] (1961), *Cérémonial Nocturne* [Night Ceremonies] (1966), *La Truie* [The Sow] (1972), and *Le Rat Kavar* [Kavar the Rat] (1975). Owen is also the author of two genre novels: *Le Livre Interdit* [The Forbidden Book] (1944) and *Le Jeu Secret* [The Secret Game] (1950).

In Owen's stories, the focus is on fear itself. It is the ultimate expression of despair that the characters face when they finally succumb to supernatural events beyond mortal comprehension. Throughout his works, the author used the same style and methods that he used when he was writing Agatha Christie-like detective novels: an objective, methodical approach, starting with ordinary, mundane events, such as marital discord or business disputes, and then bringing in not a murder but a vampire, or a ghoul, or a ghost seeking revenge from beyond the grave.

Meanwhile, during this period, Franz Hellens continued to be one of Belgium's most prolific genre contributors with *Contes Choisis* [Selected Tales] (1956), *Les Yeux du Rêve* [The Eyes of the Dream] (1964), *Herbes Méchantes* [Bad Herbs] (1964) and *Le Dernier Jour du Monde* [The Last Day of the World] (1967).

Another prolific author whose career had begun before the war was Robert Poulet with *L'Enfer-Ciel* [The Heaven-Hell] (1952), *La Lanterne Magique* [The Magic Lantern] (1956) and *Les Sources de la Vie* [The Sources of Life] (1967).

New Belgian genre authors who appeared during the 1950s and 1960s included Monique Watteau, who made a remarkable beginning with *La Colère Végétale* [The Vegetable Wrath] (1954), a novel about the revolt of the vegetable kingdom. The author's subsequent novels, such as *La Nuit aux Yeux de Bête* [The Night with Eyes of Beasts] (1956), *L'Ange à Fourrure* [The Angel With Fur] (1958) or *Luciferian - Je Suis le Ténébreux* [I Am The Dark One] (1962), all expanded on the theme of metamorphosis and devolution, creating strange interactions between man and animal, and animal and vegetal. In her works, devolution is not a fall from grace from the presumably superior status of humanity, a mere degenerescence, but on the contrary a wonderful transformation from one state into another, that can be interpreted as a liberation, a transition towards a new form of happiness.

Anne Richter (not to be confused with the French-Canadian writer) liked to blur the boundaries between men and animals. Her first collection, *La Fourmi a fait le Coup* [The Ant Did It] (1955), established the interdependence of all living things. The passage from one form to another was also depicted as a liberation. In another collection, *Les Locataires* [The Tenants] (1967), she showed that the *fantastique* is only a natural extension of reality, and there can be no happiness unless one submits willingly to the supernatural.

A writer obsessed with the triumph of the *fantastique* over the mundane was Jean Muno, whose classic novel, *L'Hipparion* (1962), set the stage for a confrontation between the imaginary and the real, not to the latter's advantage. His subsequent works, such as *L'Homme qui s'efface* [The Man Who Disappeared] (1963), and two later collections of short stories, *Histoires Singulières* [Singular Tales] (1979) and *Histoires Griffues* [Clawed Tales] (1985), only continued to explore this theme.

This notion of imagining other forms of reality is a recurrent theme in the Belgian *fantastique*. Two more examples are *Octobre, Long Dimanche* [October, Long Sunday] (1957), in which writer Guy Vaes imagined the plight of a man whose rhythm of life is so different that it is no longer possible for him to speak or even see his surroundings; and *La Longueur du Temps* [The Length of Time] (1968), in which author Albert Dasnoy, with great stylistic precision, studied the notion of schizoid realities.

Other notable Belgian authors of the period included:

Raymond Mottart, with *Bételgeuse* (1956).

José Hervyns, with *Cette Race Indécrottable* [That Incorrigible Race] (1956).

Paul Bay, with *Descendit aux Enfers* [Descending to Hell] (1958), in which Jesus visits a futuristic hell which is portrayed as a science fiction Metropolis.

Bernard Manier, with *Histoires d'Ailleurs et de Nulle Part* [Tales of Elsewhere and Nowhere] (1961).

Pierre Nothomb, with *Le Prince du Dernier Jour* [The Prince of the Last Day] (1960) and *Les Miracles* [The Miracles] (1962).

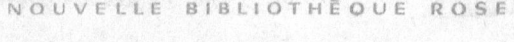

NOUVELLE BIBLIOTHÈQUE ROSE

FANTÔMETTE
CONTRE LE GÉANT

PAR
GEORGES CHAULET

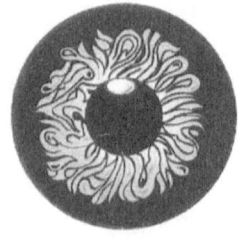

terreur en plein
soleil

B.-R. BRUSS
super luxe fleuve noir

The 1970s

The political and sociological upheavals caused by the notorious "events" of May 1968 created a virtual cultural revolution and a sharp shift to the left in France's cultural scene. Beginning in May 1968, a period of civil unrest occurred throughout France, lasting some seven weeks and punctuated by demonstrations, general strikes, as well as the occupation of universities and factories. At the height of events, the economy came to a halt. The protests reached such a point that political leaders feared civil war or revolution; the national government briefly ceased to function after President Charles de Gaulle secretly fled to West Germany. The protests inspired a generation of art in the form of films (e.g.: François Truffaut's *Baisers volés* and Jean-Luc Godard's *Tout Va Bien*), songs, graffiti, poster art, and books.

This period of transformation ended in the early 1980s, after the full impact of the Left's election to power in 1981, a factor which paradoxically broke its stranglehold on culture.

Fantastique Populaire

The *Angoisse* imprint of Éditions Fleuve Noir continued publishing horror novels until 1974, and was then followed by their *Horizons de l'Au-Delà* [*Horizons From Beyond*] imprint, which mostly reprinted earlier titles, until 1985. Among the authors introduced in *Angoisse* during its last few years were a number of distinguished science fiction writers from the *Anticipation* imprint who dabbled with horror, such as:

G.-J. Arnaud, who penned such classics as *Le Dossier Atrée* [The Atreus File] (1972) and *La Dalle aux Maudits* [The Slab of the Accursed] (1974). The author later became one of the leading contributors to Anticipation with his *Ice Company* series (see *The Handbook of French Science Fiction*). He had previously written a dozen mysteries for Hachette (1952-54), Ferenczi (1959-60) and L'Arabesque (1972-79), using the pseudonyms of "Saint-Gilles" and "Georges Murey", and over seventy-five novels for Fleuve Noir *Special-Police* imprint (1960-88). These mysteries were often very gothic, featuring pseudo-fantasy elements, and a deep sense of paranoia and unreality. Their protagonists were often women trapped in unrelentingly evil schemes. They were influenced by the writings of Georges Simenon and the films of Hitchcock. Some of Arnaud's thrillers could easily be labeled as *fantastique*.

"Paul Béra" (a pseudonym of Paul Bérato), also well known in science fiction under the other pseudonym of "Yves Dermèze", chronicled the adventures of *Léonox*, starting with *Léonox, Monstre des Ténèbres* [Leonox, Monster of Darkness] in 1971. The character subsequently appeared in five more novels, the last, *L'Être Mystérieux* [The Mysterious Being] under the pseudonym of "John Luck" published in 1977 for the short-lived fantasy series of the *Le Masque* imprint of the Librairie des Champs-Élysées. The series featured the adventures of humans who are the agents of rival supernatural powers beyond human ken.

Other *Angoisse* writers included:

Pierre Pelot, writing under the pseudonym of "Pierre Suragne", with *La Peau de l'Orage* [The Skin of the Storm] (1973), *Duz* (1973) and *Je suis la Brume* [I Am the Mist] (1974).

Jean-Pierre Andrevon, writing under the pseudonym of "Alphonse Brutsche", with *Un Froid Mortel* [A Deadly Cold] (1971) and *Le Reflux de la Nuit* [The Reflux of Night] (1972).

"Max-André Rayjean" (a pseudonym of Jean Lombard), with six novels featuring the occult detective Henri Gil, including *Dans les Griffes du Diable* [In the Clutches of the Devil] (1971) and *La Malédiction des Vautours* [The Curse of the Vultures] (1972).

Gabriel Jan, with *Au Seuil de l'Enfer* [On the Threshold of Hell] (1973) and one more novel.

Dominique Rocher, with ten novels, including *Les Voyances du Docteur Basile* [The Visions of Dr. Basile] (1970).

"Agnès Laurent" (a pseudonym of Hélène Simart), with six novels including *Le Sang des Étoiles* [The Blood of the Stars] (1973).

"Michel Saint-Romain" (a pseudonym of André Rocher, Dominique's husband), with four novels including *Le Monstre de Mes Nuits* [The Monster of My Nights] (1971) and *L'Enfant Muet* [The Dumb Child] (1972).

"Anthony Feek" (a pseudonym of Auguste Franco), with two novels including *Cimetière pour Femme Seule* [Cemetery foer a Single Woman] (1974).

"Éric Verteuil" (a pseudonym of the writing team of Alain Bernier & Roger Maridat), with *Au bout... la Mort* [In the End... Death] (1973).

Chris Burger, with two novels, *Incubation* (1974) and *Le Sorcier* [The Wizard] (1975).

Conversely, the first writer to have introduced horror to the *Anticipation* was Robert Clauzel, whose brand of horror relied on a mixture of Lovecraftian-like forces from beyond and Dean Koontz-like scientific projects. In *L'Horreur Tombée du Ciel* [The Horror That Fell from the Sky] (1971), an alien germ threatens to engulf Earth; in *La Terrible Expérience de Peter Home* [The Dreadful Experiment of Peter Home] (1973), the experiments of a modern-day Prometheus might destroy the world; in *Le Nuage qui Vient de la Mer* [The Cloud Which Came from the Sea] (1974), mysterious aliens manipulate a small corner of England to test our ability to deal with incomprehensible cosmic forces released accidentally in our universe.

Other horror imprints of the 1970s included:

La Bibliothèque de l'Étrange [*The Library of the Strange*], published by Galliéra.

Terrific, published by Monnet, which released works by Agnès Laurent, a series of horror thriller by "Maïk Vegor" (a pseudonym of Jacques Coutela), as well as a series of novels by Maurice Périsset, a writer whose genre career spanned several decades, from his classic *Les Eaux Noires* [The Black Waters] (1946) to *Le Jeu de Satan* [The Game of Satan] (1972) and *Le Visage Derrière la Nuit* [The Face Behind the Night] (1973).

Mémoires d'Outre Ciel [Memoirs from Beyond the Sky], published by Garry from 1979 to 1982. Its catalog included several genre novels by authors such as:

Jacques Hurtaud's *La Révolte des Arbres* [The Revolt of the Trees] (1979) and *Ombre* [Shadow] (1979).

Bastien Dorion's *Le Fantôme de Sang* [The Phantom of Blood] (1980) and *Les Orgues de l'Infini* [The Organs of Infinity] (1982).

Jean Scapin's *La Maison du Frisson* [House of Shivers] (1982).

Jean Mauhourat's *Le Singe Jaune* [The Yellow Monkey] (1982).

Plus books by Belgian writer Jean Sadyn (see below), Robert Clauzel (under the pseudonym of "Roy Morrisson"), Gabriel Jan (under the pseudonym of "Yann Delmon"), Maurice Limat (under the pseudonym of "Lionel Rex"), and others.

Finally, one should include here a series of horror thrillers such as *La Baie des Trépassés* [The Bay of the Trespassed] (1973) and *Robinson Cruauté* [Robinson Cruelty] (1974) written by Catherine Arley and published by Eurédif in the mid-1970s.

Fantastique Littéraire

The "events" of 1968 were indeed reflected in French literature, with the publishing of left-wing ideological novels, feminist books and post-*nouveau roman* works. Traditional fantastic subjects (such as vampires, ghosts, etc.) were increasingly relegated to the field of popular literature or used for satirical purposes.

The New Surrealists

A number of authors, generally considered to be mainstream writers, continued to follow in the footsteps of the Surrealists, and wrote what would otherwise be considered genre novels, published by mainstream houses.

One of the very best was Georges-Olivier Châteaureynaud who displayed the combined influences of both Borges and Kafka. His works were remarkable because of their macabre beauty and romantic nature. In *Les Messagers* [The Messengers] (1974), two men, a master and his disciple, carry a mysterious message to a no less mysterious recipient and undergo several severe trials in their strange journey. Eventually, the Master dies and the Disciple is expected to carry on without ever learning the purpose of his mission. Explanations are not necessary for they would destroy this fine allegory. *La Belle Charbonnière* [The Beautiful Coal Lady] (1976) was a collection of pseudo-medieval legends, one about eternal youth, the other challenging the very concept of gravity. *Le Verger* [The Orchard] (1978) took place in a mysterious concentration camp; there, a child finds a path to a secret orchard that only he can reach, but he eventually chooses to die with the other inmates rather than suffer the curse of being alone in his private paradise. Another notable work of the period was *Mathieu Chain* (1978).

Another remarkable author in this neo-surrealist category was Michel Tournier who, in *Vendredi, ou Les Limbes du Pacifique* [Friday, or Limbo of the Pacific] (1967), rewrote the classic novel *Robinson Crusoe*. Here, Friday is the incarnated double of Robinson, the fruit of his union with the Land. Robinson becomes like Prospero, and Friday serves as his Ariel— or Caliban. The author continued to display his amazing blend of myth and parable in *Le Roi des Aulnes* [The King of the Elms] (1970), *Pierrot ou les Secrets de la Nuit* [Pierrot, or The

Secrets of the Night] (1979) and *Le Vol du Vampire* [The Vampire's Flight] (1981), using classic images to propose a new place for man in the universe. In his works, we exist between myth and reality, and legends can only help us find our place in the cosmic order.

The fantastic works of Hubert Haddad also relied on revisited mythology, but in a more explicit and romantic fashion: *Un Rêve de Glace* [A Dream of Ice] (1974), *La Cène* [The Last Supper] (1975), *Les Grands Pays Muets* [The Great Silent Countries] (1978), *La Rose de Damoclès* [The Rose Of Damocles] (1982) and *Les Effrois* [The Fears] (1983) are among his most notable works.

Another author whose works re-examined the fundaments of mythology was Jean Cayrol, with his series *Histoire d'une Prairie* [Tale of a Field] (1969), *Histoire d'un Désert* [Tale of a Desert] (1972), *Histoire de la Mer* [Tale of the Sea] (1973), *Histoire de la Forêt* [Tale of a Forest] (1975), *Histoire d'une Maison* [Tale of a House] (1976) and *Histoire du Ciel* [Tale of the Sky] (1979).

The tradition of the absurdist novel inherited from the surrealists could be found in the works of Jean-Marie Le Clézio, the author of surreal novels such as *Haï* (1971), *Les Géants* [The Giants] (1973), which is set in a nightmarish shopping center, *Voyages de l'Autre Côté* [Journeys to the Other Side] (1975), in which the hero undergoes various metamorphoses before being transported into another universe, and *L'Inconnu sur la Terre* [The Unknown Man on Earth] (1978). The author's works displayed an amazing ability to translate madness and aberrations in mundane terms, and open windows into other realities.

Among other writers published by mainstream houses who incorporated into their works elements belonging to the surreal or the *fantastique* were:

Jean-Charles Rémy, with *La Randonnée* [The Journey] (1970) and *L'Arborescence* (1977), in which a bureaucrat is slowly metamorphosed into a sequoia, also displayed influences ranging from both Borges to Matheson.

Claude Louis-Combet, with *Infernaux Paluds* [Infernal Paluds] (1970) and *Voyage au Centre de la Ville* [Voyage to the Center of Town] (1974).

Maurice Pons, who mastered the art of blending the surrealist approach with the classic themes of the *fantastique* in *Rosa* (1967), which features a prostitute who magically dispatches all her unhappy clients into her womb; *Mademoiselle B.* (1973), a surreal vampire story, and *La Maison des Brasseurs* [The Brewers' House] (1978), where each chapter ends with the description of a painting in which the action takes place.

Patrick Ravignant, with *Idiot Cherche Village (Le Livre du Chaos)* [Idiot Seeks Village (The Book of Chaos)] (1976), an apocalyptic novel filled with philosophical questions, depicting an esoteric quest which becomes a battle for the ultimate truth; *La Comtesse des Ténèbres* [The Countess of Darkness] (1979); and *Les Empires Secrets de Napoléon* [Napoleon's Secret Empires] (1979).

Mario Mercier, one of the editors of the magazine *Horizons du Fantastique*, who also directed two genre films, *La Goulve* (1971) and *La Papesse* (1974), wrote three novels mixing classic genre themes such as vampires and necrophilia with erotic and esoteric elements: *La Cuvée de Singes* [A Bucketful of Monkeys] (1970), *Le Nécrophile* (1970), and *L'Odyssée Fantastique d'Arthur Dément* [Arthur Dement's Fantastic Odyssey] (1976).

Syrian-born Kamal Ibrahim, with *Celui-ci, Celui-moi* [This One, This Me] (1971), *Corps en Friche* [Fallow Bodies] (1974) and *Le Voyage de Cent Mètres* [The 100-Meter Journey] (1979).

Gilbert Lascault, with *Un Monde Mimé* [A Mimed World] (1975), *Voyage d'Automne et d'Hiver* [Travel in Autumn and Winter] (1979), *Destinée de Jean-Simon Castor* [The Destiny of Jean-Simon Castor] (1981), *420 Minutes dans la Cité des Ombres* [420 Minutes in The City of Shadows] (1988) and *Enfers Bouffons ou la Nuit de Satan Dément* [Jesting Hells, or The Night of the Mad Satan] (1996).

Finally, Pierre Gripari continued to produce a series of remarkably surreal books, such as a wonderful collection of genre stories, *L'Arrière-Monde* [The Backworld] (1972), and the novel *Gueule d'Aminche* (1973), a translation of the Gilgamesh story as a gangster saga set in a fictional Mediterranean republic. Other notable books of the period included *Rêveries d'un Martien en Exil* [Dreams of a Martian in Exile] (1976) and *Pedigree du Vampire* [Pedigree of the Vampire] (1977).

Other Mainstream Authors

Writers who simply sought to modernize classic genre themes included:

Jacques Sadoul, with his trilogy of the *Domain of R.*, comprised of *La Passion Selon Satan* [The Passion According To Satan] (1960), *Le Jardin de la Licorne* [The Garden of the Unicorn] (1977) and *Les Hautes Terres du Rêve* [The High Country of Dreams] (1979), which drew its inspiration from a variety of classic sources, ranging from Lovecraft to the author's notorious knowledge of alchemy and sorcery.

Writer/filmmaker Pierre Kast, with a classic vampire novel *Les Vampires de l'Alfama* [The Vampires of the Alfama] (1975), originally a film project and one of the first modern vampire novels to present vampires as romantic heroes.

Yves Olivier-Martin, with *Isolina* (1968).

Hubert Monteilhet, with *Les Pavés du Diable* [The Devil's Cobblestones] (1970), *Non-Sens* [Nonsense] (1971), *Les Bourreaux de Cupidon* [Cupid's Executioners] (1972), *Esprit, es-tu la?* [Spirit, Are You There?] (1977), *Un Métier de Fantôme* [A Ghostly Business] (1979) and *Les Queues de KallInaos* [The Tails of the KallInaos] (1981).

Michel Treignier, with *Spectrales* (1974) and *Le Chemin des Abîmes* [The Path to the Abyss] (1976), published by *Marabout*.

Pierre-Jean Rémy, whose *Une Figure dans la Pierre* [A Figure in Stone] (1976), *Cordélia, ou l'Angleterre* [Cordelia, or England] (1979) and *Pandora* (1980) were modern gothic fantasies.

Henri Gougaud, with *Départements et Territoires d'Outre-Mort* [Departments and Territories Beyond Death] (1977).

Paul Wagner's poetic *L'Enfant et les Magiciens* [The Child and the Sorcerers] (1977), in which a couple of sorcerers attempt to transplant the soul of their deceased child into the body of an orphan.

Jacques Hamelink, with *Horror Vacui* (1970), a collection of horror tales.

Corsican writer Jean-Claude Rogliano, whose *Le Berger des Morts* [The Shepherd of the Dead] was a classic Corsican gothic novel written directly in Corsican in 1975 (under the title *Mal'Concilio*) and translated and published in French in 1980.

Pierre Ferran with *Sans Tambour Ni Trompette* [With Neither Drum Nor Trumpet] (1979) struck an original note.

Finally, in a satirical vein, Claude Klotz, also a mainstream writer of note under the pseudonym of "Patrick Cauvin", wrote a modern, satirical prehistoric novel, *Les Innommables* [The Unmentionables] (1971), and a remarkably funny novel about Dracula being forced to move to Paris and become a horror film star, *Paris-Vampire* (1974). The latter was made into a 1976 feature film entitled *Dracula Père et Fils*, starring Christopher Lee. Another notable genre novel was *Les Aventures Fabuleuses d'Anselme Levasseur* [The Fabulous Adventures of Anselme Levasseur] (1976).

Female Authors

Female authors continued to excel in the traditional realms of the *fantastique*.

Pierrette Fleutiaux's works were praised by Julio Cortazar, who wrote an introduction to one of her collections.

These included *Histoire du Gouffre et de la Lunette* [The Story of the Pit and the Spyglass] (1967), *Histoire de la Chauve-Souris* [The Story of the Bat] (1975), *Histoire du Tableau* [The Story of a Painting] (1977) and *Métamorphoses de la Reine* [Metamorphosis of the Queen] (1984), In her stories, reality is ultimately less fulfilling than the darkness, which must be embraced. Her revisited fairy tales were dark, erotic, full of strange things waiting for the opportunity to grab us. She has often been compared to Kafka and Poe.

Gabrielle Wittkop also displayed a fine taste for the morbid and clinical horror in books such as *Le Nécrophile* (1972) and *La Mort de C. Christian* [The Death of C. Christian] (1975). Later works included *Les Rajahs Blancs* [The White Rajahs] (1986), *Hemlock* (1988) and the collection, *Les Départs Exemplaires* [Exemplary Departures] (1996).

Jehanne Jean-Charles wrote a number of Poe-inspired stories collected in *Les Plumes du Corbeau* [The Raven's Feathers] (1973), *La Mort, Madame* [Death, Madam] (1974) and *Vous avez dit Horrible?* [Did You Say Awful?] (1980).

Jeanne Champion chronicled the supernatural events happening in a small French village in *Vautour-en-Privilège* [Vulture-In-Privilege] (1973), hallucinatory remembrances of things past in *Dans les Jardins d'Esther* [In Esther's Garden] (1975) and penned a remarkable gothic murder mystery taking place in a monastery in *Les Gisants* [The Tombs] (1977).

Yvonne Caroutch wrote literary genre novels suffused with esoteric themes, such as *Le Gouvernement des Eaux* [The Government of Waters] (1970) and *La Voie au Coeur de Verre* [The Way of the Heart of Glass] (1972).

In the same vein, Sarane Alexandrian with *L'Oeuf du Monde* [The Egg of the World] (1975) contemplated the ability of the human mind to control space and time. Also notable was her *Les Terres Fortunées du Songe* [Dream's Happy Lands] (1979).

Odile Marcel made a mark with the poetic *L'Eau qui Dort* [Sleeping Water] (1977) and *L'Amazonie* (1981).

Finally, Suzy Morel blended legends and romanticism with such intimate novels as *L'Enfant Cavalier* [The Child Rider] (1977), *Les Pas d'Orphée* [Orpheus' Steps] (1982), *Le Chemin des Loups* [The Wolves' Path] (1985) and *L'Office des Ténèbres* [The Office of Darkness] (1989).

In addition to Nathalie C. Henneberg and Julia Verlanger already mentioned, other notable female authors of the period included: Christia Sylf, with her collection *La Patte de Chat* [The Cat's Paw] (1974), Nicole Avril and Claire Bonnafé, who will all be reviewed under Fantasy below.

Fantasy

Christia Sylf's novels were a breath of pure fresh airt in the relatively new domain of heroic-fantasy. *Kobor Tigan't* (1969) and its sequel, *Le Règne de Ta* [The Reign of Ta] (1971), took place thirty thousand years ago, during the reign of the Giants, a mythical pre-Atlantean race which preceded ours. The novel told of the conflict between the sorcerous Queen-Mother, Abim, and her daughters Opak, who rules Kobor Tigan't, the five-leveled City of the Giants, and her sister, Ta. The world of Kobor Tigan't is inhabited by a race of reptilian bisexual humanoids, the T'los, who are used as sex slaves by the Giants. The novels also features the crystal-like Elohim, messengers of mysterious alien powers, dragons, and a host of other fantastic creatures. The *Kobor Tigan't* novels are clearly fantasy, yet are hard to compare to anything published in England or America, before or after. They contain numerous erotic scenes as well as esoteric elements that one rarely finds in the more literary worlds of Tolkien or the savagery of *Conan*. They are written in a rich, colorful prose, and even include a glossary of the language of the Giants.

Sylf continued her saga with *Markosamo le Sage* [Markosamo the Wise] (1973), this time with a story featuring the reincarnations of all her principal characters, but taking place twenty thousand years ago, during the age of Atlantis. A fourth volume, *La Reine au Coeur Puissant* [The Strong-Hearted Queen] (1979), carried on with a tale taking place in Ancient China two thousand years ago. The author had announced the publication of five more volumes in her series: *La Geste d'Amoïnen* [The Saga of Amoinen], taking place in Nordic Finland; *Amiona la Courtisane* [Amiona the Courtesan], taking place in Renaissance Venice; *Ertulie de Fons l'Abîme* [Ertulia of Fons-l'Abîme], taking place during the reign of the Louis XIV; and the two-volume *L'Apocalypse de Kébélé* [Kebele's Apocalypse], featuring her immortal narrator and taking place in the far future. Unfortunately, these works were never published due to the author's passing away in 1980.

Charles Duits belonged to the same rich and colorful tradition of fantasy world-building as Flaubert and Sylf. With *Ptah Hotep* (1971) and *Nefer* (1978), the author wrote a prodigious fantasy saga taking place on a parallel Earth with two moons—Athenade and Thana—during the time of Ancient Egypt and the Roman Empire. *Ptah Hotep* was the story of the ascension of a young prince to the throne of Caesar. *Nefer*, which takes place several centuries later, tells of the adventures of a young Egyptian priest who falls in love with a sacred prostitute. The supernatural was featured discreetly in the novels, but was an integral part of the author's intensely spiritual "otherworld" rather than an artificial literary device to be exploited for cheap thrills. Even the erotic passages were an integral part of the magic. Duits was a friend of André Breton and the Surrealists. A gifted poet and a man who had experimented with peyote, he was also influenced by *The Thousand And One Nights* and the Indian *Ramayana*. *Ptah Hotep* and *Nefer* are prodigious descriptions of alternate realities, comparable to no other fantasy works in the Anglo-Saxon tradition.

Jean Tur created a Polynesian-like world of island empires, lost on a vast Pacific-like ocean, in a world that never was. In his series, *Memoirs of the Arkonn Tecla*, that began with *L'Archipel des Guerrières* [The Archipelago of the Warrior-Women] (1973) and continued with *La Harpe des Forces*

[The Harp of Power] (1974) and *Sterne Dorée* [Golden Sterne] (1976), the author narrated in painstaking detail the story of a peace expedition led by the Arkonn Tecla, a warrior prince of the Mavae Empire, who has been sent to the neighboring Aginn Archipelago to cement an alliance. The Aginn turned out to be fierce Amazon-like women, and by the end of the third volume, Tecla had only begun entreaties with them. The sea-faring world created by the author—perhaps the lost Empire of Mû?—owed nothing to the modern world as we know it. The first-person narration device is both poetic and epic, with many erotic scenes devoted to Tecla's tumultuous love life. As with Duits, the role of magic here is sparse, the supernatural powers manifesting themselves during a religious ceremony in the form of a celestial harp.

Yves and Ada Rémy wrote a baroque and colorful type of fantasy. In their collection, *Les Soldats de la Mer* [The Soldiers from the Sea] (1968), and their novel, *Le Grand Midi* [The Great South] (1971), they chronicled the tales of a mysterious neverland dubbed the "Federation", through its myths, legends and military history.

Another author that dabbled with fantasy was Christian Charrière, who wrote novels that would fit well between the high fantasy of a William Morris and the Symbolist literature of the previous century. *L'Enclave* [The Enclave] (1971), *Mayapura* (1973) and *Le Sîmorgh* (1977) were all anachronistic quests taking place in imaginary lands. *Mayapura* is an imaginary city that could just as well be located on Jack Vance's *Dying Earth*. The Simorgh is a colorful bird gifted with the curse of prophecy; whoever follows him, or so say the legends, can, after a perilous journey, find a land of paradise. Both novels created their own supernatural mythology, filled with religious icons, talking skeletons, animated stones giving birth to monsters, and monuments carved with secret symbols.

Other notable literary works of high fantasy written during the decade included:

Nicole Avril's *Les Gens de Misar* [The People of Misar] (1972), about a fantasy city located in an imaginary world.

René Barjavel's collaboration with Olenka de Veer, *Les Dames à la Licorne* [The Ladies of the Unicorn] (1974), and its sequel, *Les Jours du Monde* [The Days of the World] (1977).

Claire Bonnafé's poetic *Le Bruit de la Mer* [The Sound of the Sea] (1978).

Dominique Roche and Charles Nightingale's *Sous l'Araignée du Sud* [Under the Southern Spider] (1978), a fantasy odyssey mixing Tolkienesque and Lovecraftian themes.

Finally, in 1980, the writing team of Marcelle Perriod & Jean-Louis Fraysse, using the pseudonym of "Michel Grimaud", also known for their YAs and science fiction works, penned one magistral high fantasy novel for *Présence du Futur*: *Malakansâr*, sub-titled *L'Éternité des Pierres* [The Eternity of Stones]. It was a literary work of classic fantasy, telling the story of the dramatic quest by three characters for the eponymous mythical city through the Lands of the Morning and the Lands of the Evening.

The 1970s were also when British and American fantasy began to appear in France. Tolkien's *The Hobbit* had been translated in 1967, but had remained generally unnoticed. *The Lord of the Rings* was first published in 1972, but did not immediately impact the field as it had done in England and America. Robert E. Howard's *Conan* had had two volumes published in 1972, but had made no major impact. It was only in 1980 that the *Conan* saga, helped by the release of the 1982 film, became a best-selling phenomenon. More influential were the works of Jack Vance, (the *Cugel* and *Planet of Adventure* sagas), Michael Moorcock's *Elric* (translated in 1969), Philip José Farmer's *World of Tiers* (translated in 1969), and Fritz Leiber's *Fafhrd and Gray Mouser* stories (translated in 1970).

In the early 1970s, under the editorship of Alain Dorémieux, *Fiction*, which had published Vance, Leiber and Farmer, began publishing some heroic-fantasy short stories by French writers Jean-Pierre Fontana and Daniel Walther.

Fontana, using the pseudonym "Guy Scovel", embarked on *La Geste du Halaguen* [The Saga of the Halaguen], a Vance-inspired saga, that was eventually collected in 1975 by *Marabout*. The book described the battle between the brave warrior Silgan and the barbarian chief known only as the "Sequençaire" to protect the Kingdom of Occitanie. The universe it described was more science-fantasy rather than pure sword & sorcery. Silgan's world was eventually revealed to be a huge, star-traveling worldship out of control, and Silgan himself the reincarnation of his pilot. *La Geste du Halaguen* was expanded in 1997 by the author wirth the publication by L'Atalante of *Naalia de Sanar*, a prequel telling the origins of Silgan.

Another regular contributor to *Fiction*, Jean-Pierre Andrevon, wrote *Les Hommes-Machines contre Gandahar* [The Machine Men vs. Gandahar] (1969), another science-fantasy also owing much to Vance taking place on the colorful, peaceful world of Gandahar. Gandahar is a lost Earth colony inhabited by a gentle medieval society which uses ecologically-friendly technology. In the novel, Gandahar is invaded by robotic Machine Men who turn out to have been sent from its future. The heroic Sylvin Lanvere, Queen Ambisextra's knight, saves the day. The novel became the basis for the eponymous 1987 animated feature by René Laloux, released in the United States as *Lightyears*. The author returned to the colorful world of Gandahar with *Gandahar et l'Oiseau-Monde* [*Gandahar and the World-Bird*] (1997), published in a YA imprint, in which the planet is revealed to be a giant bird's egg.

At *Anticipation*, Pierre Barbet followed Kurt Steiner's ground-breaking *Ortog et les Ténèbres* [Ortog and the Darkness] (1969) (see above) with *À Quoi Songent les Psyborgs?* [What Do Psyborgs Dream About?] (1971), in which his Galactic Temporal Investigator Setni explored a planet where a trio of powerful, disembodied brains have recreated the fantasy legends of Amadis of Gaul for their own entertainment. The author continued to mine this vein with *La Planète Enchantée*

[The Enchanted Planet] (1973) and *Vénusine* (1977), the latter written under the pseudonym "Olivier Sprigel". He also penned a historical fantasy, *L'Empire du Baphomet* [The Empire of the Baphomet] (1972), in which a stranded alien attempts to manipulate the Templar Knights to take over the world during the Crusades.

Also at *Anticipation*, the writing team of Jean-Louis & Doris Le May flirted with fantasy with *Les Créateurs d'Ulnar* [The Creators of Ulnar] (1972), in which space explorers acquire god-like powers on the planet Ulnar, recreate a fantasy world and end up waging an apocalyptic war.

In 1976, publisher Librairie des Champs-Élysées was the first to offer a short-lived imprint of fantasy novels, with translations of Robert E. Howard, Gardner Fox and Fritz Leiber, as well as reprints of Nathalie C. Henneberg, and two collection of previously published fantasy stories by Julia Verlanger, *Les Portes Sans Retour* [The Gates of No Return] (1976) and *La Flûte de Verre Froid* [The Flute of Cold Glass] (1976).

Under the pseudonym of "Gilles Thomas", Verlanger then contributed the remarkable *Magie Sombre* [Dark Magic] (1977) to Fleuve Noir. In it, an eager young man finds an old book of spells and, after having adapted the spells to replace medieval ingredients with modern ones (the blood of a salamander is replaced with engine oil), he acquires the power to control demons. But he quickly discovers the evil that he has unwittingly unleashed upon the world and must join forces with the benevolent "Lords of the Fern" to banish the demons.

Occult & Esoterism

Esoteric fiction and pseudo-documentary books continued to be a staple of publishing throughout the 1970s. In 1968, Publisher J'ai Lu launched a new paperback imprint entitled *L'Aventure Mystérieuser* [The Mysterious Adventure which eventually would grow to include a total of 183 titles, before being canceled in 1996.

This imprint was devoted to the Occult, UFOs, Esotericism, the enigmas of History such as Templar Knights and secret societies, paranormal phenomena, parapsychology, alchemy, etc. It enjoyed considerable success during the 1970s, as a result of a new wave of interest in fantastic realism. So med olfg the major authors it published included Gérard de Sède, Jacques Bergier, T. Lobsang Rampa, Guy Tarade, Robert Charroux, Charles Berlitz, Ferdinand Ossendowsky, Jean Sendy, Camille Flammarion, Robert Tocquet, Belline, Jacques Sadoul, etc.

Jean Markalé proved to be a worthy successor of Anatole Le Braz with works like *La Tradition Celtique en Bretagne Armoricaine* [Celtic Tradition In Armorican Britanny] (1975), *Histoire Secrète de la Bretagne* [Secret History of Britanny] (1977), *Merlin l'Enchanteur* [Merlin the Enchanter] (1981) and *Le Graal* [The Grail] (1982). The author brought to light not only Celtic myths and legends, but also other myths connected with the Templars, the Cathars and other medieval elements.

Yann Brékilien also continued Le Braz' work on Breton legends with *Récits Vivants de Bretagne* [Living Tales of Britanny] (1979), *La Reine Sauvage* (1980), *Les Cavaliers du Bout du Monde* [The Riders of World's End] (1990) and *Le Druide* [The Druid] (1994).

Finally, Jean-Paul Bourre made his mark on the field with works dealing with witchcraft and magic, such as *Les Sectes Lucifériennes Aujourd'hui* [Luciferian Sects Today] (1978), before contributing more recent works about vampires such as *Dracula et les Vampires* [Dracula and the Vampires] (1981), a fictionalized essay painting vampires as Initiates looking for immortality.

The YAs

Throughout the 1970s, Georges Chaulet continued to produce *Fantômette* novels, as well as several other popular children's and YAs adventure series, such as *Béatrice, Candy, Étincelle, Le Petit Lion* [The Little Lion], *Le Prince Charmant* [Prince Charming], *Les Quatre As* [The Four Aces], most of which contained genre elements, as well as novelizations of *Inspector Gadget*.

René Guillot was another writer who alternated between children's fantasies, such as *Kiriki* (1970) and *L'Extraordinaire Aventure de Messire Renart* [The Extraordinary Adventure of Sir Renart] (1972), and YA adventures, such as *Le Chef au Masque d'Or* [The Chief with a Golden Mask] (1973) and *Le Chevalier Sans Visage* [The Faceless Knight] (1973).

Michèle Angot updated fairy tales with *Les Contes de la Lune Bleue* [Tales of the Blue Moon] (1970), *Les Contes de la Lune Rousse* [Tales of the Rust Moon] (1970) and *La Grotte aux Fées* [The Fairies' Cave] (1971).

Henri Gougaud also combined fairy tales and folk legends with more modern sensibilities in collections such as *Contes de la Huchette* [Tales from the Hutch] (1973), *L'Arbre à Soleil* [The Sun Tree] (1979), *L'Arbre aux Trésors* [The Treasure Tree] (1987), *L'Arbre d'Amour et de Sagesse* [The Tree of Love and Wisdom] (1992).

Philippe Dumas penned several delightful collections of modern fairy tales, such as *Le Professeur Ecrouton-Creton* (1977), *Contes à l'Envers* [Inside-Out Tales] (1977), *La Petite Géante* [The Little Giantess] (1979) and *Ondine au fond de l'Eau* [Ondine Underwater] (1979).

Finally, the success of Pierre Gripari's *Contes de la Rue Broca* [Tales of Broca Street] (1967) led him to embark on a series of modern fairy tales such as *Histoire du Prince Pipo, de Pipo le Cheval et de la Princesse Popi* [Tale of Prince Pipo, Pipo the Horse and Princess Popi] (1976), *Nanasse et Gigantel* (1977), *La Sorcière de la Rue Mouffetard* [The Witch of Mouffetard Street] (1980), *Le Gentil Petit Diable* [The Kind Little Devil] (1980), *La Patrouille du Conte* [The Fairy Tale Patrol] (1983), which easily made him the contemporary equivalent of Marcel Aymé.

In the YA field, "Michel Grimaud" (see above) turned out a number of juvenile fantasies (as well as science fiction novels) such as *Amaury, Chevalier Cathare* [Amaury, Cathar Knight] (1971), *La Ville sans Soleil* [The City Without Sun] (1973), *La Terre des Autres* [The Others' Land] (1973), *Le Peuple de la Mer* [The People of the Sea] (1974) and the prehistoric saga of *Rhôor l'Invincible* [Rhoor the Invincible], published by Alsatia in 1971.

Michel Cosem wrote *Haute Erre* [High Wandering] (1972), *La Chasse Artus* [The Artus Hunt] (1974) and *Alpha de la Licorne* [Alpha of the Unicorn] (1979).

Xavier Armange wrote *L'Arbre de l'An Bientôt* [The Tree of Next Year] (1979).

Belgian Fantastique

In 1969, writer Jean-Baptiste Baronian, himself a noted genre author, took over the editorship of *Marabout* and expanded their *fantastique* imprint by introducing a number of new authors who continued the traditions and styles of Jean Ray and Thomas Owen.

Baronian himself was the author of *Scènes de la Vie Obscure* [Scenes of the Dark Life] (1977) and *Le Diable Vauvert* [The Devil Vauvert] (1979), as well as a number of remarkable anthologies and an authoritative *Panorama de la Littérature Fantastique de Langue Française* [Panorama of Fantastic Literature in the French Language] (1978).

Among the most notable authors published by *Marabout* were:

Gérard Prévot, with *Le Démon de Février* [The February Demon] (1970), *Celui Qui Venait De Partout* [That Which Came from Everywhere] (1973), *La Nuit du Nord* [The Night of the North] (1974) and *Le Spectre Large* [The Large Spectre] (1975). A surrealist writer in the tradition of Sternberg, the author depicted a world where everyday life is *fantastique*. In his universe, dark men moved like grim specters through the cold, wind-swept cities of Flanders. The world order was always susceptible to crumble and be replaced by evil and chaos.

Jean Sadyn, with *La Nuit des Mutants* [The Night of the Mutants] (1970), which straddled science fiction and horror. The author went on to to write *Haute Magie* [High Magic] (1980) and *Cosmos* (1982) for the *Mémoires d'Outre-Ciel* imprint (see above), before eventually turning to spinning yarns derived from Flemish folklore such as *Fables et Contes Flamands* [Fables & Flemish Tales] (1993) and *Flandres Fantastiques* [Fantastic Flanders] (1994).

Gaston Compère, with *La Femme de Putiphar* [Putiphar's Wife] (1975) which sublimated the familiar certainties of ordinary life, then proceeded to destroy them with a sarcastic, laser-sharp wit. The author's vision of what dwells within the human spirit was that of a surgeon of the soul. He also penned *Sept Machines à Rêver* [Seven Dreaming Machines] (1974), a collection of tales where the burlesque competed with derision, in a manner that was equally joyful and scary, scandalous and serious. Later, notable works included *La Constellation du Serpent* [The Constellation of the Snake] (1983) and *Les Eaux de l'Achéron* [The Waters of the Acheron] (1985).

Jean-Paul Raemdonck, with *Han* (1972), a chaotic novel full of arresting images.

Daniel Mallinus, with *Myrtis & Autres Histoires de Nuit & de Peur* [Myrtis & Other Tales of Night & Fear] (1973), a collection of fear stories cleverly reworking classic themes.

Jean-Pierre Bours, with *Celui Qui Pourrissait* [He Who Rots] (1977), a collection of genre stories centered around the theme of searching for one's true identity.

Marabout eventually ceased publication in 1981. Other Belgian fantastique writers of the 1970s included:

Gabriel Deblander, the author of numerous short stories published in *Fiction* in the 1960s and collected in *Le Retour des Chasseurs* [The Return of the Hunters] (1970). The author later penned *L'Oiseau sous la Chemise* [The Bird Under the Shirt] (1976), a novel dealing with ancient folk legends.

Georges Thinès was another notable Belgian author with *L'Oeil de Fer* [The Eye of Iron] (1977) and *Les Objets vous trouveront* [Objects Will Find You] (1979). In his stories, every seemingly ordinary day became a prodigious field of dreams filled with unexpected surprises, impossible probabilities and strangely behaving objects. Later works included *Le Désert d'Alun* [The Alun Desert] (1986) and *La Face Cachée* [The Hidden Face] (1994).

The 1980s & 1990s

The third and last section of the Panorama runs from the early 1980s to the end of the 1990s and of the 20th century.

With the advent of the 1980s, films such as George Romero's *Dawn of the Dead* (1978), John Carpenter's *Halloween* (1978), David Cronenberg's *Scanners* (1981), and many others, as well as cheap Italian "rip-offs" of such works, became a definite influence in shaping the forms of modern French horror fiction. The translation and success of Anglo-Saxon authors such as Stephen King, and Robert E. Howard, Dean Koontz and Clive Barker, as well role-playing games, such as *Dungeons & Dragons*, and R. L. Stine's *Goosebumps* series (*Peur Bleue* in French) had a powerful impact on the French literary marketplace.

Several dedicated popular horror imprints were launched during these two decades:

Fantastique/Science Fiction (1979-88) by Nouvelles Éditions Oswald reprinted classic works by William Hope Hodgson, Abraham Merritt, John Buchan, Talbot Mundy, Robert E. Howard, H. Rider Haggard, Clark Ashton Smith, but also French works by B.-R. Bruss, Marc Agapit, Jean Ray, Jean-Pierre Fontana, and Daniel Walther.

Les Fenêtres de la Nuit [*The Windows of Night*] (1980-83) by Seghers.

Paniques [*Panics*] (1981-86) by Presses de la Cité, which published works by Frank de Felitta, F. Paul Wilson and John Saul.

Épouvante [Horror] (1977-99), *Ténèbres* [Darkness] (1996-2000) and *Fantasy* (1998-ongoing), by J'ai Lu, edited by Jacques Sadoul, which published works by Stephen King, Dean R. Koontz, Peter Blatty and Peter Straub.

Terreur [*Terror*] (1989-2003) by Presses-Pocket, edited by Patrice Duvic, which published works by Thomas Harris, James Herbert, Ramsay Campbell, Dean Koontz, Anne Rice and Graham Masterton, with a few French authors such as Pierre Pelot and Jeanne Faivre d'Arcier.

Spécial Fantastique [*Special Fantastic*] (1987-88) by Albin Michel which translated works by Clive Barker and James Herbert.

Présence du Fantastique [*Presence of the Fantastic*] (1989-98) by Denoël, edited by Jacques Chambon, which published works by Robert Holdstock, Lisa Tuttle, Richard Matheson and K. W. Jeter, and also French authors such as Serge Brussolo, Jean-Marc Ligny, Anne Duguël and a series of anthologies by Alain Dorémieux, entitled *Territoires de l'Inquiétude* [*Territories of Worry*].

French horror novels were mostly published by Éditions Fleuve Noir, first sporadically in the early 1980s in their classic *Anticipation* imprint (Serge Brussolo and Joël Houssin), then in a dedicated imprint called *Gore* started in 1985 by editor Daniel Riche, which also published translations of Herschell Gordon Lewis, Shaun Hutson and Joe Russo. *Gore* was taken over in 1989 by Juliette Raabe, who then edited the short-lived *Angoisses* [*Anguishes*] imprint in 1993-94, which was almost immediately replaced by the *Frayeurs* [*Scares*], edited by writer/filmmaker Jean Rollin from 1994 to 1996.

Another short-lived French horror imprint of the late 1980s was *Media 1000*, which introduced the adventures of Michael Honaker's ghost-busting *Commander Ebnezer Grimes*, whose adventures were later continued at *Anticipation*.

Finally, Serge Brussolo was granted his own horror imprint by publisher Gérard de Villiers from 1990 to 1992.

Fantastique Populaire

If France has its Clive Barker, it is undoubtedly Serge Brussolo, an amazingly prolific writer who has written well over a hundred novels, in various popular genres ranging from science fiction to horror, fantasy, crime, etc. Like filmmaker David Cronenberg, the author appears fascinated by the notion of infinite mutations of the flesh, and like Clive Barker, he displays a dark and radical vision, unafraid of delving into the extremes of pain and organic horror. At *Anticipation*, his horror novels included: *Le Puzzle de Chair* [The Jigsaw of Flesh] (1983), about radical organ transplants; *Les Semeurs d'Abîmes* [The Abyss Sowers] (1983), which took place in the same universe, and was about living, symbiotic tattoos; *La Colère des Ténèbres* [The Wrath of Darkness] (1986), which featured a disease that made human bones as fragile as glass, a werewolf and diamond-hard locusts; *Catacombes* [Catacombs] (1986), the grim story of a mad sculptor and his female model in a haunted house; *Docteur Squelette* [Doctor Skeleton] (1987), also about a mutation of the human bones; *La Nuit du Venin* [The Night of the Poison] (1987), about a carnivorous micro-organism; *Les Animaux Funèbres* [The Funeral Beasts] (1987) and *L'Ombre des Gnomes* [The Shadow of the Gnomes] (1987), both taking place in a sun-baked, Central American village, overrun by necrophagic monkeys.

In his own imprint, Brussolo published a number of powerful, morbid horror novels such as *Cauchemar à Louer* [Nightmare for Rent] (1990), a variation on the *Hell House* theme; *La Meute* [The Pack] (1990), about the crazy son of a mad hunter who sacrifices girls to his father's hunting trophies; *Les Bêtes* [The Beasts] (1990), a gory novel about men turning into animals; *Les Démoniaques* [The Demoniacals] (1991), a superb gothic novel about an ancient, cursed book; *Krucifix* (1990); *Les Emmurés* [Walled Up] (1991); *Les Rêveurs d'Ombre* [The Dreamers of Shadows] (1991); *Le Vent Noir* [The Black Wind] (1991); and *Les Inhumains* [The Inhumans] (1992).

Other Brussolo works included *La Nuit du Bombardier* [The Night of the Bomber] (1989), which takes place in a city haunted by the memory of a a plane which crashed there, killing thousands; the wreck of the plane was, itself, inhabited by a vampiric lifeform; *Boulevard des Banquises* [Ice Shelf Boulevard] (1990), which takes place in a strange city located near the arctic circle, whose sadomasochistic residents once wrecked ships, was about the grisly revenge exacted by their long-dead victims; both were published by Denoël. Other novels works published in Anticipation included *Abîmes* [Abyss] (1993); *De l'Autre Côté du Mur des Ténèbres* [On the Other Side of the Wall of Darkness] (1993), about nightmares breaking through into the real world; and a trilogy entitled *Les Brigades du Chaos* [The Brigades of Chaos] (1995-97), which takes place in a future Los Angeles where the dead have returned to life, and objects are inhabited by strange new life.

Joel Houssin was another prolific writer who began his literary career in the late 1970s with several excellent science-fiction novels. He then became a best-selling author with a series of detective thrillers featuring a tough cop nicknamed the Dobermann. The author's first horror novel published at *Anticipation* was *Angel Felina* (1981), which featured a virus that caused a bloody revolt of animals. *Le Pronostiqueur* [The Handicapper] (1981) begins with a man receiving letters advising him of the winner of tomorrow's races and ends up with the revelation of horrible human experiments. *Lilith* (1982) was about the spirit of a panther-like entity who possessed people and forced them to kill. *Le Chasseur* [The Hunter] (1983) was a monstrous gestalt being created by handicapped children whose home had been destroyed. *Voyeur* (1983) was a Cronenberg-type story in which a new synthetic biological organism infects people, making them commit acts of sexual perversion and cannibalism. Finally, *Les Vautours* [The Vultures] (1984) was a horror thriller about organ transplants.

In 1985, Houssin had two more horror novels published in the *Gore* imprint: *L'Autoroute du Massacre* [Massacre Highway], about a cannibal family which waylaid travelers, as in Wes Craven's *The Hills Have Eyes*, and *L'Écho des Suppliciés* [The Echo of the Tortured], about the terrible, ritual revenge exacted by the dead innocents slaughtered throughout history on the descendants of their torturers.

Both authors won critical recognition and commercial success. Their books caught the media's attention. Their works, which were stylish and original, compared favorably with those of their American and British counterparts. However, the power of their gut-twisting imagery was also what separated them from the literary establishment.

Michel Honaker's first three novels, *Le Démon du Bronx* [The Demon of the Bronx], *D'Argile et de Sang* [Of Clay and Blood] *and La Maison des Cauchemars* [The House of Nightmares], all published in 1988 by *Media 1000*, featured the character of a grim devil-hunter named Commander Ebenezer Graymes. The series was continued at Anticipation with six more titles published in 1990-91. The author also penned an excellent vampire novel, *Terminus Sanglant* [Bloody Terminus], published by *Gore* in 1988.

Thanks to the editorship of Daniel Riche, many other renowned authors contributed to *Gore*. Among these were:

Pascal Marignac, also known under the pseudonyms of "Kââ", "Corsélien" and "Béhémoth" wrote *L'État des Plaies* [The State of the Wounds] (1987) about a cannibal monster; and *Bruit Crissant du Rasoir sur les Os* [The Grating Sound of Razor over Bones] (1988).

"Jean Mazarin", also known under the pseudonyms of "Charles Nécrorian" and "Emmanuel Errer" (all pseudonyms of René-Charles Rey) wrote *Blood Sex* (1985), about a horror writer who needs to kidnap and torture victims in order to fuel his imagination; *Impacts* (1986); and *Skin Killer* (1987), about a serial killer who skinned his victims.

G.-J. Arnaud penned *Le Festin Séculaire* [The Secular Feast] (1985), about a living house feeding on human flesh; and *Grouillements* [The Swarming] (1986), about humans living in symbiosis with worms.

Pierre Pelot, wrote *Aux Chiens Écrasés* [The Run-Over Dogs] (1987).

André Ruellan writing as "Kurt Steiner", penned *Grand Guignol 36-88* (1988).

Christian Vilà, wrote *Clip de Sang* [Bloody Video Clip] (1985) ,about a devil-worshipping rock star; *L'Océan Cannibale* [The Cannibal Ocean] (1987), about an underwater monster; and together with Jean-Pierre Hubert usinfg the pseudonym of "Jean Viluber", *Coupes Sombres* [Dark Cuts] (1987) and *Greffes Profondes* [Deep Grafts] (1990).

Daniel Walther, wrote *La Marée Purulente* [The Foul Tide] (1986), about an evil spirit using leprosy to attack the world.

Jean-Pierre Andrevon, wrote *Cauchemars de Sang* [Bloody Nightmares] (1986), the tale of a bloody revenge.

Claude Ecken, wrote *La Peste Verte* [The Green Plague] (1987), about a mad doctor spreading contagious diseases.

Emmanuel Jouanne teamed up with Jacques Barbéri to pen *Rêve de Chair* [Dream of Flesh] (1988).

Bruno Lecigne teamed up with Sylviane Corgiat and Thierry Bataille to pen the *Immolations* series (1987-88).

The writing team of Alain Bernier and Roger Maridat, who began their career under the pseudonym of "Éric Verteuil" in 1974 in the classic *Angoisse* imprint of Fleuve Noir, moved to *Gore* with *Horreur à Maldoror* [Horror in Maldoror] (1987), about a madwoman who creates a living horror museum. They went on to publish over half-a-dozen novels, including *Monstres sur Commande* [Monsters to Order] (1988), *Les Horreurs de Sophie* [The Horrors of Sophie] (1989) and *Le Tour du Monde en Quatre-Ving Cadavres* [Around the World with Eighty Corpses] (1990).

New authors included:

"Gilles Bergal" (a pseudonym of Gilbert Gallerne), with *Cauchemar à Staten Island* [Nightmares in Staten Island] (1987), about sewer monsters, and *Camping Sauvage* [Savage Camping] (1989).

Yves Ramonet, who used the pseudonym "Axelman", with *La Massacreuse* [The Massacror] (1988), *Aux Morsures Millénaires* [At the Millenial Bites] (1989) and *Dunes Sanglantes* [Bloody Dunes] (1990).

Norbert Moutier, under the pseudonym of "Norbert Mount", with *Neige d'Enfer* [Hellish Snow] (1988) *and L'Équarisseur de Soho* [The Soho Equerry] (1990).

Fétidus, with *La Mort Putride* [Putrescent Death] (1989).

"François Sarkel" (a pseudonym of de Jean-Pol Laselle, who also used the pseudonym of "Brice Tarvel") with *La Chair sous les Ongles* [The Flesh under the Nails] (1990).

"Mort Humann" (a pseudonym of André Jammet), with *Fantôme de Feu* [Ghost of Fire] (1989) and *Horrific Party* (1990).

François Darnaudet and Catherine Rabier with *Collioures Trap* (1989) and *Andernos Trap* (1990).

Gilles Santini, with *Morte Chair* [Dead Flesh] (1989) and *Éventrations* [Disembowelings] (1990), etc.

In 1993, the short-lived *Angoisses* (plural) imprint only published nine novels, by Jean-Pierre Andrevon, Kââ, Jean Mazarin, François Sarkel, Jean Rollin, and "Axelman", plus *Magna Mater* (1994) by Laurent Fétis, about a young girl from Brazil who uses her evil powers to destroy the Earth.

In 1994, Rollin launched the *Frayeurs* imprint, sub-titled a "blood-red series for your white nights", which published such notable authors as:

Rollin himself contributed his pulp-like series, *Les Deux Orphelines Vampires* [The Two Orphan Vampire Girls], which started with the eponymous novel in *Angoisses* in 1993 and continued in *Frayeurs* with Anissa (1994), *Les Voyageuses* [The Travelers] (1995), *Les Pillardes* [The Looters] (1995) and *Les Incendiaires* [The Female Arsonists] (1995).

"Anne Duguël", a prolific children's book author under the pseudonym of "Gudule" (see below) (a pseudonym of Anne Carali), penned *Asylum* (1994), about a child gifted with psychic powers who avenges his parents' murder; *Gargouille* [Gargoyle] (1995), about a catholic girls' school; *Lavinia*

(1995), a mixture of political fiction and horror and *La Baby-Sitter* (1995). She continued her production at *Présence du Fantastique* with *Le Chien qui Rit* [The Laughing Dog] (1995) and *La Petite Fille aux Araignées* [The Little Girl with Spiders] (1995).

Kââ wrote *Criant de Vérité* [Screaming with Truth] (1995), about a sect of mad sculptors who use human limbs for their works.

Science fiction writer Serge Lehman contributed *Le Haut-Lieu* [The High Place] (1995), by about a cursed apartment.

Frayeurs also introduced a number of new writers such as:

Alain Venisse, with *Le Clown de Minuit* [The Midnight Clown] (1994), about a murderous phantom that appears in the guise of a clown; *Symphonie pour l'Enfer* [Symphony for Hell] (1994), a Lovecraftian homage; and *Dans les Profondeurs du Miroir* [In the Depths of the Mirror] (1994), a novel about an evil doppelganger.

"Lori Anh" (a pseudonym of Sandra Vo-Anh) penned *Dégénérescence* (1994), about a girl pursued by a half-plant, half-human mutant.

Félix Brenner wrote *L'Araignée de Yoshiwara* [Yoshiwara's Spider] (1994), a vampiric tale recast as a Japanese legend.

Anissa Berkani-Rohmer, wrote *Catacombes* [Catacombs] (1995), about a monster prowling the Paris catacombs.

Pascal Françaix wrote *Le Cercueil de Chair* [The Coffin of Flesh] (1995) and *Kamarde* (1995), an interesting supernatural variation on the Frankenstein theme.

Bernard Florentz wrote *La Femme Morte* [The Dead Woman] (1994), a doomed love story, and *La Correction* (1994), a tale of revenge.

Other notable genre works published elsewhere included the following:

In 1979, Jean-Pierre Andrevon published *Les Revenants de l'Ombre* [The Shadow Ghosts], a novel in which nazis fought zombies; he then revised the novel in 1989 for publisher NéO, and again in 1997 for *Présence du Fantastique*.

In 1983, Pierre Pelot wrote *La Nuit sur Terre* [Night on Earth] for Denoël, a superb novel of suspense and terror in which a young woman is lured to a deserted mountain house by a religious sect. It was reprinted by Presses-Pocket in 1997.

Michel Pagel's *Sylvana* (1989), published by Anticipation, was an excellent novel about vampires; *Nuées Ardentes* [Fiery Clouds] (1997), was also another notable book.

Jean-Marc Ligny wrote *Yoro Si* (1991), the beautiful story of a young European musician confronted with African magic in the state of Burkina Faso ("yoro si" means *nowhere* in the local language). In *La Mort Peut Danser* [Death Can Dance] (1994), the author mixed modern rock 'n' roll with celtic fantasy, in what is now considered a cult book. Both novels were published by *Présence du Fantastique*.

In 1993, Alain Dorémieux wrote a hauntingly beautiful ghost novel, *Black Velvet*, also published by Denoël.

Brigitte Aubert staked out the niche claimed in the United States by Thomas Harris with *The Silence of the Lambs*. She penned a series of harrowing thrillers featuring mysterious serial killers, such as *Les Quatre Fils du Dr. March* [The Four Sons of Dr. March] (1992), in which the killer was one of four brothers; *La Mort des Bois* [Death in the Woods] (1996), in which the protagonist is a blind, speechless quadriplegic; and the colorful *Requiem Caraïbe* (1997). Her *Ténèbres sur Jacksonville* [Darkness over Jacksonville] (1994) and its sequel, *La Morsure des Ténèbres* [The Bite of Darkness] (1999) are an *Evil Dead*-type story about zombies terrorizing a New Mexico town. With about twenty novels published, she has become the flagship author of the *Seuil Police* imprint; her novels have been translated in seventeen languages, including in the United States, and she appears as the great revelation of the 1990s in the field.

The theme of the elusive serial killer was also featured in *Monsieur Malaussène*, a 1995 novel with genre elements by mainstream thriller writer Daniel Pennac. His *Messieurs les*

Enfants [Mister Children] (1997), was about children and adults trading places, and featured a very modern ghost.

Nicolas Kieffer, in *Peau de Lapin* [Rabbit Skin] (1994), wrote a thriller with fantasy elements taking place in a mysterious Colorado lunatic asylum where the patients may not be insane but in contact with other realities.

Yvon Hecht, in *Helena Von Nachtheim* (1996), penned a gothic vampire story.

Another notable gothic vampire series was Jeanne Faivre d'Arcier's *Rouge Flamenco*.

Jean-Jacques Nguyen penned several Lovecraft-inspired short-stories collected in *Rêves d'Arkham* [Arkham Dreams] (1996), as well as other genre stories gathered in *Rêves d'Ailleurs* [Elsewhere Dreams] (1997).

Philippe Ward's (a pseudonym of Philippe Laguerre) *Artahe* (1997)[166] was a novel about the modern-day worshippers of an ancient bear-god spirit.

The literary pastiches of René Réouven, the French equivalent of Philip Jose Farmer, brought together popular fiction characters as diverse as Sherlock Holmes, Dupin, Captain Nemo, as well as real-life characters such as Vidocq, Jack the Ripper and Poe. His novels included *Élémentaire, mon cher Holmes* [Elementary, My Dear Holmes] (1982), *Le Bestiaire de Sherlock Holmes* [Sherlock Holmes' Bestiary] (1987), *Le Détective Volé* [The Stolen Detective] (1988), in which Holmes investigates the *Purloined Letter* case, *Les Passe-Temps de Sherlock Holmes* [Sherlock Holmes' Passtimes] (1989), *Histoires Secrètes de Sherlock Holmes* [Secret Tales of Sherlock Holmes] (1993) and *Voyage au Centre du Mystère* [Journey to the Center of Mystery] (1995), an homage to Jules Verne.

Another author of literary pastiches was Belgian writer Yves Varende, the author of *Sherlock Holmes Revient* [Sherlock Holmes Returns] (1996), *Le Requin de la Tamise* [The

---

[166] Black Coat Press, ISBN 978-1-61227-767-7.

Shark of the Thames] (1996) and *Le Tueur dans le Fog* [The Killer in the Fog] (1997).

François Rivière, a renowned essayist, also paid homage to the classics in novels such as *Le Manuscrit d'Orvileda* [The Orvileda Manuscript] (1980), *Profanations* (1982), a tale of the desecration of a sacred Indian site, *Tabou* [Taboo] (1985), *Julius Exhumé* [Julius Exhumed] (1990) and *Kafka* (1992), which incorporated a variety of influences, ranging from Agatha Christie to H. P. Lovecraft, German cinema to Hollywood.

In 1997, Francis Valéry, also a renowned critic and editorialist, created the shared-world series of the *Agence Arkham*, a group of investigators of the supernatural. The series was short-lived but included Valéry's *Les Messagers de Saumwatu* [The Messengers of Saumwatu] (1997), Roland C. Wagner's *Le Nombril du Monde* [The Navel Of The World] (1997) and François Darnaudet's *Daguerra* (1997).

In the same vein, publisher Khom-Heidon released several shared-world horror series such as the three-volume *Scales* (1996-97) by "G. Elton Ranne" (the pseudonym of Gérard & Anne Guéro); and the three-volume *Nightprowler* (1996-97) by Christian Jacq.

Fantastique Littéraire

The fantastique, in all its diversity of expression, has continued to be well represented among the works published by mainstream publishers and generally deemed to be part of so-called mainstream literature during the last two decades. By necessity, considering the lack of historical perspective, we shall refrain from classifying authors too specifically, following instead a chronological perspective and providing a potpourri-like selection of some of the most interesting works.

Fréderic Tristan, a renowned and prolific author whose genre career could easily said to have begun as early as 1959 with his novel *Le Dieu des Mouches* [The God of the Flies], returned with *Les Tribulations Héroïques de Balthasar Kober*

[The Heroic Tribulations of Balthasar Kober] (1980), a picaresque novel, then embarked on a series of strikingly original esoteric novels, each depicting an initiatic, spiritual journey. In *Les Tribulations*, a divinely inspired madman seeks the Light by exploring the secrets of kabbala and alchemy. *L'Histoire Sérieuse et Drolatique de l'Homme sans Nom* [The Serious and Funny Tale of the Nameless Man] (1980) features a nameless adventurer who has lived for centuries. Other notable works in this vein include *L'Oeil d'Hermès* [The Eye of Hermes] (1982), *Naissance d'un Spectre* [Birth of a Spectre] (1983), *Le Fils de Babel* [The Son of Babel] (1985), *Le Singe Égal du Ciel* [The Ape the Equal of Heaven] (1986), *L'Ange dans la Machine* [The Angel in the Machine] (1989) and *Le Dernier des Homme*s [The Last Man] (1993).

Jean-Pierre Hubert, Hubert Haddad and Georges-Olivier Châteaureynaud, already mentioned in our previous section, continued to pen finely-crafted, literary fantasies. The former with novels such as *La Ville sans Miroir* [The City Without Mirrors] (1984), *Oholiba des Songes* [Oholiba of the Dreams] (1989), *L'Âme de Buridan* [Buridan's Soul] (1992) and *La Falaise de Sable* [The Sand Cliff] (1997). The latter two with works like *La Faculté des Songes* [The Faculty of Dreams] (1982), *Le Congrès de Fantômologie* [The Congress of Phantomology] (1985), *Le Jardin dans l'Île* [The Garden in the Island] (1989), *Le Château de Verre* [The Glass Castle] (1994) and *Les Messagers* [The Messengers] (1996).

Michel Tournier also continued to produce notable YA works (see below), as well as remarkable genre novels such as *Le Crépuscule des Masques* [The Twilight of the Masks] (1992) and *Le Miroir à Deux Faces* [The Mirror with Two Faces] (1994).

Claude Louis-Combet offered such fine works as *Le Roman de Mélusine* [The Novel of Melusine] (1986), *Figures de Nuit* [Night Figures] (1988) and *Augias et Autres Infâmes* [Augias & Other Infamous Actions] (1993).

Jean-Marie Le Clézio contributed *La Genèse* [Genesis] (1987) and *L'Étoile Errante* [The Wandering Star] (1992).

Mainstream novelist Jean d'Ormesson penned the notable *Histoire du Juif Errant* [Story of the Wandering Jew] (1991).

René Réouven, the author of several Holmesian pastiches (see above), also wrote science fiction novels under the name of René Sussan. Under that pseudonym, he published *Les Insolites* [Strange Tales] (1984), a collection of fantastical and science fiction tales which won the 1985 French Science Fiction Grand Prize. As Réouven, he wrote *Les Grandes Profondeurs* [The Lower Depths] (1991) and *Les Survenants* [The Overghosts] (1996), a prodigious novel about a man stalked by another version of himself from a "what if" reality. With Donna Sussan, he also co-authored *Les Nourritures Extra-Terrestres* [Extra-Terrestrial Food] (1994), which won the 1995 Grand Prize of Imagination.

Roger Vrigny made a remarkable appearance with *Un Ange Passe* [An Angel Passes] (1979), the striking tale of an exterminating angel, followed by *Accident de Parcours* [Accident in Transit] (1985), a collection of three fantastic stories. Other notable works include *Le Garçon d'Orage* [The Storm Boy] (1994) and *Instants Dérobés* [Purloined Moments] (1996).

Pierre-Jean Rémy, wrote some wonderful modern, gothic fantasies, such as *Cordélia, ou l'Angleterre* [Cordelia, or England] (1979) and *Pandora* (1980).

Georges de Lorzac penned *La Loque à Terre* [The Wreck of a Tenant] (1980), the surreal tale of a man trapped in a high-rise staircase.

François Sonkin published *Le Petit Violon* [The Small Violin] (1981), a remarkable collection of fantastic tales.

Gérard Macé penned several short stories that read like prose poems, collected in *Bois Dormant* [Sleeping Woods] (1983), *Les Trois Coffrets* [The Three Boxes] (1985), *Vies Antérieures* [Previous Lives] (1991) and *L'Autre Hémisphère du Temps* [The Other Half of Time] (1995).

Sony Labou Tansi (a pseudonym of Marcel Ntsoni) is a Congolese author whose first novel, *Conscience de Tracteur*

[Tractor Consciousness] (1979) dealt with a sentient tractor in his native Africa. Other notable works by him include *Les Sept Solitudes de Lorsa Lopez* [The Seven Solitudes of Lorsa Lopez] (1985) and *Les Yeux du Volcan* [The Eyes of the Volcano] (1988).

Belgian writer Alain Berenboom is another notable author, with works such as *La Position du Missionnaire Roux* [The Red Missionary Position] (1989), *La Table de Riz* [The Rice Table] (1992) and *La Jerusalem Captive* [Captive Jerusalem] (1997).

Finally, Jeremy Bérenger is a poet of the supernatural. His *Allison la Sybilline* (1994) and *La Rousseur des Bananes à l'Été finissant* [The Redness of Bananas at the End of Summer] (1997) are written in a flamboyant style that perfectly transcribes his rich imagination. In *Allison*, as in most of his writings, the author was inspired by a story of his own life. The result is an endearing and gripping tale of a man who has fallen in love with a woman which he cannot have and who will, eventually, become his writing muse.

Female Authors

Notable women writers included:

Danièle Sallenave, with *La Vie Fantôme* [The Ghost Life] (1986) and *Les Trois Minutes du Diable* [The Devil's Three Minutes] (1994), in which the world stops every day for three minutes.

Isabelle Hausser, with *Célubée* (1986).

Florence Trystram with *Lancelot* (1987)

Colette Fayard, *with Les Chasseurs au Bord de la Nuit* [The Hunters at the Edge of Night] (1989), *Par Tous les Temps* [At All Times] (1990) and *Le Jeu de l'Éventail* [The Game of the Fan] (1992).

Katherine Quénot, with *Rien que des Sorcières* [Nothing but Witches] (1993), the tale of three women with strange powers, and *Blanc comme la Nuit* [White as Night] (1993).

Jeanne Faivre d'Arcier, one of the very few French authors published by Presses-Pocket, mined the vein exploited by Anne Rice with *Rouge Flamenco* [Flamenco Red] (1993) and *La Déesse Écarlate* [The Scarlet Goddess] (1997), two very colorful gothic novels about vampires.

Laurence Cossé, with *Le Coin du Voile* [The Corner of the Veil] (1996), in which a priest discovers an unarguable proof of the existence of God, but the world cannot live with it.

Marie Darrieussecq, one of 1996's literary successes, with *Truisme*, an allegorical novel in which a woman is gradually changing into a sow.

Fantasy

Heroic-Fantasy thrived in the 1980s and 1990s as never before, but mostly following the well-established templates of Tolkien, Howard, Moorcock and the TSR role-playing games *Dragonlance* and *Dungeons & Dragons*.

Also, in 1995, both David Eddings and Robert Jordan were translated in dedicated fantasy imprints like *Fantasy* and *Dark Fantasy* at Presses-Pocket, edited by Jacques Goimard, and Fantasy at J'ai Lu, edited by Jacques Sadoul.

Nevertheless, one of the first dedicated heroic-fantasy imprints of the 1980s was the short-lived *Plasma*, edited by Bruno Lecigne, which published a series of novels taking place in the shared world of the *Cycle des Chimères* [The Saga of the Chimeras]. Among these were:

Le Titan de Galova [The Titan of Galova] (1983) and *Océane* (1983), by Lecigne and Sylviane Corgiat.

Jean-Marc Ligny's *Succubes* [Succubi] (1983), which was revised in 1990 for an *Anticipation* reprint, along with its sequel, *Sorciers* [Wizards].

Jean-Pierre Hubert's *Séméla* (1983).

Alain Paris' *Chasseur d'Ombres* [Shadows Hunter] (1983).

Jean-Pierre Vernay's *Le Sang des Mondes* [The Blood of the Worlds] (1983).

Another short-lived heroic-fantasy imprint was *Temps Futurs* [Future Times], which published translations of Michael Moorcock's *Eternal Champion* stories and Stephen R. Donaldson's *Thomas Covenant* saga. The French "star" of the imprint was Francis Berthelot with the novel *Khanaor* (1983), comprised of two separate books, *Solstice de Fer* [Iron Solstice] and *Équinoxe de Cendre* [Ash Equinox], which were also revised for a 1986 *Anticipation* reprint.

In the mainstream, renowned writer René Barjavel penned a brilliant retelling of the saga of Merlin with *L'Enchanteur* [The Enchanter] (1984), which became a bestseller.

Another mainstream success was Bernard Simonay, published by the Éditions du Rocher. His novels *Phénix* (1986), and its sequel *Graal* (1988), were science-fantasies not unlike Fred Saberhagen's *Swords* or Michael Moorcock's *Runestaff* series, taking place in a pseudo-medieval future Europe where post-nuclear technology has become like magic. In *Phénix*, the brother and sister team of Dorian and Solyane must find the secret of their origins as well as save their peaceful kingdom of Syrdahar. *Graal* took place twenty years later when Solyane must defeat an evil Prophet. The author continued his prolific production with *La Malédiction de la Licorne* [The Curse of the Unicorn] (1990), *La Porte de Bronze* [The Gate of Brass] (1994), and the three-volume series *Les Enfants de l'Atlantide* [The Children of Atlantis] (1994-96).

In the mid-1980s, *Anticipation* began to regularly publish works of heroic-fantasy, and in 1992, eventually created its own dedicated sub-imprint, *Legend*. Its major authors were:

Hugues Douriaux quickly became one of *Legend*'s most prolific and popular writers. He was the author of numerous multi-volume, sprawling sagas, as well as many stand-alone novels. The author began his career with a post-nuclear science-fantasy saga entitled *Un Homme Est Venu...* [A Man Came...], originally published in the *Grands Romans* imprint of Fleuve Noir in 1981, and reprinted in *Anticipation* as six volumes in 1987 and 1988. It was followed by *Le Chemin des Mondes* [The Path of Worlds] (1982). His major herpoic-fantasy series included: *La Biche de la Forêt d'Arcande* [The Doe from the Forest of Arcande] (3 volumes; 1988); *Les Chroniques de Vonia* [The Chronicles of Vonia] (7 volumes; 1989-90); *Les Fleurs et le Vent* [The Flowers and the Wind] (3 volumes; 1991); *L'Anneau-Feu de Gundhera* [The Fire-Ring of Gundhera] (5 volumes; 1992-93); and *La Porte de Flamme* [The Gate of Fire] (3 volumes; 1994-95).

Under the pseudonym of "Gilles Thomas", and until her death in 1985, Julia Verlanger continued to produce heroic-fantasy works such as *La Croix des Décastés* [The Cross of the Outcasts] (1977), *D'un Lieu Lointain Nommé Soltrois* [From a Far Away Place Called Solthree] (1979), *La Porte des Serpents* [The Gate of Serpents] (1980) and *Les Cages de Beltem* [The Cages of Beltem], a novel first published in condensed form in 1982, and reissued as two volumes, *Acherra* and *Offren*, in 1995.

Daniel Walther contributed the science-fantasy trilogy of *Swa*, comprised of *Le Livre de Swa* (1982), *Le Destin de Swa* (1982) and *La Légende de Swa* (1983), to *Anticipation*, as well as *Nocturne sur Fond d'Epées* [Nocturne on a Field of Swords] (1984) to publisher NéO.

André Caroff penned the heroic fantasy saga of the *Reds* (4 volumes; 1983), in which Hem-The-Red frees an occupied Europe from the tyrannic Masters.

Alain Paris & Jean-Pierre Fontana created the *Chroniques de la Lune Rouge* [Chronicles of the Red Moon] (4 volumes; 1984-87), detailing the adventures of the warrior Zarko in a post-cataclysmic Central/South America that had reverted to savagery.

Paris alone wrote the *Chroniques d'Antarcie* [Chronicles of Antarcia] (3 volumes; 1985-87), the story of the ancient civilization that thrived in Antarctica ten thousand years ago; followed by the *Pangea* trilogy (1989); and finally by his masterpiece, *Le Monde de la Terre Creuse* [The World of the Hollow Earth] (10 volumes; 1988-91), a prodigious saga taking place in an alternate reality where the Nazis have won World War II, and where the world may really be hollow. The series also became a popular role-playing game. Single heroic-fantasy novels included *Ashermayam* (1986), in which a warrior-wizard fought a female demon; and *Le Dieu de la Guerre* [The God of War] (1989).

After writing esoteric pseudo-documentary books such as *Quand l'Atlantide resurgira* [When Atlantis Will Rise Again] (1979), *Châteaux Forts Magiques de France* [Magical Castles of France] (1982) and *Vercingétorix et les Mystères Gaulois* [Vercingetorix & The Gallic Mysteries] (1983), Roger Facon wrote a number of heroic-fantasy novels for *Anticipation*, such as *Par Le Sabre des Zinjas* [By the Sword of the Zinjas] (1986) and *Les Compagnons de la Lune Blême* [The Fellowship of the Wan Moon] (1992).

Bruno Lecigne & Sylviane Corgiat penned *Le Jeu de la Trame* [The Game of the Weave] (4 volumes; 1986-88), the tale of the quest of the warrior Keido for the thirty-nine major arcana of the magic Game of the Weave which he needed in order to return his dead sister to life.

Pierre Bameul, who had written *Par Le Royaume d'Osiris* [By the Kingdom of Osiris] (1981) for OPTA, wrote a saga entitled *Pour Nourrir le Soleil* [To Feed the Sun] (2 volumes; 1986) for *Anticipation*. It told the story of a parallel universe in which the Viking warrior Arne Marsson became Quetzalcoatl and conquered the Aztec Empire.

Popular horror writer Serge Brussolo contributed two heroic-fantasy novels with strong horror elements: *Le Tombeau du Roi Squelette* [The Tomb of the Skeleton King] (1988) and *Le Dragon du Roi Squelette* [The Dragon of the Skeleton King] (1989), in which legless Shagan, Junia the giantess, who carried him on her back, and their master, the smith-sorcerer Massalian, teamed up to face the demonic hordes of the Skeleton King. The author also wrote the more literary medieval saga of *Hurlemort - Le Dernier Royaume* [DeathScream - The Last Kingdom] (1993). Finally, using the pseudonym of "Kitty

Doom", he was also the author of two dark fantasies, *L'Empire des Abîmes* [The Empire of the Abyss] (1997) and *Les Invisibles* [The Invisible Ones] (1997), published by *Présence du Futur*.

Michel Pagel wrote *L'Ange du Désert* [The Desert Angel] (2 volumes; 1985-86), which took place in a barbaric world where a biker nicknamed "Angel" searched for the mythical city of Lankor; and *Les Flammes de la Nuit* [The Flames of Night] (4 volumes; 1986-87), where the Sorceress Rowena, who had once been banished from the Kingdom of Fuinor, a hollow-Earth-type world, eventually returns to conquer it. *L'Antre du Serpent* [The Lair of the Serpent] (1990) and *Le Refuge de l'Agneau* [The Refuge of the Lamb] (1991) formed a novel entitled *Les Antipodes* [The Antipodean]. Writing under the pseudonym of "Félix Chapel", the author also penned the series *L'Oiseau de Foudre* [The Bird of Lightning] (5 volumes; 1990-91).

Jean-Claude Dunyach penned *Le Jeu des Sabliers* [The Game of the Hourglasses] (2 volumes; 1987-88), which featured four characters who were incarnations of a tarot-like set of cards searching for three hourglasses supposed to confer immortality. He also penned *La Guerre des Cercles* [The War of the Circles] (1995).

Belgian author Alain le Bussy created the adventures of *Yorg*, another barbarian in a post-cataclysmic Earth (6 volumes; 1995). He was also the author of *Chatinika* (1995), and *Le Dieu Avide* [The Hungry God] (1996), the first volume of a new heroic-fantasy series

Claude Castan penned the tetralogy of *Galaë* (1996). In it, young Celian was raised by a friend of his dead mother, eventually learned that his father was the King of the Elves, and that only he could save the kingdom from a cataclysmic war.

Phil Laramie (a pseudonym of Xavier Snoeck) wrote the *Akantor* series (2 volumes; 1986-87).

Jean-Christophe Chaumette penned *Le Neuvième Cercle* [The Ninth Circle] (6 volumes; 1990-91) and *Le Niwaâd* (1997).

Manuel Essard wrote *La Forteresse Pourpre* [The Purple Fortress] (1993).

G. Elton Ranne wrote *La Mâchoire du Dragon* [The Jaws of the Dragon] (1996).

Christophe Loubet wrote *La Saga des Bannis* [The Saga of the Banished] (Nos 17, 18; 1997).

Finally, Valérie Simon penned *Arkem, La Pierre des Ténèbres* [Arkem, The Stone of Darkness] (2 volumes; 1997).

The same publishing group which controlled Fleuve Noir also financed Éditions Vaugirard, which published translations of E. C. Tubb's *Dumarest*, Warren Murphy & Richard Sapir*'s The Destroyer* and "Jeffrey Lord"'s (a pseudonym of Roland J. Green, Ray Nelson, and Manning Lee Stokes) *Richard Blade* series, featuring the titular MI6A's special agent who was teleported into a random alternate dimension at the beginning of each novel and forced to rely on his wits and strength.

The *Richard Blade* series was carried on in French from 1983 to 2012 (first by Plon, then Presses de la Cité, Vaugirard and finally Vauvenargues) after it ended in the original English-language edition. The French authors included Richard D. Nolane (a pseudonym of Olivier Raynaud), Gérald Moreau, Thomas Bauduret (using the pseudonym of "Patrick Eris", Raymond Audemard, "Philippe Randa", Patrice Roger-Chantin, Frédéric Szczepaniak, Arnaud Dalrune, Yves Chéraqui, Christian Mantey, Paul Couturiau, Olga Tormes, Yves Bulteau, Didier Le Grais, Nadine Monfils, Jean-Manuel Moreau (using the pseudonym of : Nemo Sandman"), Stéphane Arlann, Paul-Gaspard Julien, and Pascal Candia. One of the characteristics of the French series was the frequent tongue-in-cheek tone, the punish titles, occasionally developing into a parody of the original series. The numbering of the French series carried on where the English one left off, starting with #38 and ending in 2012 with #206.

Vaugirard dedicated an entire paperback imprint to the adventures of *Rohel Le Conquérant* [Rohel the Conqueror], another sprawling science-fantasy saga created by writer Pierre Bordage. In this series, the hero, Rohel the Vioter, was forced to travel from world to world, seeking the sword Lucifal to avenge his people, the Genesians of Antiter, who were murdered by the evil Garloups [Werwolves]. The Garloups originally came from within a black hole, and took Rohel's true love, the beautiful Saphyr, prisoner. Rohel stole the ultimate equation, the Mentral, which controlled the passage between the worlds, from the Jahad, the fanatical worshippers of the One True Oak. The Rohel saga was comprised of three "Cycles" of five volume each: Dame Asmine of Alba (1992-94), Lucifal (1995-96) and Saphyr of Antiter (1996-97).

New publisher L'Atalante, which released Bordage's notable space opera trilogy, *Les Guerriers du Silence* [The Warriors of Silence] (1993-95), also published Gilles Servat's heroic-fantasy trilogy, *Les Chroniques d'Arcturus* [The Chronicles of Arcturus] (1996-97). Mostly known as a Breton singer and lyricist, the author came to write novels to tell the longer stories that he could not tell in songs. His *Arcturus* novels, based on the ancient legends of Britanny, were filled with epic and sensual scenes, larger-than-life characters. The first novel told of how Skinn Mac Dana came to the world of Bré, and of his fight for survival.

Other L'Atalante heroic-fantasy works included Jean-Pierre Fontana's revised *Halaguen* saga (1997) (see above).

Other recent notable genre works included:

Two heroic-fantasy novels written in Occitan by Joan-Frédéric Brun, *Lo Retrach dau Dieu Negre* (1987) and *Septembralas* (1994).

Michel Novy's *Le Châtiment des Rois Frères* [The Punishment of the Brother Kings] (1994), the beautiful, poetic tale of two brothers, one good and one evil, who fought for a kingdom. The story was epic and reminiscent of the classic fairy tales.

Hervé Carn's *Issek* (1997).

"Harry Morgan"'s (a pseudonym of Christian Wahl) baroque *La Reine du Ciel* [The Queen of the Sky] (1997), published by Rivages in their new *Fantasy* imprint.

Also in 1997, renowned science fiction writer Ayerdhal (a pseudonym of Marc Soulier) published *Parleur, ou La Chronique d'un Rêve Enclavé* [Speaker, or The Chronicle of An Embedded Dream] at J'ai Lu. It was a unique political fantasy with no supernatural or magical elements, in which a group of revolutionaries attempted to resist the encroachments of the medieval authorities.

In 1995, new publisher, Mnemos launched an entire line of heroic-fantasy novels written by young French authors. Among these were:

Mathieu Gaborit, with *Les Chroniques du Crépusculaire* [Chronicles of Twilight] (3 volumes; 1995-96), which starred a young female magician called Agone; and the saga of the city of *Abyme* [Abyss], a mix of fantasy and film noir (2 volumes; 1996).

David & Isabelle Collet, with the *Nephilim* series (3 volumes; 1995-96), based on a French role-playing game. The Nephilim were body-snatching entities which have plagued Mankind since the dawn of time. They were fought by an occult alliance of Templar Knights, and alchemists.

Sébastien Pennes's trilogy *Le Cycle des Phénix* [The Cycle of the Phenix] (3 volumes; 1995-96) also took place in the *Nephilim* universe.

Pierre Grimbert, with the award-winning *Le Secret de Ji* [The Secret of Ji] (4 volumes; 1996-97), a series of novels in which the heroes were heirs to a mysterious magical secret.

Editor Stéphane Marsan's *Les Carnets de la Constellation* [The Notebooks of the Constellation] (3 volumes; 1996) took place in the universe of the Guild, a series of island kingdoms located on a vast ocean; the novels dealt with the changes created by the emergence of a new continent.

Laurent Kloetzer, with *Mémoire Vagabonde* [Wandering Memory] (1997) and *La Voie du Cygne* [The Way of the Swan] (1999).

Erik Wietzel, with *La Porte des Limbes* [The Gate of Limbo] (1997).

In 1997, Mnemos created a new imprint, *Daemonicon*, featuring three more heroic-fantasy sagas, *L'Éclipse des Dragons* [The Eclipse of Dragons] by "Duncan Eriksson" (a pseudonym of Fabrice Colin), *L'Âme des Rois Nains* [The Soul of the Dwarf Kings] by "William Hawk" (A pseudonym of Mathieu Gaborit) and *Le Sanctuaire des Elfes* [The Sanctuary of The Elves] by "Edwyn Kestrel" (a pseudonym of Stéphane Marsan), in reality French writers using English-sounding pseudonyms in order to boost sales—a sad commentary on the growing preponderance of Anglo-Saxon authors in the genre.

The same editorial policy was followed by publisher Khom-Heidon for a series by Christian Jacq entitled *Chroniques des Sept Cités* [Chronicles of the Seven Cities] (1997); and another by Bernard Rastouin entitled *Shaan - Le Cercle des Réalités* [The Circle of Realities] (1996-97).

Stéphane Marsan left Mnemos in 2000 and went on to launch a new publishing house, Bragelonne, entirely dedicated to fantasy, publishing David Gemmell, Andrzej Sapkowski and Terry Goodkind.

The YAs

The field of children's books and YA literature virtually exploded in the 1980s and 1990s, and genre works became superabundant, especially after the successful translations of American series like R. L. Stine's *Goosebumps*.

We are providing here a selection of the major writers with selected works, starting with previously mentioned authors:

The writing team using the pseudonym of "Michel Grimaud" contributed books for children such as *Les Contes de la Ficelle* [Tales from the String] (1982), YA fantasies such as the remarkable *L'Enfant de la Mer* [The Child from the Sea]

(1986) and *Le Coffre Magique* [The Magical Chest] (1990), as well as more modern horror-slanted thrillers such as *L'Assassin crève l'Écran* [The Murderer Steps through the Screen] (1991) and *L'Inconnu dans le Frigo* [The Stranger inside the Refrigerator] (1997).

Michel Tournier penned *La Fugue du Petit Poucet* [Tom Thumb's Escape] (1988), as well as the delightful *Les Contes du Medianoche* [Tales from the Medianoche] (1989) and *Le Medianoche Amoureux* [The Medianoche in Love] (1989).

Another mainstream writer, Robert Escarpit, the author of the classic *Contes de la Saint Glinglin* [Tales of Any Saint] (1973), returned to the field with a vengeance with *L'Enfant qui Venait de l'Espace* [The Child Who Came from Outer Space] (1984), *Tom, Quentin et le Géant Bila* [Tom, Quentin and Bila the Giant] (1994), *Hugo, Charlie et la Reine Isis* [Hugo, Charlie and Queen Isis] (1995) and *La Poudre du Père Limpinpin* [The Powder of Father Limpinpin] (1996).

Through the 1980s and 1990s, Jean-Pierre Andrevon diversified his career further, producing crime thrillers, adventure novels and YA novels, as well as horror, fantasy and science fiction. Among his best YAs were the fantasy, *La Fée et le Géomètre* [The Fairy and the Surveyor] (1981), contrasting the fairy people and the modern, materialistic world; *Le Grand Combat Nucléaire de Tarzan* [Tarzan's Great Nuclear Fight] (1986), *Le Chevalier, l'Autobus et la Licorne* [The Knight, The Bus & The Unicorn] (1987), *Le Jour du Grand Saut* [The Day of the Great Jump] (1997), *La Bête sur le Parking* [The Beast on the Parking Lot] (1997) and a sequel to his classic 1970s fantasy, *Gandahar et l'Oiseau-Monde* [Gandahar and the World-Bird] (1997) for the new *Vertige* imprint (see above).

Jean-Marc Ligny published *Les Ailes Noires de la Nuit* [The Black Wings of Death] (1995).

Michel Cosem wrote *Le Chapeau Enchanté* [The Enchanted Hat] (1984) and *Le Chemin du Bout du Monde* [The Path at the End of the World] (1993).

Xavier Armange contributed *Dragon d'Ordinaire* [Ordinary Dragon] (1985) and a series of novel entitled *Cache-Cache* [Hide-&-Seek] (1986).

Other YA series included:

Basile (1995-96) by Véronique Le Normand.

Lapoigne (1995-97), a juvenile fantasy/thriller saga by Thierry Jonquet.

Abdallah (1995-97) by Paul Thiès.

A special mention goes to the wonderful *Jonathan Cap* series (1986-90) by François Rivière, which wonderfully blended YA adventure and old-fashioned pulps with *Le Labyrinthe du Jaguar* [The Jaguar's Labyrinth] (1986), *La Samba du Fantôme* [The Ghost's Samba] (1986), *La Clinique du Docteur K.* [Dr.K's Clinic] (1986), *Jonathan Cap contre les Chevaliers de Satan* [Jonathan Cap vs. Satan's Knights] (1986), *Les Formules de Zoltan* [Zoltan's Formulas] (1986) and *Le Spectre du Mandarin* [The Mandarin's Ghost] (1988).

New author François Sautereau switched from science fiction with *La Cinquième Dimension* [The Fifth Dimension] (1979) to magical realism, with *Léonie et la Pierre de Lumière* [Leonie & The Stone of Light] (1980) and *Nicolas et la Montre Magique* [Nicolas & The Magic Watch] (1981). The author's novels were elaborate fantasies, remarkable for their sense of detail and exotism. Other noteworthy titles included *L'Héritier de la Nuit* [The Night Heir] (1985), *La Cité des Brumes* [The City of Mists] (1986) and *La Forteresse de la Nuit* [The Fortress of Night] (1989).

Evelyne Brisou-Pellen wrote YA fantasies in a style not unlike that of Ursula K. Le Guin's *Earthsea* novels. Notable titles included *La Porte de Nulle Part* [The Gate of Nowhere] (1980), *La Cour aux Étoiles* [Courtyard of the Stars] (1982), *La Grotte des Korrigans* [The Korrigans' Cave] (1985), *Le Maître de la Septième Porte* [The Master of the Seventh Gate] (1986) and *Le Défi des Druides* [The Challenge of the Druids] (1988).

Odile Weulersse penned action-oriented, YA adventures with solid plots and exotic locales. Notable titles included Le

Messager d'Athènes [The Messenger from Athens] (1985), *Le Secret des Catacombes* [The Secret of the Catacombs] (1986), *Le Cavalier de Bagdad* [The Rider of Baghdad] (1988) and *L'Aigle de Mexico* [The Eagle from Mexico] (1992).

Béatrice Tanaka used classic fairy tales to create new, colorful tales, aimed at younger audiences. Notable titles included *Ytch et les Choumoudoux* [Ytch and the Choomoodoos] (1982), *La Princesse aux Deux Visages* [The Princess with Two Faces] (1987), *Trois Sorcières* [Three Witches] (1988) and *La Quête du Prince de Koripan* [The Quest of the Prince of Koripan] (1992).

Évelyne Reberg similarly relied on classic fairy tales and folk legends for her inspiration. Notable titles included *Le Dragon Chanteur* [The Singing Dragon] (1980), *La Princesse Muette* [The Silent Princess] (1980) and *La Machine à Contes* [The Storytelling Machine] (1981).

Michèle Kahn's modern fairy tales were more somber and reflective, yet shone with a special poetic light. Notable titles included *De l'Autre Côté du Brouillard* [On the Other Side of the Fog] (1980), *Contes du Jardin d'Eden* [Tales of the Garden of Eden] (1982) and *De l'Autre Côté du Miroir* [On the Other Side of the Mirror] (1985).

Christian Poslaniec's books were filled with a strange sense of humor and a weird notion of reality. Notable titles included *Histoires Horribles et Pas si Méchantes* [Awful & Not So Nasty Tales] (1986), *L'Escargot de Cristal* [The Crystal Snail] (1986), *Le Marchand de Mémoire* [The Memory Merchant] (1988), *Le Treizième Chat Noir* [The Thirteenth Black Cat] (1992) and *Le Jour des Monstres* [The Day of the Monsters] (1994).

Jean Alessandrini's brand of juvenile *fantastique* relied on a slightly surrealist conception of the adventure novel. Notable titles included *Le Prince d'Aéropolis* [The Prince of Aeropolis] (1986), *Le Détective de Minuit* [The Midnight Detective] (1987) and *La Malédiction de Chéops* [The Curse of Cheops] (1989).

The prolific "Gudule" (another pseudonym of Anne Carali), also knew how to take classic concepts such as monsters, witches and devils, and give them a weird, modern twist. Notable titles included *Prince Charmant Poil aux Dents* [Prince Charming My Foot] (1987), *Agence Torgnole, Frappez Fort!* [Slap Agency, Hit Harder!] (1990), *L'École qui n'existait pas* [The School That Did Not Exist] (1994), *Le Dentiste est un Vampire* [The Dentist is a Vampire] (1996), *La Sorcière est dans l'École* [The Witch Is in the School] (1996), *Le Manège de l'Oubli* [The Merry-Go-Round of Oblivion] (1997), *Bonjour, Monsieur Frankenstein* [Hello, Mr. Frankenstein] (1997), to name but a few titles amongst her outstanding production.

Jean-Louis Craipeau followed in the same vein with *L'Oeil de Belzébuth* [Beelzebub's Eye] (1986), *L'Ogre-Doux* [The Sweet Ogre] (1989), *Le Dragon Déglingué* [The Broken Dragon] (1989), *La Sorcière des Cantines* [The Witch of the Cantina] (1997) and *Dracula fait son Cinéma* [Dracula Makes a Movie] (1997).

So did Alain Surget with *Gare à la Bête!* [Beware The Beast!] (1989), *Le Fils des Loups* [The Son of Wolves] (1989), *L'Abominable Gosse des Neiges* [The Abominable Snow Kid] (1990), *Le Bal des Sorcières* [Witches' Ball] (1994) and *Le Gouffre aux Fantômes* [The Ghost Pit] (1994).

Marie Farré was another proponent of the updating of classic monsters, with *Papa est un Ogre* [Dad Is an Ogre] (1983), *Mon Maître d'École est le Yéti* [My Principal Is the Yeti] (1984) and *Mon Oncle est un Loup-Garou* [My Uncle Is a Werewolf] (1985).

Others in this genre included:

Olivier Cohen, with *Je m'appelle Dracula* [My Name Is Dracula] (1987) and *La Fiancée de Dracula* [The Bride of Dracula] (1988).

Martine Bourre, with *Ne Dérangez pas les Dragons!* [Don't Disturb the Dragons!] (1988).

Philippe Barbeau, with *L'Ami de l'Ogre* [The Ogre's Friend] (1990).

Stories leaning more towards horror and the more traditional types of fantastique included:

Yak Rivais' *Les Sorcières sont N.R.V.* [The Witches Are Annoyed] (1988), *Les Contes du Miroir* [Tales of the Mirror] (1988) and *Contes du Cimetière après la Pluie* [Tales from the Cemetery after the Rain] (1997).

Hervé Fontanières, with *Rendez-vous en Enfer* [Rendez-vous in Hell] (1997), which takes place on a lonely lighthouse.

Éric Sanvoisin, with *Bizarre le Bizarre* (1996) and *Les Chasseurs d'Ombre* [The Shadow Hunters] (1997).

Jacques Barnouin delighted younger readers with the nocturnal tales of *Le Fantôme Sparadrap et Autres Histoires Sans Sucre* [The Band-Aid Ghost & Other Sugarless Stories] (1984) and *Bonjour, la Nuit!* [Hello, Night!] (1985).

So did Yves-Marie Clément with *Le Petit Dragon qui Toussait* [The Little Dragon Who Coughed] (1996).

Lorris Murail was a noted science fiction writer and scholar who contributed *Le Marchand de Cauchemars* [The Nightmare Peddler] (1990) and *La Poubelle d'Ali-Baba* [Ali-Baba's Dustbin] (1991); while Marie-Aude Murail wrote *Graine de Monstre* [Monster Seed] (1986), *Le Visiteur de Minuit* [The Midnight Visitor] (1988) and *Le Docteur Magicus* (1988).

Finally, heroic-fantasy began to make an appearance among juvenile novels with Éric Bisset's *Le Grimoire d'Arkandias* [The Grimoir of Arkandias] (1997) and numerous, young adult genre novels written by Michel Honaker, with the trilogy *Le Chevalier de Terre Noire* [The Knight of Blackland] (1996); *Le Chant de la Reine Froide* [The Song of the Cold Queen] (1996), *La Cantate des Anges* [Angels' Cantata] (1996), *La Symphonie du Destin* [The Symphony of Fate] (1996), *Nocturne pour une Passion* [Nocturne for a Passion] (1996), *Les Héritiers du Secret* [The Heirs of the Secret] (1996), and *La Flûte Enchantée* [The Enchanted Flute] (1997).

The author also contributed some young adult horror novels, such as *Magie Noire dans le Bronx* [Black Magic in the Bronx] (1996), a reworking of his first *Commander* novel,

Le Démon du Bronx [The Demon of the Bronx] (1988), *La Créature du Néant* [The Creature from the Void] (1997) and *Rendez-Vous à Apocalypse* [Rendezvous at Apocalypse] (1997).

Afterword: 2022

The previous pages were written as the 20th century came to an end. We weren't able to entirely update this book by devoting as much time and space to the last twenty years as we did with the earlier decades, which were written in the late 1990s. However, it is fair to ask what major changes, significant events and new names appeared in French fantasy and supernatural fiction since we brought the original project to a close in 2000.

Here is, then, a brief overview of what we consider to be important occurrences in the field during the last two decades.

First and foremost, book publishing in general took a hit after the economic downturn of 2009. Also, the massive advent of Twitter, Instagram, Facebook, Youtube, Tiktok and other social media, as well as streaming networks like Netflix, has cannibalized precious time that might otherwise have been used to read books, purchasing power that might otherwise have been used to buy them, and even the space necessary to discuss them. It is no exaggeration to say that the art of the book review is. if not totally dead, but on its last legs; besides, even excellent reviews no longer seem to impact sales, as readers are too busy or too distracted to follow up and buy the reviewed item. Yes, there are still best-sellers racking in the big bucks, but what used to be known as the midlist is now gone.

In terms of major influences during the last two decades on French fantasy and supernatural fiction, one must include the *Harry Potter* and *Twilight* book series, "bit-lit," the French term for urban fantasy, which after a quick surge in popularity declined sharply in the late 2010s, *The Da Vinci Code* (whose concepts, ironically, were borrowed from French sources), *Game of Thrones* (mostly the HBO TV series), and

The Lord of the Rings films. Fantasy (as well as *noir* thrillers, but these are not our object here) were by far the most successful genres of the last two decades.

Fantasy propelled new publisher Bragelonne to a level of commercial success that turned it into a real powerhouse.[167] They won the World Fantasy Award in 2011. But that success mostly benefited American and British authors such as Terry Gemmell, David Goodkind and Robert Jordan. They published such notable French authors as Pierre Bordage with *Arkane* (2017-18); Mathieu Gaborit, with *Les Chroniques des Féals* (2001-02); and Pierre Pevel, with the *Ambremer* (2003-04) and *Haut Royaume* [High Kingdom] (2013-21) cycles

Publisher Mnemos increased its number of translations, but in 2009 created the *Dédales* sub-imprint whose purpose was to find new French talents. They had already introduced such notable French authors as Mathieu Gaborit, Laurent Kloetzer and Erik Wietzel in the 1990s; they added Frédéric Delmeulle, with *La Parallèle Vertov* (2010); and Justine Niogret, with *Chien du Heaume* [Helmet Dog] (2009-11).

Publisher L'Atalante, which had already published Pierre Bordage, Jean-Claude Dunyach and Roland C. Wagner (who passed away in 2012), as well as Terry Pratchett, introduced Anne Fakhouri, with *Le Clairvoyage* [Clearjourney] (2008) and *La Brume des Jours* [The Mist of the Days] (2009); and Régis Goddyn, with *Le Sang des Sept Rois* [The Blood of the Seven Kings] (2013).

Other publishers ineluctably mirrored this evolution, concentrating on translations, novelizations and fantasy of various kinds. In 2013, the name "Fleuve Noir" disappeared entirely, the company being folded into its parent, Univers Poche, rebranding itself as *Outrefleuve*, but no longer playing a major role in the genre. The remaining publishers still laboring in the field included J'ai Lu, Denoël (with their *Lunes d'Encre* [Inky Moon] imprint started in 1999), Pocket and

---

[167] In 2022, Bragelonne was bought by mega-publisher Hachette.

Pocket Junior/Jeunesse (YAs), Albin Michel's *Imaginaire* (started in 2018), plus a number of smaller presses, the most notable being Au Diable Vauvert, Callidor, Critic, Leha, Les Moutons Electriques, La Volte, and Le Chat Noir.

One notable exception was *Rivière Blanche*, the French-language imprint of Black Coat Press, founded by Jean-Marc Lofficier in 2004 and edited by Philippe Ward until 2019. Rivière Blanche published books harking back to the style of the old Fleuve Noir's *Angoisse* imprint, mixing "old" authors with "new" ones. The former included Gilles Bergal; André Caroff (who passed away in 2009); Max-André Rayjean; and Kurt Steiner (who passed away in 2016); and the latter, Dumé Antoni, with *Le Serpent Autour de l'Etoile* [The Snake Around the Satar] (2020); Charlotte Bousquet, with *Lettre aux Ténèbres* [Letters to the Darkness] (2008); Cathy Coopman, with the *Susylee* series (2013-17); Lionel Davoust, with *L'Importance de ton Regard* [The Importance of Your Glance] (2010); Sébastien Gayraud, with *Galerie Noir* (2019); Justine Niogret, with *Vers le Pays Rouge* [Towards the Red Country][(2019); Micky Papoz, with *Au Seuil de l'Enfer* [On the Threshold of Hell] (2011) and *Le Cahier Gainé de Noir* [The Blackbound Notebook] (2017); Catherine Robert, with *Thanateros* (2018); and Serge Rollet, with *Le Dieu Sans Nom* [The Nameless God] (2015); as well As French-Canadian author Fréderick Durand, with *Quand s'éteindra la dernière chandelle* [When The Last Candle Goes Out] (2015). As of mid-2022, Riviere Blanche had published 159 volumes belonging to the *fantastique*.

In addition to the names mentioned above, other notable authors included Paul Béorn, with *La Pucelle de Diable Vert* [The Maiden of the Green Devil] (2010) and *Calame* (2019); Georgia Caldera, with *Les Larmes Rouges* [The Red Tears] (2011-15) and *Les Brumes de Cendrelune* [The Mists of Moonash] (2019-21); Morgane Caussarieu, with *Je suis ton Ombre* [I Am Your Shadow] (2014) and *Vertèbres* (2021); Fabien Cerutti, with *Le Batard de Kosigan* [The Bastard of Kosigan] (2014-19); Fabien Clavel, with *Nephilim-L'Hepta*

(2003) and *La Nireide* (2022); Patrick K. Dewdney, with *Le Cycle de Syffe* (2018-21); Claire Duvivier, with *Un Long Voyage* [A Long Voyage] (2020); Estelle Faye, with *La Voix des Oracles* [The Voice of the Oracles] (2014-16); Jean-Philippe Jaworski, avec *Les Rois du Monde* [The Kings of the World] (2013-21); Christian Léourier, with *La Lyre et le Glaive* [The Lyre and the Sword] (2019-20); Jean-Luc Marcastel, with the *Louis le Galoup* series (2005-10) and *Frankia* (2009); Cassandra O'Donnell , with the *Rebecca Kean* series (created in 2011); Carina Rozenfeld, with *La Quête des Livres Mondes* [The Quest for the World-Books] (2008-12) and *Doregon* (2010-12); Adrien Tomas, with *Les Six Royaumes* [The Six Kingdoms] (2011-123) et *Le Vaisseau d'Arcane* [The Ship from Arcane] (2020-22); and Aurélie Wellenstein, with YA fantasies such *Le Roi des Fauves* [The King of the Beasts] (2015), *Les Loups Chantants* [The Singing Wolves] (2016) and *Chevaux de Foudre* [Thunder Horses] (2017).

Across the centuries, the children of Madame d'Aulnoy and Paul Féval are still embarking on fantastic quests, encountering unimaginable monsters, adding new fears to ancient terrors, and continuing the exploration of the infinite mindscapes of imagination.

Index

Adam, Paul, 111, 127
Aesop, 17
Agapit, Marc, 200, 201, 255
Alain, Jean-Claude, 225
Alain-Fournier, 169
Albaret, d', 26
Albaret, Laurent, 176
Albertus Magnus, 29
Alessandrini, Jean, 280
Alexandrian, Sarane, 24, 242
Allain, Marcel, 134, 139, 162
Andersen, Hans Christian, 118
Andrau, Marianne, 216
Andrevon, Jean-Pierre, 234, 247, 260, 261, 262, 278
Angot, Michèle, 250
Anh, Lori, 262
Antoni, Dumé, 287
Apollinaire, Guillaume, 151, 166
Aragon, Louis, 167
Arbos, Ange, 200
Arlann, Stéphane, 274
Arley, Catherine, 236
Arlincourt, Charles-Victor d', 58
Arly, Dominique, 205
Armange, Xavier, 251, 279
Arnaud, G.-J., 233, 234, 259
Arnoux, Alexandre, 181
Arrabal, Fernando, 208
Arras, Jehan d', 19
Artaud, Antonin, 168
Arthaud, Émile, 63
Asselineau, Charles, 103
Aubert, Brigitte, 263
Audemard, Raymond, 274
Aulnoy, Marie-Catherine d', 34, 35, 36, 41, 120, 121, 225, 288
Aurembou, Renée, 225
Aveline, Claude, 165
Avril, Nicole, 243, 245
Axelman, 261
Ayerdhal, 276
Aymé, Marcel, 8, 176, 250
Bacon, Roger, 29
Baïf, Jean-Antoine de, 24
Balazard, Simone, 217
Balzac, Honoré de, 51, 52, 56, 57, 58, 64, 66, 73, 75, 77, 115, 122, 124, 126, 148
Bameul, Pierre, 272

Banville, Théodore de, 55, 120
Barbeau, Philippe, 281
Barbéri, Jacques, 260
Barbet, Pierre, 247
Barbey d'Aurevilly, Jules-Amédée, 109, 110, 126
Barbier, Jules, 101
Barbot de Villeneuve, Gabrielle-Suzanne, 42, 43
Barjavel, René, 246, 270
Barker, Clive, 255, 256, 257
Barnouin, Jacques, 282
Baronian, Jean-Baptiste, 251
Bataille, Félix-Henri, 128
Bataille, Henry (Léo Taxil), 128
Bataille, Thierry, 260
Bauche, Henri, 164
Baudelaire, Charles, 52, 102, 103, 109, 113, 118, 124, 166
Bauduret, Thomas, 274
Bay, Paul, 230
Bazire d'Amblainville, Gervais, 26
Béalu, Marcel, 210, 211, 215, 227
Beauplan, Amédée de, 101
Beauvoir, Simone de, 193, 214
Bechtel, Guy, 201
Becker, Benoît, 202

Beckford, William, 39, 47
Bédier, Joseph, 13
Béhémoth, 259
Bélen, 217
Béliard, Octave, 147
Belline, 249
Benoît, Pierre, 170, 171, 172, 173, 174
Béorn, Paul, 287
Béra, Paul, 234
Bérard, Cyprien, 53, 54
Béraud, Antoine, 54
Berbiguier, Alexis-Vincent, 128
Berenboom, Alain, 268
Bérenger, Jeremy, 268
Bergal, Gilles, 260, 287
Bergier, Jacques, 222, 223, 249
Berkani-Rohmer, Anissa, 262
Berlioux, E. F., 172
Berlioz, Hector, 100
Berlitz, Charles, 222, 249
Bernanos, Georges, 110, 170, 188, 205, 213
Bernanos, Michel, 194, 205, 213
Bernard, Pierre-Joseph, 26
Bernède, Arthur, 160, 161
Bernier, Alain, 235, 260
Berthelot, Francis, 270
Berthoud, S. Henry, 97, 98, 99, 118, 219
Bertrand, Aloysius, 113, 118
Bessière, Richard, 204

Bettencourt, Pierre, 208
Beucler, André, 214
Bhély-Quénum, Olympe, 220
Bierce, Ambrose, 163, 211
Bignon, Jean-Paul, 40
Binet, Alfred, 164
Bisset, Éric, 282
Blanchot, Maurice, 209
Blanzat, Jean, 220
Blatty, Peter, 255
Blau, Alfred, 101
Blau, Édouard, 152
Blavatsky, Helena, 222
Block, Aloysius, 63
Blondel, Roger, 194, 200, 209
Bloy, Léon, 107
Blyton, Enid, 224
Bodel d'Arras, Jean, 19
Bodin, Jean, 28
Boguet, Henri, 28
Boileau, Pierre, 196
Boileau-Narcejac, 197
Bois, Jules, 126
Bonnafé, Claire, 243, 246
Bonneau, Albert, 147
Bordage, Pierre, 275, 286
Borel, Petrus, 61, 98
Borges, Jorge Luis, 195, 214, 237, 238
Boron, Robert de, 14, 16, 117
Bosschère, Jean de, 188
Boucher de Perthes, Jacques, 62
Boulenger, Jacques, 16

Bouquet, Jean-Louis, 196, 214
Bourgeois, Albert, 63
Bourges, Élémir, 112, 126
Bourre, Jean-Paul, 249
Bourre, Martine, 281
Bours, Jean-Pierre, 252
Bousquet, Charlotte, 287
Boussenard, Louis, 147
Boutet, Frédéric, 123, 175
Brékilien, Yann, 249
Brenner, Félix, 262
Bressy. Eugène, 220
Breton, André, 67, 100, 116, 118, 152, 153, 167, 215, 244
Brion, Marcel, 211, 215
Brisou-Pellen, Evelyne, 279
Brosses, Marie-Therèse de, 217
Brown, Fredric, 209
Brun, Joan-Frédéric, 275
Bruss, B.-R., 194, 200, 209, 255
Brussolo, Serge, 256, 257, 258, 272
Brutsche, Alphonse, 234
Buchan, John, 255
Bulteau, Yves, 274
Bulwer-Lytton, Edward, 103
Burger, Chris, 235
Burroughs, Edgar Rice, 115, 155
Butor, Michel, 193
Buzzati, Dino, 195, 214

Byron (Lord), 47, 53, 54, 91, 108, 109, 114, 156
Cabell, James Branch, 152
Caesar, Julius, 118
Cahusac, Louis de, 26
Caillois, Roger, 213
Caldera, Georgia, 287
Calvino, Italo, 214
Campbell, Ramsay, 256
Camus, Albert, 159, 193
Candia, Pascal, 274
Cardoze, Jules, 90
Carn, Hervé, 275
Caroff, André, 202, 204, 205, 271, 287
Caroutch, Yvonne, 242
Carré, Michel, 100, 101
Carrère, Jean, 182
Carrière, Jean-Claude, 201, 202
Cars, Guy des, 225
Casanova, Giacomo, 115
Cassan, Marguerite, 217
Cassou, Jean, 176
Castan, Claude, 273
Caumont de La Force, Charlotte-Rose, 37
Caussarieu, Morgane, 287
Cauvin, Patrick, 241
Caylus, Philippe de, 42
Cayrol, Jean, 193, 238
Cazotte, Jacques, 44, 45, 46, 47, 93
Céline, Louis-Ferdinand, 159
Cendrars, Blaise, 167
Certon, Erik J., 206

Cerutti, Fabien, 287
Chabar, Jacques, 225
Chaine, Pierre, 164
Chambon, Jacques, 256
Champagne, Maurice, 147
Champion, Jeanne, 242
Champreux, Maurice, 160
Champsaur, Félicien, 182
Chapel, Félix, 273
Charles, Frédéric, 197
Charpentier, Louis, 223
Charrière, Christian, 245
Charroux, Robert, 223, 249
Chasles, Philarète, 60, 77
Châteaureynaud, Georges-Olivier, 194, 237, 266
Chatrian, Alexandre, 97
Chaulet, Georges, 226, 249
Chaumette, Jean-Christophe, 274
Chauveau, Léopold, 17
Chéraqui, Yves, 274
Chevrier, Martine, 217
Choisy, Camille, 163
Choquart, Alphonse, 63
Chrétien de Troyes, 13, 14, 116
Chrétien des Croix, Nicolas, 25
Christie, Agatha, 265
Claretie, Jules, 125
Claris de Florian, Jean-Pierre, 47
Claudel, Paul, 113
Clauzel, Robert, 235, 236

Clavel, Fabien, 287
Clément, Yves-Marie, 282
Clouzot, Henri-Georges, 197
Cocteau, Jean, 159, 168, 195, 201, 224
Cohen, Olivier, 281
Coleno, Alice, 224
Colin, Fabrice, 277
Collet, David & Isabelle, 276
Collin de Plancy, Jacques, 115
Compère, Gaston, 252
Cooper, Fenimore, 60
Coopman, Cathy, 287
Corgiat, Sylviane, 260, 269, 272
Corneille, Pierre, 25
Corsélien, 259
Cortazar, Julio, 195, 241
Cosem, Michel, 251, 278
Cossé, Laurence, 269
Couturiau, Paul, 274
Couvreur, André, 142
Craipeau, Jean-Louis, 281
Craven, Wes, 259
Crevel, René, 169
Cronenberg, David, 255, 257, 258
Cyrano de Bergerac, Savinien de, 46
D.L. (Comtesse), 38
Dalens, Serge, 226
Dalrune, Arnaud, 274
Danchet, Antoine, 26
Dante Alighieri, 18

Danville, Gaston, 105
Dard, Frédéric, 197
Darnaudet, François, 261, 265
Darrieussecq, Marie, 269
Dasnoy, Albert, 230
Daudet, Léon, 175
David, Jean, 205
Davoust, Lionel, 287
De la Halle, Adam, 18
De la Salle, Antoine, 16
Deblander, Gabriel, 215, 252
Debresse, Pierre, 226
Deharme, Lisa, 215
Delmeulle, Frédéric, 286
Delmon, Yann, 236
Demade, Paul, 130
Demolder, Eugène, 129
Dermèze, Yves, 234
Descartes, René, 33
Deschamps, Émile, 127, 128
Desnos, Robert, 169
Devaulx, Noël, 212
Dewdney, Patrick K., 288
Dhôtel, André, 212
Dib, Mohammed, 221
Dickens, Charles, 210
Diderot, Denis, 33, 42
Donaldson, Stephen R., 270
Doom, Kitty, 273
Dorémieux, Alain, 214, 246, 256, 263
Dorion, Bastien, 236
Dornay, Jules, 55

Dos Passos, John, 159
Douriaux, Hugues, 270
Doyle, Arthur Conan, 73, 137, 185
Drowin, Michel, 214
Du Bartas, Guillaume, 24
Ducasse, Isidore, 60, 109
Duclos, Charles, 39
Ducray-Duminil, François-Guillaume, 53
Duguël, Anne, 256, 261
Duits, Charles, 244, 245
Dujardin, Édouard, 113
Dulac, Germaine, 196
Dumas, Alexandre, 46, 55, 65, 66, 67, 90, 92, 133, 134, 135, 159, 224, 227
Dumas, Philippe, 250
Dunan, Renée, 176
Dunsany (Lord), 152
Dunyach, Jean-Claude, 273, 286
Durand, Frédérick, 287
Duras, Marguerite, 193
Duvic, Patrice, 256
Duvivier, Claire, 288
Eaubonne, Françoise d', 216
Ecken, Claude, 260
Eddings, David, 269
Eddison, E. R., 152
Eekhoud, Georges, 130
Éluard, Paul, 169
Epheyre, Charles, 125
Erasmus, 23, 29
Erckmann, Émile, 97
Erckmann-Chatrian, 97, 227
Eriksson, Duncan, 277
Errer, Emmanuel, 259
Escarpit, Robert, 278
Escoula, Yvonne, 216
Esquiros, Alphonse, 63
Essard, Manuel, 274
Ewers, H. H., 129, 227
Facon, Roger, 272
Fagnan, Marie-Antoinette, 38
Faivre d'Arcier, Jeanne, 256, 264, 269
Fakhouri, Anne, 286
Falques, Marianne-Agnès, 39
Farmer, Philip José, 246, 264
Farré, Marie, 281
Farrère, Claude, 150, 174
Faulkner, William, 159
Fayard, Colette, 268
Faye, Estelle, 288
Feek, Anthony, 235
Felitta, Frank de, 255
Fernez, André, 227
Ferran, Pierre, 241
Fétidus, 261
Fétis, Laurent, 261
Feuillade, Louis, 160
Féval, Paul, 67, 68, 69, 70, 71, 72, 73, 74, 75, 76, 77, 79, 117, 133, 134, 135, 159, 160, 227, 288
Flamel, Nicolas, 29

Flammarion, Camille, 124, 249
Flanders, John, 183, 184
Flaubert, Gustave, 64, 94, 102, 119, 133, 181, 244
Fleutiaux, Pierrette, 241
Flor O'Squar, Charles-Marie, 129
Florentz, Bernard, 262
Foleÿ, Charles, 164
Foncine, Jean-Louis, 226
Fondal, Mik, 226
Fontana, Jean-Pierre, 246, 247, 255, 271, 275
Fontanières, Hervé, 282
Forneret, Xavier, 113
Fort, Charles, 103
Fox, Gardner, 248
Françaix, Pascal, 262
France, Anatole, 111, 122, 150
France, Marie de, 18
Franju, Georges, 160, 197
Frédérique, André, 208
Freud, Sigmund, 166
Froissart, Jean, 16
Frondaie, Pierre, 175
Fuzelier, Louis, 26
Gaborit, Mathieu, 276, 277, 286
Galland, Antoine, 39, 40
Galli de Bibbiéna, Jean, 47
Galopin, Arnould, 155
Garcia-Marquez, Gabriel, 195
Gardner, John, 76
Garnier, Charles-Georges-Thomas, 46
Gauthier, Georges, 199
Gautier de Coincy, 19
Gautier, Judith, 122
Gautier, Théophile, 19, 64, 94, 95, 101, 122, 124, 163, 227
Gay, Sophie, 94
Gayraud, Sébastien, 287
Gemmell, David, 277
Gemmell, Terry, 286
Gennari, Geneviève, 216
Georges-Méra, Robert, 198
Gestelys, Léo, 165, 198
Ghelderode, Michel de, 8, 188, 227
Gheusi, Pierre-Barthélemy, 152, 153
Giffard, Pierre, 147
Girardin, Delphine de, 94
Girardin, Émile de, 94
Giraudoux, Jean, 168
Gobineau, Joseph, 113
Godard, Jean-Luc, 233
Goddyn, Régis, 286
Goethe, Johann Wolfgang von, 92, 151
Gogol, Nikolai, 96
Goimard, Jacques, 269
Goncourt, Edmond de, 133, 150
Goodkind, David, 286
Goodkind, Terry, 277
Gougaud, Henri, 241, 250
Gourmont, Rémy de, 110

Gozlan, Léon, 63, 79
Gracq, Julien, 168, 206, 215
Gramont, Louis de, 101
Grandjean, Georges, 174
Grazzini, Anton Francesco, 93
Gréban, Arnoul, 19
Green, Roland J., 274
Grimaud, Michel, 246, 251, 277
Grimbert, Pierre, 276
Grimm (Brothers), 98
Gripari, Pierre, 7, 210, 240, 250
Guaïta, Stanislas de, 126
Gudule, 261, 281
Guéroult, Constant, 90
Gueulette, Thomas-Simon, 40
Guieu, Jimmy, 205, 224
Guillot, René, 250
Guiraud, Alexandre, 62
Guyon, Charles, 181
Haddad, Hubert, 238, 266
Haggard, H. Rider, 135, 146, 171, 172, 173, 255
Hamelink, Jacques, 241
Haraucourt, Edmond, 149, 155
Hardellet, André, 221, 222
Harris, Thomas, 256, 263
Hart Milman, Henry, 93
Hausser, Isabelle, 268
Hecht, Yvon, 264
Hellens, Franz, 189, 227, 229

Hello, Ernest, 107
Henneberg, Charles, 218
Henneberg, Nathalie C., 216, 218, 219, 243, 248
Hennique, Léon, 125
Herbert, James, 256
Hersart, Théodore, 116, 117
Hervyns, José, 230
Hetzel, Pierre-Jules, 172
Hitchcock, Alfred, 197, 234
Hodgson, William Hope, 143, 162, 175, 255
Hoffmann, E. T. A., 8, 51, 60, 64, 66, 91, 92, 94, 100, 101, 102, 113, 129, 135, 160, 210
Holberg, Ludwig, 115
Holdstock, Robert, 256
Homer, 182
Honaker, Michel, 90, 256, 259, 282
Houdar de la Motte, Antoine, 26
Houdenc, Raoul de, 16
Houssin, Joël, 256, 258
Hoveyda, Fereydoun, 215
Howard, Robert E., 8, 119, 152, 195, 246, 248, 255, 269
Hubert, Jean-Pierre, 130, 238, 240, 260, 266, 269
Hugo, Victor, 51, 58, 64, 113, 124
Humann, Mort, 261
Hunt, Robert, 98

Hurtaud, Jacques, 236
Hutson, Shaun, 256
Huysmans, Joris-Karl, 110, 127
Ibrahim, Kamal, 239
Jacob, Max, 169
Jacq, Christian, 265, 277
James, Henry, 166
Jan, Gabriel, 235, 236
Janin, Jules, 60, 79, 98
Jarry, Alfred, 120, 149, 151, 166, 206
Jaworski, Jean-Philippe, 288
Jean-Charles, Jehanne, 238, 242
Jeancourt, Auguste, 62
Jeanne, René, 34
Jeter, K. W., 256
Jodorowsky, Alexandro, 208
Jonquet, Thierry, 279
Jordan, Robert, 269, 286
Joseph-Renaud, Jean, 163
Jouanne, Emmanuel, 260
Jouvin, Jack, 163
Joyce, James, 159
Julien, Paul-Gaspard, 274
Kââ, 259, 261, 262
Kafka, Franz, 195, 237, 242
Kahn, Gustave, 112
Kahn, Michèle, 280
Kaplan, Nelly, 217
Kardec, Allan, 124, 126, 222
Kast, Pierre, 240

Keller, David H., 199, 204
Keller, Dominique H., 204
Kieffer, Nicolas, 264
King, Stephen, 163, 195, 255
Kloetzer, Laurent, 276, 286
Klotz, Claude, 194, 241
Koontz, Dean, 235, 255, 256
Kumel, Harry, 185
L'Estoille (Comte de), 118
L'Héritier de Villandon, Marie-Jeanne, 34
La Chave, Clément de, 125
La Fontaine, Jean de, 35
La Garde, Marcellin, 129
La Hire, Jean de, 134, 141, 155, 160
La Houssaye, Noël de, 221
La Madelène, Jules de, 100
La Porte, Joseph de, 42
Labou Tansi, Sony, 267
Laboulaye, Édouard-René de, 120
Lacour, José-André, 202
Lacroix, Paul, 59, 66, 67
Laloux, René, 208, 247
Lamerlière, Eugène de, 59
Lamothe-Langon, Étienne-Léon de, 55, 56
Lancre, Pierre de, 28
Lang, Fritz, 161
Laramie, Phil, 273

Lascault, Gilbert, 239
Lassailly, Charles, 63
Laurent, Agnès, 235
Lautréamont, 60, 109, 166
Lautrec, Gabriel de, 111, 149
Lazare, Bernard, 113
Le Bourguignon, Alain, 113
Le Braz, Anatole, 98, 100, 219, 249
le Bussy, Alain, 273
Le Clézio, Jean-Marie, 238, 266
Le Faure, Georges, 147
Le Grais, Didier, 274
Le Guin, Ursula K., 279
Le May, Jean & Doris, 248
Le Normand, Véronique, 279
Le Rouge, Gustave, 134, 143, 155, 160, 162, 167
Le Valois d'Orville, Adrien-Joseph, 26
Lebègue, Raymond, 25
Leblanc, Maurice, 134, 136, 137, 138, 160, 197
Lecigne, Bruno, 260, 269, 272
Legué, Gabriel, 148
Lehman, Serge, 262
Leiber, Fritz, 152, 246, 248
Leiris, Michel, 169
Lemercier de Neuville, Louis, 107
Léourier, Christian, 288
Leprince de Beaumont, Jeanne-Marie, 42, 43
Leprince, X. B., 226
Lermina, Jules, 105
Leroux, Gaston, 8, 124, 134, 135, 136, 146, 160
Lesage, Alain-René, 40, 46
Letailleur, Édouard, 165
Leuven, Adolphe de, 101
Level, Maurice, 149, 175
Lévi, Éliphas, 106, 123, 124, 126, 222
Levin, Ira, 110
Lewis, Herschell Gordon, 256
Lewis, Matthew, 48, 51, 52, 227
Ligny, Jean-Marc, 256, 263, 269, 278
Limat, Maurice, 204, 236
Limbour, Georges, 169
Lintot, Catherine de, 41
Livet, Guillaume, 144
Lobsang Rampa, T., 249
Lofficier, Jean-Marc, 287
Lombrosi, Cesare, 144
Lomon, Charles, 152, 153
London, Jack, 146
Lord, Virginia, 199
Lorde, André de, 145, 163, 164
Lorrain, Jean, 110, 123, 127
Lorris, Guillaume de, 18
Lorzac, Georges de, 267

Loubet, Christophe, 274
Louis-Combet, Claude, 239, 266
Louÿs, Pierre, 148
Lovecraft, H. P., 28, 102, 103, 173, 183, 187, 195, 200, 235, 240, 246, 262, 264, 265
Lubert, Marie-Madeleine de, 41
Luck, John, 234
Luitz-Morat, 196
Lulle, Raymond, 29
Mac Orlan, Pierre, 170
Macé, Gérard, 267
Machard, Raymonde, 196
Maeterlinck, Maurice, 111, 188, 189
Magden, Henry, 171
Magre, Maurice, 154, 155, 177, 178, 179, 180
Maillart, Jehan, 188
Mailly, Louis de, 38, 40
Maindron, Maurice, 147
Mallarmé, Stéphane, 111, 113, 166
Mallinus, Daniel, 252
Malory, Thomas, 15
Malraux, André, 159
Manier, Bernard, 230
Mantey, Christian, 274
Marcastel, Jean-Luc, 288
Marcel, Odile, 242
Mardrus, Joseph-Charles, 181
Marès, Roland de, 130
Maridat, Roger, 235, 260

Marignac, Pascal, 259
Markalé, Jean, 16, 249
Marmontel, Jean-François, 26
Marsan, Stéphane, 276, 277
Masterton, Graham, 256
Matheson, Richard, 195, 212, 214, 217, 238, 256
Matip, Benjamin, 221
Maturin, Charles-Robert, 51, 52, 57, 58, 227
Mauckner, Walter, 199
Mauclair, Camille, 112
Mauhourat, Jean, 236
Maupassant, Guy de, 64, 102, 103, 145, 174
Maurey, Marcel, 196
Maurey, Max, 145, 196
Mauriac, André, 110
Maurois, André, 214
Mayer, Charles-Joseph de, 44
Mazarin, Jean, 259, 261
Mélesville, 101
Mendès, Catulle, 104, 120, 121, 122, 123, 127
Méon, D.-M., 17
Mercier, Louis-Sébastien, 44
Mercier, Mario, 239
Mérimée, Prosper, 64, 95, 96, 211
Merritt, Abraham, 255
Méténier, Oscar, 145
Mettais, Hippolyte, 119
Michaux, Henri, 189

Michel, Francisque, 13
Michelet, Victor-Émile, 148
Milton, John, 99, 150
Mirbeau, Octave, 148
Mistral, Frédéric, 100
Mockel, Albert, 187
Monfils, Nadine, 274
Monmouth, Geoffrey of, 13
Montalvo, Garcia Rodriguez, 25
Monteilhet, Hubert, 240
Montesiste, Laurent, 107
Montfaucon de Villars, Pierre-Henri de, 46
Montignac, Georges, 164
Moorcock, Michael, 13, 246, 269, 270
Moore, Catherine L., 152
Moréas, Jean, 108
Moreau, Gérald, 274
Moreau, Jean-Manuel, 274
Morel, Suzy, 243
Morgan, Harry, 276
Morris, William, 115, 152, 245
Morrisson, Roy, 236
Mottart, Raymond, 230
Mount, Norbert, 261
Mourguet, Laurent, 145
Moutier, Norbert, 261
Mouton, Eugène, 107
Mundy, Talbot, 255
Muno, Jean, 230
Murail, Lorris, 282
Murail, Marie-Aude, 282

Murat, Henriette-Julie de, 36, 37, 41, 120
Murelli, Jean, 205
Murey, Georges, 234
Murphy, Warren, 274
Musset, Alfred de, 91
Mysor, Fernand, 174
Nabokov, Vladimir, 195
Narcejac, Thomas, 196
Nécrorian, Charles, 259
Nelson, Ray, 274
Nerval, Gérard de, 47, 51, 64, 66, 91, 92, 93, 95, 96, 97, 166, 170, 210, 213, 227
Nevers-Severin, 196
Newton, Isaac, 33
Nightingale, Charles, 246
Nimal, Henri de, 129
Niogret, Justine, 286, 287
Nizerolles, René-Marcel de, 147
Nodier, Charles, 54, 91, 94, 97, 114, 152, 211, 213
Nolane, Richard D., 274
Nolant de Fatouville, 40
Nonon, Charles, 196
Nostradamus, 29
Nothomb, Pierre, 230
Novy, Michel, 275
O'Donnell, Cassandra, 288
Olivier-Martin, Yves, 240
Omessa, Charles & Henri, 181
Ormesson, Jean d', 267

Ossendowsky, Ferdinand, 249
Owen, Thomas, 203, 228, 251
Pagel, Michel, 263, 273
Païen de Maisières, 16
Papoz, Micky, 287
Papus, 126
Paradis de Moncrif, François-Augustin de, 39
Paré, Ambroise, 23
Paris, Alain, 269, 271
Paroutaud, Jean Marie Amédée, 209
Pauwels, Louis, 222, 223
Pays, Jean-François, 225
Péladan, Joséphin, 124, 126
Pellegrin (Abbott), 26
Pelot, Pierre, 234, 256, 260, 263
Pennac, Daniel, 263
Pennes, Sébastien, 276
Péret, Benjamin, 169
Périsset, Maurice, 236
Pérochon, Ernest, 175
Perrault Darmancourt, Pierre, 35
Perrault, Charles, 27, 34, 35, 121, 177, 183, 225
Petis de la Croix, François, 40
Pevel, Pierre, 286
Peyramaure, Michel, 226
Pieyre de Mandiargues, André, 211, 227

Pigault-Lebrun, Charles, 53
Pixérécourt, Guilbert de, 53
Pliya, Jean, 220
Poe, Edgar Allan, 8, 51, 60, 64, 73, 91, 101, 102, 103, 104, 105, 108, 109, 133, 135, 145, 149, 160, 175, 183, 210, 227, 242, 264
Poittevin, Alfred de, 63
Polanski, Roman, 208
Polidori, John William, 53, 91
Pons, Maurice, 239
Ponson du Terrail, Pierre-Alexis, 79, 80, 81, 82, 85, 87, 88, 89, 137, 227
Poslaniec, Christian, 280
Potocki, Jan, 48, 65
Poujol, Adolphe, 63
Poulet, Robert, 189, 229
Pourrat, Henri, 183
Pratchett, Terry, 286
Préchac, Jean de, 38
Prêtre, Marcel G., 197
Prévot, Gérard, 251
Prieur, Jean, 224
Prudhomme, Jean, 176
Puig, Franc, 206
Pushkin, Alexander, 96
Puvis de Chavannes, Pierre, 126
Quénot, Katherine, 268
Quinault, Philippe, 26

Quinet, Edgar, 65, 117, 151
R'Hoone (Lord), 56
Raabe, Juliette, 256
Rabbe, Alphonse, 63
Rabelais, François, 29, 210
Rabier, Catherine, 261
Rabou, Charles, 77
Rachilde, 127
Racine, Jean, 26
Radcliffe, Ann, 51, 52, 58, 60, 68, 69, 70
Raemdonck, Jean-Paul, 252
Rameau, Jean, 26
Ramonet, Yves, 261
Randa, Peter, 205
Randa, Philippe, 274
Ranne, G. Elton, 265, 274
Raspe, Rudolf Erich, 95
Rastouin, Bernard, 277
Ravignant, Patrick, 221, 239
Ray, Jean, 8, 183, 184, 185, 186, 187, 214, 227, 251, 255
Rayjean, Max-André, 234, 287
Reberg, Evelyne, 280
Redon, Jean, 197, 206
Régnier, Henri de, 16, 156
Régnier-Bohler, Danielle, 16
Rehm, Pierre-Louis, 150
Rémy, Jean-Charles, 238
Rémy, Pierre-Jean, 110, 241, 267
Rémy, Yves & Ada, 245
Renard, Christine, 215, 216
Renard, Maurice, 17, 108, 134, 142, 214
Rendell, Ruth, 200
Réouven, René, 194, 264, 267
Resnais, Alain, 207
Restif de la Bretonne, Nicolas-Edmé, 43, 93
Reverdy, Pierre, 169
Reveroni Saint-Cyr, Jacques-Antoine, 53
Rex, Lionel, 236
Rey, Stéphane, 228
Rice, Ann, 95, 256, 269
Richaud, André de, 212
Riche, Daniel, 256, 259
Richepin, Jean, 105, 151
Richet, Charles, 125
Richter, Anne, 229
Rimbaud, Arthur, 111, 113, 166, 168
Rivais, Yak, 282
Rivière, François, 265, 279
Rivière, Henri, 125
Robbe-Grillet, Alain, 8, 193, 207
Robert, Catherine, 287
Robert-Dumas, Charles, 150
Robitaillie, Henriette, 225
Roche, Dominique, 246

Rocher, Dominique, 235
Roger-Chantin, Patrice, 274
Rogliano, Jean-Claude, 241
Rohmer, Sax, 142
Rollet, Serge, 287
Rollin, Jean, 256, 261
Ronsard, Pierre de, 24
Rosny Aîné, J.-H., 108, 111, 123, 134
Rotrou, Jean de, 26
Rousseau, Jean-Jacques, 39
Roussel, Raymond, 151
Roze, Jean Baptiste Marie, 20
Rozenfeld, Carina, 288
Ruellan, André, 199, 217, 260
Russell, Eric Frank, 103
Russo, Joe, 256
Ryner, Han, 156
Saberhagen, Fred, 270
Sade, Donatien Alphonse François de, 52, 53, 61, 109, 166, 211
Sadoul, Jacques, 224, 240, 249, 255, 269
Sadyn, Jean, 236, 252
Sagan, Françoise, 193
Saint-Aubin, Horace de, 57, 115
Saint-Cloud, Pierre de, 17
Saint-Exupéry, Antoine de, 183
Saint-Georges, Henri de, 106
Saint-Gilles, 234
Saintine, Xavier-Boniface de, 61, 62
Saint-Martin, Louis-Claude de, 45, 47, 58
Saint-Pol Roux, 126
Saint-Romain, Michel, 235
Saintyves, Pierre, 183
Sallenave, Danièle, 268
Sand, George, 64, 97, 219
Santini, Gilles, 261
Sanvoisin, Éric, 282
Sapir, Richard, 274
Sapkowski, Andrzej, 277
Sardou, Victorien, 153
Sarkel, François, 261
Sarraute, Nathalie, 193
Sartre, Jean-Paul, 193
Sattler, Roger, 199
Saul, John, 255
Saurat, Denis, 224
Sautereau, François, 279
Sazie, Léon, 139
Scapin, Jean, 236
Schneider, Marcel, 213
Schultz, Friedrich, 37
Schuré, Édouard, 125
Schwob, Marcel, 111, 149, 170
Scott, Walter, 58, 59, 101, 114
Scovel, Guy, 247
Scribe, Eugène, 55, 61, 101

Sède, Gérard de, 222, 223, 249
Ségur (Comtesse de), 120
Ségur, Nicolas, 182
Seignolle, Claude, 219, 227
Sendy, Jean, 249
Servat, Gilles, 275
Sévestre, Norbert, 143, 144
Shakespeare, William, 15, 120, 201
Shaver, Richard S., 222
Shelley, Mary, 54, 201, 227
Silvestre, Armand, 100, 101
Simenon, Georges, 234
Simon, Valérie, 274
Simonay, Bernard, 270
Smith, Clark Ashton, 152, 173, 203, 255
Sobra, Adrien, 200
Sonkin, François, 267
Sorr, Angelo de, 106
Soulié, Frédéric, 60, 61, 79, 227
Soupault, Philippe, 167
Souvestre, Pierre, 134, 139
Sprenger, Jakob, 27, 28
Sprigel, Olivier, 248
Steiner, Kurt, 199, 217, 247, 260, 287
Sternberg, Jacques, 207, 214, 215, 251
Stevenson, Robert Louis, 110, 111, 170
Stiernet, Hubert, 130
Stine, R. L., 195, 255, 277
Stoker, Bram, 55, 227
Stokes, Manning Lee, 274
Straub, Peter, 255
Sue, Eugène, 60, 64, 90, 109, 134, 151, 159, 227
Supervielle, Jules, 168, 189
Suragne, Pierre, 234
Surget, Alain, 281
Sussan, Donna, 267
Sussan, René, 267
Svenn, Patrick, 205
Swedenborg, Emmanuel, 45, 58
Swift, Jonathan, 96
Sylf, Christia, 243, 244
Szczepaniak, Frédéric, 274
Talbert, Michel, 194, 205
Tanaka, Béatrice, 280
Tarade, Guy, 224, 249
Tarvel, Brice, 261
Tasso, Torquato, 25
Taxil, Léo, 128
Terrasson, Jean, 46
Tessin, Carl Gustaf, 39
Thévenin, René, 147
Thiaudière, Edmond, 107
Thiès, Paul, 279
Thinès, Georges, 253
Thiry, Marcel, 228
Thomas, Gilles, 248, 271
Tocquet, Robert, 249

Toesca, Maurice, 214
Tolkien, J. R. R., 8, 243, 246, 269
Tomas, Adrien, 288
Topor, Roland, 208, 215
Tormes, Olga, 274
Tournier, Michel, 237, 266, 278
Toussaint-Merle, Jean, 54
Trassard, Jean-Loup, 220
Treignier, Michel, 240
Tristan, Frédéric, 13, 166, 265
Truffaut, François, 233
Trystram, Florence, 268
Tubb, E. C., 274
Tur, Jean, 244
Tuttle, Lisa, 256
Tyssot de Patot, Simon, 65, 115
Tzara, Tristan, 166
Ulbach, Louis, 96
Urfé, Honoré d', 25
Valade, Frédéric, 90
Valéry, Francis, 265
Valorbe, François, 209
Van Gennep, Arnold, 183
Van Lerberghe, Charles, 187
Van Offel, Horace, 188
Vance, Jack, 152, 189, 245, 246, 247
Varende, Yves, 264
Veer, Olenka de, 246
Vegor, Maïk, 235
Velez de Guevara, Luis, 46

Venisse, Alain, 262
Verlaine, Paul, 111
Verlanger, Julia, 215, 216, 243, 248, 271
Vernay, Jean-Pierre, 270
Verne, Jules, 85, 108, 115, 133, 134, 144, 146, 210, 224, 264
Vernes, Henri, 227
Vernoy de Saint-Georges, Jules-Henri, 101
Verteuil, Éric, 235, 260
Véry, Pierre, 164, 214
Vian, Boris, 193, 206
Vignon, Claude, 106
Vilà, Christian, 260
Villeneuve, Arnauld de, 29
Villiers de l'Isle-Adam, Auguste de, 103, 124
Viluber, Jean, 260
Voltaire, 40, 54, 96, 210
Von Daniken, Erich, 222, 223
Voragine, Jacques de, 20
Vrigny, Roger, 267
Wagner, Paul, 241
Wagner, Richard, 16, 51, 108, 126
Wagner, Roland C., 265, 286
Waldor, Mélanie, 62
Walpole, Horace, 52
Walther, Daniel, 246, 255, 260, 271
Walton, Evangeline, 199
Wandrei, Donald, 199

Ward, Philippe, 264, 287
Warren, Raoul de, 197
Watteau, Monique, 229
Wellenstein, Aurélie, 288
Wells, H. G., 141
Weulersse, Odile, 279
Wiegant, Christiane, 196
Wietzel, Erik, 277, 286
Wilde, Oscar, 108, 124
Willy, 127
Wilson, F. Paul, 138, 255
Wittkop, Gabrielle, 242
Yarbro, Chelsea Quinn, 95
Yourcenar, Marguerite, 221
Zola, Émile, 109, 133, 159

www.ingramcontent.com/pod-product-compliance
Lightning Source LLC
Chambersburg PA
CBHW030135170426
43199CB00008B/72